The Glitter & The Gold

Fashioning America's Jewelry

The Glitter & The Gold

FASHIONING AMERICA'S JEWELRY

Ulysses Grant Dietz

Jenna Weissman Joselit

Kevin J. Smead

Janet Zapata

THE NEWARK MUSEUM

The Glitter & The Gold: Fashioning America's Jewelry has been published to accompany the exhibition of the same name, shown at The Newark Museum from May 7 through November 2, 1997. The exhibition, this publication and related public programs are made possible through the generosity of The National Endowment for the Humanities, The Geraldine R. Dodge Foundation, The Andrew W. Mellon Foundation, Krementz & Co., PNC Bank, Tiffany & Co. and The New Jersey Council on the Humanities.

The Newark Museum receives operating support from the City of Newark the State of New Jersey, and the New Jersey State Council on the Arts/Department of State. Funding for acquisitions and activities other than operations must be developed from outside sources.

ISBN 0-932828-35-3 (hc)
ISBN 0-932828-34-5 (pbk)

Library of Congress Cataloging-in-Publication Data
    The Glitter & the gold: fashioning America's jewelry / Ulysses
    Grant Dietz . . . [et al.].
        p. cm.
    Includes bibliographical references and index.
    ISBN 0-932828-34-5 (alk. paper) ISBN 0-932828-35-3 (hc)
    1. Goldwork—Newark—History. 2. Jewelry making—New
    Jersey—Newark—History. I. Dietz, Ulysses G. (Ulysses Grant),
    1955– .
    TS723.G55   1997
    739.27'09749—dc21   97-8038
                                                      CIP

Edited by
Ulysses Grant Dietz

Essays by
Ulysses Grant Dietz
Jenna Weissman Joselit
Kevin J. Smead
Janet Zapata

Photography
Richard Goodbody

Additional Photography
Armen Shamlian
Sarah Wells

Design
Antony Drobinski
Emsworth Design, Inc., New York City

Printing
Spectrum Press
Roseland, New Jersey

This book is printed on acid and elemental chlorine-free paper, containing at least 20% de-inked post-consumer waste.

Frontispiece
Fig. 30 (lower left) and Fig. 142 (upper right)

Contents

Chairman's Foreword

When my grandfather, Bernard M. Shanley, Jr., established his jewelry-manufacturing firm in 1908, Newark was at the peak of its importance as the center of solid-gold jewelry-making in America. In that same year, my grandfather celebrated his tenth wedding anniversary, and received from his wife as a gift a solid gold spectacle case with a cabochon ruby clasp (which you can see in Fig. 142 in this book). That spectacle case, the product of a newly-founded business, was one of the inspirations for this book and the exhibition it documents. Given by my aunt, Mary Shanley Dempsey, to The Newark Museum in 1980, it not only represents the remarkable quality of American-made jewelry during Newark's jewelry-making heyday, but also serves as a touchstone for a vanished era: the Gilded Age in America, when everything that could be made out of gold *was*, and when gold jewelry had become not a luxury, but a necessity, for the well-dressed American consumer. My grandfather's gold spectacle case is a piece of history in material form, a fossil, if you will, of a dinosaur long extinct. The curators of this exhibition and the authors of this book are like paleontologists, who have sifted through huge numbers of surviving historical fragments in order to put together a vivid picture of a thriving industry and a glamorous world that no longer exist. I commend them for their efforts, and I welcome you to the fascinating story of *The Glitter & The Gold*.

KEVIN M. SHANLEY
Chairman and President

Director's Foreword

The Newark Museum has long been interested in the products of New Jersey's industries, not just because of their regional importance, but because of their national influence on the design and production of American consumer goods. Since 1915, when our founding director, John Cotton Dana, mounted an exhibition on New Jersey's ceramic industry, the Museum has been interested in the way in which everyday objects are made, and how they affect and are affected by the world around us. I applaud Ulysses Grant Dietz, Curator of Decorative Arts, and Janet Zapata, guest Co-Curator of *The Glitter & The Gold*, for carrying on the tradition established here so long ago. I also thank Jenna Weissman Joselit and Kevin J. Smead for their illuminating essays, which shed important light on aspects of American culture and history that have been all but ignored until now.

In 1909, when the Museum was founded, the City of Newark was to jewelry-making what Detroit would soon become to automobile manufacturing. Unquestionably, the impact of the auto on American culture has been deeper and more radical than that of jewelry; but the pervasiveness of jewelry's influence on the American psyche should not be underestimated. By the turn of the century, gold jewelry was ubiquitous, and, moreover, essential to daily self-presentation for the average American. Jewelry, once the province of monarchs and nobles, had been appropriated by the middle class in the nineteenth century, and had become as deeply entrenched a part of American

material culture as any other domestic product, such as furniture, or ceramics, or silver. Newark made its influence felt—quite literally—in every jewelry store in every town, large and small, all across the North American continent. This book is the record of that remarkable story, and a reminder that Newark, founded as the heart of a Puritan colony in 1666, was once known to the jewelry world as "the city of gold and platinum and precious stones."

In closing, I wish to thank the National Endowment for the Humanities, without whose funding the project would not have been possible. Krementz & Co., through the personal interest of Chairman Richard Krementz, provided the critical seed money for research. Other important funders stepped forward to support the project, and were vital to our success: the Geraldine R. Dodge Foundation, The Andrew W. Mellon Foundation, PNC Bank, Tiffany & Co., and the New Jersey Council on the Humanities. We are also indebted to the City of Newark, the State of New Jersey, and the New Jersey State Council on the Arts/Department of State for their ongoing support.

MARY SUE SWEENEY PRICE
Director

7

Acknowledgments

This project really began back in 1992, during the run of a small exhibition of The Newark Museum's jewelry collection, called "Human Plumage". It was then we discovered that the elegant gold spectacle case that had come to the Museum in 1980 from the Shanley family was in fact *made* by Bernard M. Shanley, Jr.'s jewelry company. It dawned on us that there was really very little known, and nothing published, about what was made in Newark's jewelry factories, or about how these products fit into the broader scheme of jewelry in America.

Two important things happened in 1993 that shaped the course of this project. First, we visited Joseph Hammond, an avid scholar of New Jersey silver, and former director at the Monmouth County Historical Society. Joe encouraged us to forge ahead, and overwhelmed us with over one thousand carefully accumulated notecards documenting the existence of silversmiths and goldsmiths all over New Jersey—hundreds of them in Newark alone—up into the middle decades of the nineteenth century. For the first time we realized the kind of role Newark must have played in the American jewelry industry, and how much research there was to be done.

Also in 1993, The Newark Museum received as a gift from the Honorable Millicent Fenwick, just before her death, a magnificent (but unmarked) diamond and emerald two-stone ring. Mrs. Fenwick's intention was to benefit the Decorative Arts collections, and the Director Emeritus, Samuel C. Miller, with the Aquisitions Committee of the Board of Trustees, decided to sell the ring in order to establish the Millicent Fenwick Fund. This fund was used, over the next few years, to purchase Newark-made jewelry and create a core collection of important examples from Newark's major factories. We are most grateful for Mrs. Fenwick's generosity, and hope that the collection assembled by the Museum stands as a fitting memorial to a grand lady and a great New Jerseyan.

Many people deserve thanks for the assistance that has made this book, and the exhibition, possible, including funders previously mentioned. The Trustee co-chairs of the gala benefit ball, Arlene Lieberman and Christabel Vartanian, worked terribly hard with Board Chairman Kevin Shanley and their Gala Committee members to make that important and glamorous event a rousing success. Paul Vartanian, too, provided invaluable assistance. The Museum's Development Office, Director of Development Peggy Dougherty, along with Associate Directors Angela Richards and Brian Ferriso, were crucial in seeking out support for the project. Meme Omogbai, Deputy Director for Finance and Administration, handled the funding for all aspects of the project, and Toni Jones worked wonders coordinating the publication of this book and the public relations campaign with Public Relations Officer Cynthia Brown. Diane Salek faithfully volunteered her time to assist in developing the public relations materials. Of course, throughout the project we have relied on the support, encouragement, and guidance of Director Mary Sue Sweeney Price, and Ward Mintz, Deputy Director for Programs and Collections.

No project like this can succeed without the assistance of friends and volunteers who did research and provided invaluable assistance. Jenna Joselit and Kevin Smead sailed some uncharted waters to produce their landmark essays for this book, opening a window into the historical past which was long overdue. Richard Goodbody took most of the wonderful photographs in this book, and became a friend as we worked side by side for days on end. Armen Shamlian and Sarah Wells did yeoman service to provide additional photography as we, inevitably, needed it. Sheila Schwartz cast her expert editor's eye across the hundreds of pages of manuscript, and Antony Drobinski tied the entire package together with his elegant book design.

Volunteer Mimi Cohen, who did endless tasks related to the exhibition and this book, is owed a special debt of gratitude for unearthing the identity of the maker of the great testimonial medallion in Fig. 7, now known to be by Durand & Co. She also spent innumerable hours in the library counting names in the Newark City Directories, and compiling lists, not always understanding just why we asked her to do this. As Lisa Taylor Summer Interns from the Cooper-

Hewitt Museum, Stéphane Houy-Towner and Simonette Hakim dug up priceless documentary treasures relating to jewelry etiquette and wearing, providing us with a rich background for our own research.

Joshua Freeman, Joyce Jonas, Jenna Joselit, Harold Koda, Rita Moonsammy, and Annamarie Sandecki all participated in our initial scholars' advisory meeting, and helped guide the direction that the book and exhibition ultimately took. The staff at the New Jersey Historical Society in Newark provided valuable assistance in our research, allowing us to peruse the Henry Blank & Co. papers as well as the Alling Brother & Co. Hands Ledger, a uniquely important document of the early jewelry industry. In part, this project was inspired by the Historical Society's small 1979 exhibition, "Craftsmen of Elegance: The Newark Jewelry Industry." In particular, we wish to thank Hope Alswang, Director, Libby DiRosa, Curator of Collections, and Catherine Quintana, Collections Manager, for their assistance and support in providing us with loans of archival materials. Likewise, Annamarie Sandecki, Archivist for Tiffany & Co., and her staff were most helpful in letting us study and borrow things from both the permanent collection and the archives, to better understand Tiffany's ties with Newark's jewelry makers. The library of the Dallas Museum of Art kindly let us hold onto its microfilms of *The Jewelers' Circular* for years, providing us with an important research tool.

Many different people also provided us with significant nuggets of priceless information over the years, and we want to express our gratitude to them all, including Sandy Adams; Elena Alcalay; Gary Dalziel; Helga Bendix; Kathleen Bennett; Gary N. Berger; Peggy Bingel; Buddy Braun; Ruth Caccavale; Christie Cavanaugh; Joyce Chapman; Ilene Chazanof; Mr. and Mrs. Anton Civan; Nancy Cooper; William Dane; Janet, Byrd and William Drucker; Ralph Esmerian; Martha and Dean A. Fales, Jr.; Marguerite Fairbrothers; Suzanne Gandell; Cheryl Grandfield; David Hopkinson and Walter Edmondson of Church & Co.; H. Jack Hunkele; June A. Herman of Jabel, Inc.; Uve Jesse of Erwin Reu, Inc.; Nancy N. Kattermann;

Gladys and Robert Koch; Helene Konkus; Richard Krementz, Chairman of Krementz & Co.; Neil Lane; Susanne Moritz; Margarette Herpers Remington; Barbara Neiman; Andrew Nelson; Susan Newberry of the Durand-Hedden House in Maplewood, New Jersey; Dr. and Mrs. Joseph Sataloff; Donald S. Roth of Robert S. Fisher & Co., Inc.; Barbara, Neal and Stephen Schatz; Louis Scholz; Stephen Schuetz of Larter & Sons; Iris and Seymour Schwartz; Kevin Shanley; Reuben Simantov; Donald R. Tharpe; Doris Weinstein; and Christopher English Walling.

Museum staff who worked tirelessly on different aspects of the project also deserve thanks. Margaret Molnar, Associate Registrar, handled the complicated loan process with precision and tact, and Curatorial Secretary Ruth Barnet typed out the many loan forms necessary for the exhibition. Exhibitions Director David Palmer designed the exhibition at The Newark Museum; Merchandise Manager Lorelei Rowars developed the line of products related to the exhibition and the book; Museum Educator Enola Romano oversaw the educational programs related to the exhibition; Linda Nettleton, Assistant Director for Family, Youth and Adult Programs in the Education Department, worked with volunteers Marian Soloway and Doris Froelich to develop a special jewelry-related tour of the Museum's galleries; Public Programs Coordinator Jane Stein managed the public programs, and Special Events Manager Sharon Breland handled the opening receptions.

A special note of thanks goes to Ron Malick, who saved a lost manuscript from the virtual jaws of a recalcitrant hard drive.

Finally we have to thank our families, who put up with us through years of jewelry shop talk. They gave us comfort when all the glitter and all the gold got to be too much.

ULYSSES GRANT DIETZ
Curator of Decorative Arts

JANET ZAPATA,
Co-Curator, The Glitter & The Gold

NEWARK INDUSTRIAL EXHIBITION BUILDINGS,
Washington, Court and Marshall Street.

1. Industrial Exhibition Buildings, Newark, from *Holbrook's Newark City Directory*, 1874, p. 11.

The Glitter & The Gold: Fashioning America's Jewelry

ULYSSES GRANT DIETZ

In January 1929, The Newark Museum mounted an exhibition called "The Jewelry Industry in Newark." Otto Goetzke, a local jewelry maker and designer, had recently loaned his vast collection of gemstones to the Museum's science department (it would become a gift in 1953). John Cotton Dana, the Museum's founding director and also director of the Newark Free Public Library, took advantage of the loan to mount a parallel exhibition extolling the great tradition of jewelry manufacture in his home city. The exhibition proved to be a swan song; the stock market crash that October and the Great Depression that followed would cripple the city's jewelry industry and send it into a long decline. However, when the Museum exhibition opened, staff member Julia B. Smith, author of the twelve-page booklet that accompanied the exhibition, could easily claim that "Newark indeed has an enviable reputation in the jewelry industry."[1]

The fact that Newark, New Jersey, found itself the center of solid-gold jewelry production in America in 1929 was the result of a complex web of social, economic, and demographic forces that transformed the United States during the course of the nineteenth century. Between 1825 and 1900, America changed from a country dependent on Europe for its highest quality luxury goods and its mineral resources to an international economic, design, and manufacturing power, as well as a major source of metals and gemstones. From a nation of farmers and shopkeepers, America became a nation of industrialists and factory workers, two groups increasingly separated by social and economic divisions. From a nation of people who wore little more than mourning brooches and wedding rings, America was transformed into a country of ardent jewelry consumers, who wore a dizzying variety of jewelry forms as a sort of national costume. The essays in this volume will, for the first time, study these phenomena in the context of America's jewelry industry, and examine how they helped make Newark the fine jewelry capital of the United States for nearly a century.

The Emergence of Newark's Jewelry Industry

1801 is the birthdate of Newark's jewelry industry, the year historically given for the opening of the first production shop for jewelry-making in America. The proprietor of that shop was Epaphras Hinsdale. The earliest published account of the shop appeared on August 20, 1872, during the opening ceremonies of the first Newark Industrial Exhibition (Fig. 1). General Theodore Runyon, in the course of a long oration on the development of Newark's enormous and diverse industrial base, outlined the history Newark's jewelry industry:

The manufacture of jewelry was commenced here by EPAPHRAS HINSDALE, whose work became very celebrated. About the year 1813 he associated with him JOHN TAYLOR, and they conducted the business under the firm of Hinsdale & Taylor. DOWNING & PHELPS were their co[n]temporaries in the business, as were CARRINGTON and BALDWIN. Subsequently Taylor and Baldwin established the great business which by many is regarded as the foundation of the jewelry trade in this city.[2]

By 1872, the jewelry industry was already manufacturing an annual product worth $5 million, an amount matched only by Newark's other celebrated industry, that of leather-making. From a small shop founded early in the century, jewelry-making had become one of the two largest single segments of Newark's annual $70 million production.[3]

In 1882, William R. Bagnall published a brief history of Newark's jewelry industry in a remarkable thirty-nine page booklet produced for Enos Richardson & Co. (Fig. 2). He placed Epaphras Hinsdale's first small factory at "about 1790, or a little later," and reported that Hinsdale's

2. Cover of *The Manufacture of Gold Jewelry*, published by Enos Richardson & Co., Newark, 1882, The Newark Museum, Anonymous gift, 1996 (96.14)

enterprise grew until his death in 1810, when he was succeeded by his former employee and perhaps partner, Mr. Taylor.[4] Bagnall credits Taylor with the invention of various machines to speed up jewelry manufacturing. He also notes the presence of George R. Downing as a jewelry maker in Newark between 1812 and 1821, before his move to New York City.[5]

The establishment of the year 1801 as the starting date for Hinsdale's enterprise was unquestioned by the time William H. Shaw wrote of Newark's jewelry industry in his 1884 *History of Essex & Hudson Counties, New Jersey*. Shaw, like General Runyon in 1872, gives credit to Taylor & Baldwin for making Newark's name as a jewelry center. The key words in his description of the fledgling industry in Newark are "fair dealing" and "superior workmanship," the latter no doubt emphasized because the industry had to overcome a deeply entrenched prejudice against American-made luxury goods. These two characteristics, honesty and high quality, became hallmarks of Newark jewelry makers generally and were important in turning the tide in favor of homegrown goldsmithing.[6]

The significance of Hinsdale's factory was not that it produced jewelry, but that its production had a new goal: to manufacture jewelry in quantity for sale beyond local customers. This might seem self-evident from a late twentieth-century perspective, but at the time it was a remarkable breakthrough. During the period of Hinsdale's enterprise, Newark silversmiths, such as Benjamin Cleveland and Cyrus Durand, made silver spoons and shoe buckles, and

probably an occasional pair of gold cuff buttons or a mourning pin (Fig. 3). American-made jewelry in the post-Colonial period was "bespoke," or made to order. Newark, it should be remembered, was still a Puritan city at the end of the eighteenth century, despite the materialistic influence of Dutch families and the less ascetic Protestants. Bagnall notes in his 1882 history that there was limited call for jewelry in Colonial America, except among the wealthy and those who chose to imitate the life of English and European gentry.[7] Although more than a century old, Bagnall's grasp of the facts has been surprisingly well supported by more recent research. Documented examples of pre-industrial American gold jewelry are few, and usually survive with provenances in elite families.[8]

John Cunningham's 1954 volume on New Jersey's industrial history finally fit together all the pieces of the puzzle. He fixed the date of Hinsdale's shop at 1801 and underscored Hinsdale's courage in opening a shop to make jewelry at a time when those wealthy few who

3. Coin silver spoons from Newark goldsmiths. From top: tablespoon, by Benjamin Cleveland, 1810–1825, The Newark Museum, Gift of Berry B. Tracy, 1961 (61.509); teaspoon, by Benjamin Cleveland, 1810–1825, The Newark Museum, Bequest of Marcus L. Ward, 1921 (21.19a); teaspoon, by Cyrus Durand, 1800–1810, The Newark Museum, Gift of Miss Elizabeth S. Colie, 1981 (81.179); teaspoon, by Downing & Phelps, 1810–1825, The Newark Museum, Purchase 1974 Mathilde Oestrich Bequest Fund (74.146); tablespoon, mate to top spoon.

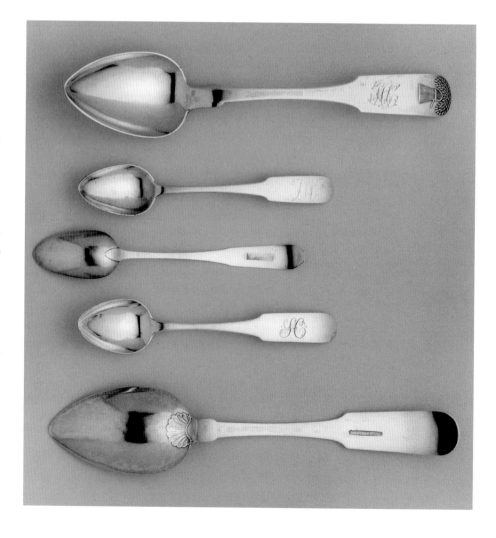

4. Toast rack, by Taylor & Hinsdale, New York, 1820–1825, silver, private collection, New Jersey.

purchased jewelry preferred to buy English- or French-made goods. Apparently Hinsdale's tactic was to set himself up in a stylish modern building and hire a staff of six—putting on a good show attracted customers. John Taylor entered the picture in 1805 as a partner and, after Hinsdale's death in 1811, took on Colonel Isaac Baldwin as his partner.[9]

If Hinsdale established the first jewelry factory in America, Taylor & Baldwin made it a thriving industry. The key elements in the success of jewelry-making in America were the ability to produce in quantity, rather than simply to order, and the creation of a market for the goods produced. If, as Bagnall asserted in 1882, Taylor was the inventive spirit who made quantity production of jewelry possible, Baldwin was the marketing partner, who could sell ready-made Newark goods to retail jewelers in the face of often crushing competition from foreign makers. Baldwin went off on sales trips to meet shopkeepers face-to-face, thus establishing a market for Newark-made jewelry where none had existed before. So it was logical for General Runyon in 1872 to praise Taylor & Baldwin as the foundation of Newark's jewelry empire. The firm introduced large-scale, machine-assisted

production to jewelry making; and it also introduced the traveling jewelry salesman, a figure who remained, throughout Newark's history as a jewelry center, a critical force in commercial jewelry production.

Another of John Taylor's important innovations was the establishment of sales outlets across the Hudson River. Even as he was working with Isaac Baldwin in Newark, he teamed up with Epaphras Hinsdale's son Horace in a New York City firm (Fig. 4).[10] At this early stage, with New York just eight miles from Newark's workshops, a Manhattan presence probably provided a distinct commercial edge for a Newark jewelry maker. From this point on, Newark's jewelry manufacturers would increasingly have showrooms and sales offices on Maiden Lane and other parts of the New York jewelry district. By 1836, when the Puritan settlement of Newark was incorporated as a city, there were perhaps six factories with one hundred people in the jewelry trade in Newark, with an annual product worth $180,000.[11]

By 1893 Newark's jewelry trade was already renowned enough to warrant an extensive article in the national trade journal, *The Jewelers' Circular and Horological Review*. The anonymous

5. Pocket watch, by Baldwin & Co., ca. 1860, gold, The Newark Museum, Gift of Helen Tufts Bailie, 1944, in memory of Daniel Durand Terrill and Matilda Hand Terrill (44.147)

Newark after assaying, a delivery system that would have been inconceivable in Colonial America, when colonists were forbidden to deal in gold or silver bullion.[14] However else the impact of the Gold Rush was felt in Newark, it undoubtedly gave a boost to the burgeoning jewelry industry by providing both plentiful raw material more cheaply and by imparting a nationalistic pride in American-made gold jewelry for the first time.

The rise of machine technology in America was as crucial to Newark's jewelry industry as the new availability of precious metals. Railroads, which had been transporting Newarkers into New York since the 1830s, were not only making it easier to get raw materials into the city, but were also enabling jewelry salesmen to travel outside the city to sell their goods. New York had always been the first stop for Newark's producers, but with the growth of the railroads in the nineteenth century, salesmen, called jobbers, could offer their goods directly all across the country.

Of equal significance was the arrival of steam-driven machinery in the jewelry factory. Pennington, Carter & Doremus, founded in 1841, became one of the first American jewelry makers to use steam power. They purchased a steam engine built by Newark inventor Seth Boyden for the New York Crystal Palace Exposition in 1853 and installed it in their Newark factory in the mid-1850s.[15] By 1878, the firm, which had become Carter, Howkins & Sloan, was reported to be the largest jewelry factory in the world, with an annual output valued at $2 million (Fig. 6).[16]

By the end of the Civil War in 1865, the jewelry manufacturing industry in Newark had reached its initial stage of maturity. Transportation, machinery, available raw materials, and a growing market had all converged to help Epaphras Hinsdale's first small shop blossom into a major national presence. Newark-made jewelry had been sold for years by major urban retailers in New York, Boston, Philadelphia, Chicago, and even San Francisco. Old Cyrus Durand, the silversmith, who had long since retired to his villa in Irvington, New Jersey, advised his son-in-law in 1864 to send his grandson Willie into the Newark jewelry business, "for all get rich that understand it. . . . I think Isaac Alling's in Newark would be a good place for him. . . ."[17]

writer confuses the Hinsdales, father and son, but continues the story of Newark's jewelry industry to the next generation. He begins with the Taylor & Baldwin partnership of 1821, and continues to John Taylor's retirement in 1842 to become a bank president. At this point, Isaac Baldwin took on his sons Horace and Wickliffe Baldwin and C.E. Chevalier to form Baldwin & Co. That firm is known today primarily for a small amount of conservative but well-made silver hollow wares, and by a single gold watch case, patented in 1858 (Fig. 5).[12]

During the 1840s, two major events had an enormous impact on the future of Newark's jewelry industry. In 1842, Congress passed a stiff tariff on imported silver, thus opening up the market for American silversmiths and jewelers for the first time. The tariffs on imports were also payable in silver or gold coin, a stipulation that provided the government with a new source of raw material that it could in turn sell to manufacturers.[13] The second major event was the discovery of gold in California in 1849. As Martha Fales has documented, there were several Newark jewelry makers who gave California addresses in the 1850–1851 city directories. Gold from the California fields was shipped directly to

However, the best work from large, well-known firms within the trade, such as Durand & Co., (founded by Cyrus Durand's nephew), Carter, Howkins & Dodd, Alling Brother & Co., and Enos Richardson & Co., was still being sold as imports from France or England. Another kind of misperception was propagated by the U.S. Census, which underreported the production of the jewelry manufacturers. According to the records of local historians, the Census accounts of 1860 and 1870 were grossly inaccurate in their reporting of the growth of Newark jewelry making. According to one locally prepared report published in the *Newark Daily Journal* in 1869, Newark jewelry makers turned out work to the value of $4,432,000, employed 1,493 people, and paid them $1,791,600. These figures topped the statistics for the entire State of New

6. Carter, Howkins & Sloan factory, Newark, ca. 1879, from *Holbrook's Newark City Directory*, 1879, p. 1107.

CARTER, HOWKINS & SLOAN,

MANUFACTURERS OF

FINE JEWELRY,

No. 1 Bond Street, New York.

MANUFACTORY. - - NEWARK, N. J.

| A. CARTER, JR., | WM. HOWKINS, | A. K. SLOAN, |
| C. E. HASTINGS, | GEO. R. HOWE, | W. T. CARTER. |

7. Testimonial medallion, by Durand & Co., 1868, gold, 3 × 1⅝ in., The Newark Museum, Gift of Vivian Sauvage and his sisters, 1937 (37.590)

Jersey compiled in the 1870 census, and the annual output in 1869 was more than thirty percent higher than that given for jewelry production in the entire nation in 1860.[18]

Statistical vagaries aside, what came through clearly was a sense of local pride in an industry that had survived a major depression in the late 1850s and a Civil War in the 1860s, and had gone on to influence the taste of a newly rich and powerful country. As William Shaw noted, "The eyes of the blind have been opened and dazzled by the brilliancy of Newark workmanship, as displayed at Tiffany's and other great jewelry bazars [sic] in New York and elsewhere."[19] The ranks of the Newark jewelry makers had been swelled by the end of the 1860s to include names that would carry on for generations to come: Champenois, Riker, Fay & Searing, Shafer & Douglas, Kerr, Richardson, Larter, Hedges, and Krementz.

Shaw's mention of Tiffany & Co. in 1884 is neither surprising nor mere bragging. Henry Herpers, in handwritten notes made about the history of his father, Ferdinand, as a jewelry maker in Newark, lists Tiffany & Co. as one of the early firms in Newark's jewelry industry.[20] Tiffany & Co. did move its manufacturing operation to Newark, but not until the 1890s, and most of the work from that factory was silverware, rather than jewelry. Little known, however, is the fact that Charles L. Tiffany, founder and owner of the firm that dominated American jewelry for most of the nineteenth century, was a partner in the Newark manufacturing firm of Durand & Co.[21] It may well be that, just as Tiffany's contracted with John C. Moore in New York to produce much of its silver, it had similar production ties with Durand in Newark. Tiffany & Co. continued to subcontract some of its jewelry production to other Newark firms long after beginning in-house production.[22]

Two specific pieces of jewelry amply demonstrate both the quality and the sense of importance that Newark jewelry makers displayed following the Civil War. On December 16, 1868, a splendid gold testimonial medal was presented to Thomas B. Peddie, mayor of Newark and three-time congressman. It is not in fact strictly a medal, but more a piece of man's jewelry, incorporating all the skills available from Newark's goldsmiths at the time (Fig. 7). A ribbon-form bar holds an elaborate monogram, and a braided chain suspends a circular plaque, on which the seal of the City of Newark is surrounded by three-dimensional chased garlands of laurel and oak. A small beehive, symbol of industry, surmounts the plaque. Although the piece is unmarked, the *Newark Evening Courier* of December 17, 1868, noted that "The whole is most artistically executed. The cost of the medal, which was manufactured by Durand, was some $250."[23] James Madison Durand had learned his trade with Taylor & Baldwin and, along with others, among them Enos Richardson, Stephen and Horace Alling, Aaron Carter, and the Baldwins, dominated Newark's jewelry industry at this period.

In 1872, James Durand was on the board of managers for the Newark Industrial Exhibition along with Horace Alling (of Alling Brother & Co.). Oscar Barnett, also a manager, was a maker of drop-presses used by jewelers. The exhibition, the first of its kind in the nation, drew publicity and famous visitors from all over the country, including Horace Greeley and President Ulysses S. Grant. Nine exhibitors related to the jewelry industry participated, including toolmakers, engravers, jeweler's bench makers, and one E.S. Nelson, a black jeweler who produced earrings.[24] However, the grandest display seems to have been Durand's own. The *Newark Daily Advertiser* reported on "the fine display of James M. Durand & Co.'s case of diamonds and exquisitely fine jewelry, valued at some $120,000." It is likely that Charles L. Tiffany supported Durand's role in this exhibition, especially in light of the quantity of diamonds displayed. The importance of Newark's jewelry industry comes into higher relief when we discover that the entire value of the goods displayed at the exhibition was $900,000.[25]

At the time of this great outpouring of industrial pride, there were reportedly thirty-nine jewelry factories in Newark.[26] It is interesting that so few of them chose to exhibit at the fair. Perhaps Durand's overweening presence discouraged smaller houses from trying to compete for attention and customers.

At the close of the 1872 exhibition, Albert Holbrook, secretary of the board of managers, and his wife were both given gifts of jewelry as thanks from the exhibitors. Mrs. Holbrook received "an elegant and costly set of jewelry valued at $125" and understandably was "very much overcome by this token of regard."[27] Holbrook himself, who was also the printer of the exhibition's commemorative catalogue, was awarded a "magnificent gold watch and chain," on the premise that "a handsome present of jewelry was worthy of the man." The presenter of the watch and chain described it to the gathered throng of Newark movers and shakers as "made in Newark, by Newark mechanics, purchased of a Newark manufacturer by the generous contributions of these exhibitors, many of whom are now before you."[28] The watch and chain were described as "quite heavy and very beautifully made," showing "elaborate design and workmanship."[29] Produced by Durand & Co., this watch and chain, whose location is now unknown, exemplified the sense of place, and of pride, that Newark's jewelry makers felt on the threshold of their greatest period of growth and influence.

Even as the great industrial exhibition was going on, a former employee of both Baldwin & Co. and Durand & Co. was changing jewelry history in his small shop on Washington Street in Newark. Ferdinand J. Herpers, Prussian by birth and trained in the jewelry shops of Pforzheim, Germany, had worked in Newark as a journeyman since 1846. He started his own shop in 1865, moving, as was the jeweler's tradition, from workbench to front office to factory ownership.[30] On September 3, 1872, during the successful run of the industrial exhibition, Herpers received a patent, among the earliest of its kind, on an improvement in diamond settings (Fig. 8). Herpers's setting was designed to increase the sparkle of diamond-set jewelry by raising the stone up and holding it nearly invisibly on tiny prongs. Herpers was the first American shop to mass produce jewelry settings with machine assistance, and his patent paved the way for the dominance of diamond jewelry in the New York factories.

As Newark's jewelry industry entered its next phase, Herpers and his other German-born contemporaries, George Krementz and Herman Unger, would gain increasing prominence. Already by 1859, Newark firms such as Alling were employing jewelers of German ancestry, a distinct switch from the native-born jewelers of English descent typical of the previous generation. In 1849–1850, there were only seventeen jewelers listed in *Holbrook's Newark City Directory* with German names, as opposed to seventy-five with names of English origin. By the 1872 directory, there were nearly three hundred jewelers with German names, compared to 459 with English names. By 1890, of the 876 people who listed themselves as jewelers or jewelry manufacturers in that year's directory, 429 had names of German origin, and 405 had names of English origin. In 1845, when Ferdinand Herpers arrived in America, he was in the vanguard. German skills and names would increasingly dominate Newark's jewelry industry during its glory years, from 1875 to 1929.

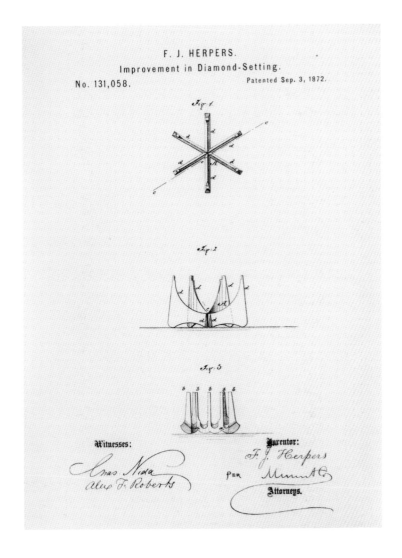

F. J. HERPERS.
Improvement in Diamond-Setting.
No. 131,058.   Patented Sep. 3, 1872.

8. Letter of patent for an improvement in diamond settings, granted September 3, 1872 to Ferdinand Herpers, Newark, The Newark Museum archives.

NOTES

1   Smith 1929, p. 4. The Goetzke exhibition was written up in *The Jewelers' Circular*, vol. 98, March 7, 1929, p. 44.

2   Reprinted in *Report and Catalogue of the First Exhibition of Newark Industries, Exclusively* (Newark: Holbrook's Steam Printery, 1882), p. 18.

3   Ibid., p. 20.

4   Bagnall 1882, p. 14.

5   Ibid., p. 16.

6   Shaw 1884, p. 601.

7   Bagnall 1882, pp. 12-14.

8   The Yale University Art Gallery has one of the finest such collections of pre-industrial American gold jewelry. Martha Gandy Fales has done extensive research into jewelry used and made in Colonial and post-Colonial America in her *Jewelry in America, 1600-1900* (Fales 1995).

9   Cunningham 1954, p. 57. Cunningham also notes Ephrais as the alternate spelling of Hinsdale's first name.

10 Fales 1995, p. 159.

11 Shaw 1884, p. 601; "Newark as a Jewelry Center," in *JCW*, vol. 44, February 3, 1902, p. 32.

12 "Progress of the Jewelry Trade in Newark, N.J.," *JCHR*, vol. 26, February 8, 1893, p. 82. The Newark Museum owns a number of silver pieces by Baldwin & Co. that were clearly modeled after New York competitors' work.

13 Charles Venable, *Silver in America, 1840-1940: A Century of Splendor*, exh. cat. (Dallas: Dallas Museum of Art, 1994), pp. 19-21.

14 Fales 1995, pp. 262, 289.

15 Cunningham 1954, p. 58.

16 Ibid.

17 Cyrus Durand to the Rev. John L. Chapman, September 13, 1864, collection of the Durand-Hedden House, Maplewood, New Jersey.

18 Shaw 1884, p. 602.

19 Ibid.

20 Herpers source files, The Newark Museum archives.

21 See "Important Partnership Change," *Press Register* (Newark), December 29, 1886, p. 1: "Mr. C.L. Tiffany has withdrawn from the well-known jewelry manufacturing firm of Durand & Co."

22 For Newark-made pieces retailed by Tiffany & Co., see Figs. 59 and 207.

23 Newark Public Library, microfilm.

24 *Report and Catalogue of the First Exhibition of Newark Industries, Exclusively*, p. 52.

25 Ibid., pp. 26, 37.

26 Shaw 1884, p. 602. "Newark as a Jewelry Center," p. 32, gives the number as thirty-two.

27 *Newark Daily Advertiser*, October 3, 1872, p. 2.

28 *Report and Catalogue of the First Exhibition of Newark Industries, Exclusively*, p. 50.

29 *Newark Daily Advertiser*, October 3, 1872, p. 2.

30 For a detailed account of the labor history of early jewelry manufacturing in Newark, see Susan Hirsch, *Roots of the American Working Class: The Industrialization of Crafts in Newark, 1800-1860* (Philadelphia: University of Pennsylvania Press, 1978).

Jewelry: The Natural Gift

JENNA WEISSMAN JOSELIT

"No other nation in the world," American fashion doyenne Muriel MacFarlane observed in 1915, "spends so lavishly upon personal adornment or so delights in the brilliancy of gems and the measure of social prestige that attaches to those who own and display them." Indeed, like many other Americans, MacFarlane confessed that she, too, could not "withstand the lure of the jewelry store."[1] *Vogue*, the bible of fashion magazines, had much the same thought. "For eight women out of ten," it related, "the lure of the jeweler's window surpasses in interest the most artfully decorated show case in the dry goods shop, or the tempting display of the costumer or milliner." "For many persons," concluded the monthly, "the subject of jewels possesses an indescribable fascination."[2]

Taking its cue from *Vogue* and other gemologically attuned periodicals, this essay explores the "lure of the jeweler's window" and, with it, the popularity of jewelry-wearing in America from the turn of the century well into the post-World War I era. During these years, the country emerged "from the lingering influences of Puritanism and provincialism" to become a citadel of consumerism.[3] Fervently embracing the "goods life," Americans, explains historian William Leach, developed a "commercial aesthetic of longing and desire."[4]

Some assuaged their hunger for material goods by purchasing "ravishing sailor suits" with attached whistles; others pined for pencil boxes.[5] "The number and variety of pencil boxes alone took one's breath away," recalled one enraptured consumer, adding that "there seemed to be no limit to the complexity of pencil boxes."[6] Still other consumers took a "public fancy to jewels."[7] Once the "ultra accoutrement of fashion" and the exclusive signature of the well-to-do, jewelry became increasingly affordable.[8] Those Americans with limited means who were said to "cod-dle a lean purse" as well as those with no financial constraints able to "indulge a fat one"—all could now find a dazzling array of items within their respective price range.[9]

That jewelry came in a wide range of styles as well as prices furthered its appeal. On the eve of World War I, as one astute student of the industry then pointed out, shoppers could easily find "vigorous" jewelry suited "to the woman of the massive type"; "intricate, oriental things" suited for the tall woman, and "fragile, tranquil ones" to suit the "delicately fashioned woman."[10] Even "mannish jewelry" (Fig. 9), traditionally eschewed by the American male, began to come into its own.[11] No longer are the "masculine members of society" neglected, observed the Bureau of Jewelry Fashions in 1917. "The unique and the unusual have been created for them in a form sufficiently conservative to appeal to the most fastidious of men, even the men who rather shy the vanities of dress, and new enough and different enough to interest the most blasé."[12]

No wonder, then, that Americans everywhere, from the most manly sort to the most fragile flower, and from Marion, Iowa, to midtown Manhattan, began eagerly to fill their jewelry boxes and adorn their persons with earrings,

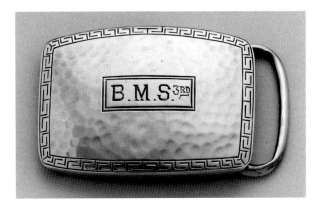

9. Man's belt buckle, by B.M. Shanley, Jr. Co., ca. 1915, gold, collection of Kevin Shanley.

10. Insect jewelry. From top: brooch of butterfly form, by A.J. Hedges & Co., 1890–1900, gold, enamel, diamonds, and demantoid garnets, private collection, Pennsylvania; segmented bracelet with winged insect, by Riker Brothers, 1890–1900, gold, diamonds, and kunzite, collection of Mr. and Mrs. Anton Civan; brooch of winged insect form, by A.J. Hedges & Co., 1890–1900, gold, enamel, diamonds, and opal, private collection.

watch chains, pocket watches, brooches, belt buckles, lavalieres, pins, and "better rosaries," many of them fashioned in Newark, America's capital of fine and affordable jewelry manufacturing, whose quality was "never questioned."[13]

Jewelry fashions, on the other hand, came and went, answerable, it seemed, only to Dame Fashion and her mercurial temperament. In the 1870s, marcasite was all the rage, only to be thoroughly eclipsed a few short years later by "interesting" insect jewelry (Fig. 10).[14] Later still, the monocle took pride of place, touted by fashion magazines as "one of the fads of the hour for both men and women"; by 1925, the same fashion pundits predicted the return of the earring, noting that "ears again are asserting themselves."[15]

Through it all, Americans democratized the wearing of jewelry, transforming a perquisite of the rich into a prerogative of the many. Advertisements, etiquette manuals, sermons, and trade journals variously abetted, encouraged, and at times even fretted over this transformation. Taken together, these texts make clear jewelry's relationship to vernacular culture, gift-giving and gender and, in the process, highlight the aesthetics of everyday life.

The Etiquette of Jewelry—Or, How Many Jewels?

Wearing jewelry was not only a keen source of pleasure and a treat for the eyes, it was also a minefield, or so etiquette writers, those "apostles of civility," would have their readers believe.[16] "One of the few ways in which a man or woman *unerringly* expresses individuality is in the use or misuse of jewelry," they trenchantly observed, hoping to replace idiosyncrasy with a universal system of gemological do's and don'ts.[17]

Heavily consulted, if not always heeded, etiquette texts provided aspiring middle-class Americans of the Gilded and Victorian ages with the logistical and social tools necessary to navigate an increasingly complex world. Rich in consumer goods and new opportunities for display, gift-giving, and social exchange, this new world beckoned with one hand and bewildered with the other. Etiquette manuals leapt into the breach, imposing a grid on the serendipity of social exchange. Unsure of how to greet a former beau while *en promenade*, why, just turn to page 329 of John Young's 1885 text, *Our Deportment, or the Manners, Conduct and Dress of the Most Refined Society*. Uncertain of what to wear to a tea party, Emily Post's *Etiquette: The Blue Book of Social Usage* would restore your sartorial confidence in no time (see under: Dress—Afternoon Tea).

Etiquette writers also sought to temper the anxieties of those whose grip on the ladder of upward mobility was anything but secure. Take, for example, Mrs. Mary F. Armstrong's *Habits and Manners* (1888). Originally written for the students at Virginia's Hampton Institute, the volume was later "adapted to general use" for members of the African-American community, now encouraged to place their faith in the "gospel of civility."[18] "Propriety of deportment on your own part," Armstrong wrote reassuringly, "will do more than anything else towards securing for you fair and proper treatment from others."[19] Similarly, immigrants to America, baffled by the nation's "zippy and exhilarating climate," turned to etiquette manuals like *Etikete* for advice.[20] Written in Yiddish, this 1912 "guide to proper behavior, politeness and good manners for men and women" taught would-be Americans to comport themselves like proper ladies and gentlemen at all times and to "value taste more than ostentation."[21]

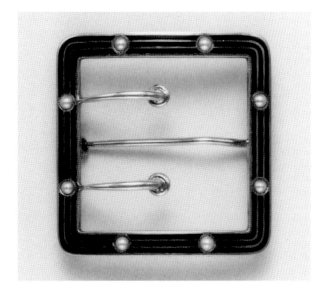

11. Buckle-form sash pin, by Riker Brothers, 1900–1910, gold, enamel, and pearls, The Newark Museum, Purchase 1993 The Millicent Fenwick Fund (93.179)

Whether intended for the newly emancipated, the newly arrived, or the nouveau riche, etiquette books took great pains to establish the appropriate "social grammar" for the wearing and exchange of jewelry.[22] A number of different factors, among them social setting, and the wearer's age, gender, and religion, supplied the "jewelry password into the sanctums of society," underscoring the belief that pins, necklaces, and chains possessed "as marked and distinct a time

and place when they should be worn as the fasts and feasts on the church calendar."[23] For starters, etiquette writers fashioned an elaborate sartorial geography of the world, making sure their readers would know how to dress properly when on the street, in the office, at church, or on the train. "To make either too much or too little of your clothes is a serious mistake, and one against which I greatly desire to help you guard yourself," Mrs. Armstrong told her readers, urging them to refrain from wearing "useless ornaments" and brightly colored attire in public. "You will find that among ladies and gentlemen a very plain reality (Fig. 11) is better than a very fine sham, and that it is good to be true in dress as well as in other things."[24]

The importance of keeping up appearances also loomed large in Hallie E. Rives' *The Complete Book of Etiquette—With Social Forms for All Ages and Occasions* (1926). True to its word (and title), Rives' guidebook even devised a highly detailed chart, several pages in length, that coordinated hats, shoes, handbags, and individual pieces of jewelry with the time of day, the occasion, and the venue. While at home, the properly accoutred woman, the chart made clear, should wear just her engagement and wedding ring; if at a lecture, though, she'd do well to don pearls and a pair of earrings; a formal luncheon, in turn, called for pearls, rings, and a set of semi-precious chains but "nothing showy."[25] "If you care to be taken for a well-bred person," wrote Emily Post, the dean of comportment, "never wear anything that is exaggerated."[26]

Age considerations also determined what constituted "correct jewelry,"[27] a point emphasized by such popular *fin-de-siècle* texts as *The Well-Bred Girl in Society*, published in 1898 by Doubleday as part of the Ladies Home Journal Girls Library. While most authorities preferred to see young girls bedecked with flowers rather than jewels, several grudgingly conceded, "It is in America alone that the matter of jewels would be likely to come up for consideration in a young girl's toilet."[28] Mindful, then, of both tradition and convention, "the well-bred girl" displayed restraint. "Excepting a string of small pearls, or some dainty brooch miniature affixed to a band of velvet around the throat, ornament . . . is almost unseen in full dress among the really well-bred people [Fig. 12]."[29]

Still, in the world of the "really well-bred," gender had the most to do with determining the limits and possibilities of the sartorially permissible. "As apparel oft proclaims the man," categorically declared one authority, "so does jewelry oft proclaim the woman," establishing in the popular mind a hard and fast distinction between male and female attire.[30] "In America men are not particularly receptive to the idea of jewelry," stated *The Complete Book of Etiquette*, furthering that distinction. "A man may go through life without possessing any valuable pieces and his friends be none the wiser."[31] Women, however,

had no such luck; "every woman," it was said, "loves good jewelry."[32] Some cultural arbiters even went a step further by insisting that "the love for gems and jewels is innate in the heart of women, be they Jewish, Mohammedan or Christian."[33] To counter, then, the ever-lurking fear of effeminacy, etiquette manuals routinely emphasized that the authentic gent was one who left jewelry-wearing to the ladies. "Jewels are an ornament to women, but a blemish to men. They bespeak either effeminacy or a love of display. . . . The best jewel a man can wear is his honor."[34]

Over time, resistance to the idea of a bejeweled man gently weakened. By the later years of the nineteenth century, the practice of men wearing some form of ornamentation was no longer *verboten*, only circumscribed. Enlisting the seemingly unassailable virtue of "good taste," etiquette arbiters began to tolerate a modicum of manly adornment. "It is not considered in good taste for men to wear *much* jewelry. They may with propriety wear one gold ring, studs, and cuff-buttons, and a watch chain. . . . Anything more is like a superabundance of ornament [Fig. 13]."[35]

12. Oval brooch or lace pin, by Kollmar, Rauch & Co., 1900–1910, gold, pearls, diamond, and sapphires, ½ × 1 in., The Newark Museum, Purchase 1995 Membership Endowment Fund (95.105.3)

13. A group of "appropriate" man's jewelry, ca. 1910–1920. Left to right: pocket knife and chain, by Thomas W. Adams & Co., gold, Gift of Ulysses Grant Dietz, 1996, in Memory of Edward Johnson Dietz (96.40.2); pair of stiff-bar cuff buttons, by Larter & Sons, gold, The Newark Museum, Gift of Frank I. Liveright, 1971 (71.314); set of shirt studs, by W.F. Cory & Brother, gold and amethyst cabochons, Gift of Katherine Kinnane, 1973 (73.509a–c); signet ring with carved intaglio seal, by Larter & Sons for Cartier, New York, gold and nephrite, Purchase 1994 Stella Goldstein Purchase Fund (94.153)

Another bit of advice: "No well-bred gentleman will load himself with jewelry. He may wear one ring, a watch chain, studs and cuff buttons."[36]

By the second decade of the twentieth century, "propriety" gave way to an entirely new set of norms. No longer was jewelry anathematized for its putative unmanliness. Instead, as the jewelry industry gleefully pointed out at the time, "there is no lack of good attractive masculine merchandise."[37] Goods ranged from sterling silver and 14-carat gold buckles "of substantial

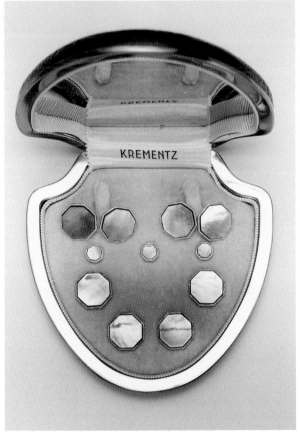

14. Man's dress set in original box, by Krementz & Co., 1940–1950, consisting of bodkin-type cufflinks, shirt studs, and vest buttons, rolled-gold plate and smoked pearl, The Newark Museum, Gift of Mr. and Mrs. Irving J. Soloway, 1993 (93.185)

quality and mannish design" ("they grip like a bulldog and release at the flip of a finger," boasted their manufacturer, the William B. Kerr Co.) to handsome onyx and platinum shirt studs, vest buttons, and matching cufflinks.[38] These items, declared their manufacturer, Krementz & Co., "are approved by Dame Fashion, for their chaste designs, eminent quality and authoritative correctness [Fig. 14]."[39] More important, the company explained, "there is a tone of distinction and refinement of finish in Krementz Evening Jewelry which makes it the first choice of men with whom correctness of dress is a principle."[40]

Even those with the most masculine and principled of jewelry wardrobes, however, had to

be constantly vigilant lest they fall prey to the siren of superabundance. "Whatever the tempting glow of gem-set cuff links, inlaid cigarette cases or gleaming rings, the man of refinement eschews them," insisted an etiquette writer of the 1920s.[41] Above all else, the proverbial man of refinement made sure to eschew diamonds. "A gentleman finds no other use for diamonds than to deck his wife and daughters with them. The man who wears diamond studs and rings is in danger of being taken for a bookmaker or a pawnbroker" or, worse still, a Jew (Fig. 15).[42]

The prospect of being mistaken for a member of the Jewish people seemed to have offended quite a number of American sensibilities as far back as the Gilded Age, inspiring commentators such as the pseudonymous Henry Lunettes, author of *The American Gentleman's Guide to Politeness and Fashion*, to offer the following helpful hint: for those few young men who insist on "sporting" a diamond or two, "never let their number induce in the minds of beholders the recollection that a travelling Jew—whether from hereditary distrust of the stability of circumstances,

15. Man's cigarette lighter to be worn as a fob, by Ronson, Inc., 1920–1930, gold, platinum, and diamonds. The Newark Museum, Gift of N.S. Rosengarten, 1991, in memory of his grandfather, Louis V. Aronson (91.100). Louis V. Aronson, the owner of the Newark-based Ronson lighter firm, would have been flouting convention in the 1920s by wearing this gold lighter with platinum-set diamonds as a watch fob.

16. Pendant in the Louis XVI style, by Sloan & Co., 1900–1910, gold, pearls, and citrine, private collection, New York City.

or from some other consideration of personal convenience, usually carries his entire fortune about his person! Better the simplest fastenings of mother-of-pearl than such staring vulgarity of display."[43]

Women, with their "innate" predisposition for gold and diamonds, simply could not make such a commitment, or so it was widely believed. Instead, they were actively encouraged to seek the counsel and the steadying hand of an Emily Post, a Hallie Rives, or a Walter Houghton, all of whom exhorted their female readers to "pursue refinement" rather than ostentation. "A lady may be covered with jewels, and yet not show the slightest good taste," chided Houghton's popular text, *American Etiquette and Rules of Politeness*, a view enthusiastically endorsed by its Yiddish counterpart which, with an uncharacteristic show of passion, denounced those who would wear an abundance of jewelry as ill-tutored and unrefined "yentas."[44]

Time and again, these tracts cautioned against succumbing to extravagance and excessive display. Always use jewelry "sparingly," and never wear diamonds during the day, they coun-

seled, urging their readers to make sure they didn't give in to the temptation to "outdazzle one's neighbor," a common enough phenomenon abroad; as *Vogue* observed, "too much jewelry [is] worn in foreign society."[45] At evening functions, reported the magazine's overseas correspondent, "few refrain . . . from overloading themselves with a variety of jewels; as many as two and three necklaces are worn by those who consider their taste beyond criticism. This weakness, combined with the lavish use of strass [glass] gems in full-dress gown embroidery is barbaric, loud and discordant." Model American women, in contrast, were ladies whose motto was moderation and whose bosoms sparkled with subtlety (Fig. 16). "Jewelry well selected and worn in the right way at the right time," they affirmed, "will often lend a much more pleasing effect than far more costly pieces worn indiscriminately and in defiance of the canons of good taste."[46]

The restraint and sense of balance allegedly characteristic of the ideal American woman not only distinguished her from her more "barbaric" European sisters, but also set her apart from the parvenu, especially the much-dreaded and much satirized parvenu of immigrant origin, with her penchant for "flashing jewelry" and "glittering tinsels."[47] Abraham Cahan's classic tale of the Eastern European Jewish experience in America, *The Rise of David Levinsky* (1917), contains an acidly rendered portrait of one such character, "Auntie Yetta whose fingers were a veritable jewelry store."[48] When in public, Yetta made a point of smoothing her hair for the sole purpose of exhibiting her rings. But then she was not alone. Another woman, "whose fingers were as heavily laden," vied with Yetta. From time to time, this other woman "would flirt her interlocked hands, in feigned absentmindedness, thus flashing her diamonds upon the people around her. At one moment it became something like a race between her and Auntie Yetta."

The sight of thousands of Auntie Yettas flaunting their newfound wealth on their fingers occasioned considerable distress among their German-Jewish coreligionists. "We must prove ourselves to be genteel, cultured and dignified . . . and teach our thoughtless sisters that ostentation is unbecoming and that modesty is a jewel," they vowed, without so much as hinting at the fact that, only a generation or two earlier, they, too, had faced similar criticism.[49] As the *American Jewess* glumly observed in 1899, "The Jewess, more than any other woman, is accused of indulging and displaying a fondness for jewels. Such censure was never justified: Jewesses do not love jewels more than any other woman and display them with no greater eagerness than others."[50] How, then, to account for this perception? "The personality of the Jewess," its champion gamely explained, "is rather showy and even a modest spread of jewelry tends to make her look vulgar."[51]

Nevertheless, many German-Jewish women made a concerted effort to "discard jewelry" and to "conquer" their affection for display.[52] Little by little, the American-Jewish woman has come to recognize the virtue of restraint, the *American Jewess* proudly affirmed at the turn of the century. "She at last realizes that golden ornaments are not becoming to her style of beauty. . . . All hail this new American beauty, who satisfied with her natural God-given endowment, discards flashing ornamentation and to a certain extent boycotts jewelry. Heaven be praised that jewels are no longer synonymous with Jewess."[53] By then, it seemed, jewelry had become everyone's cross.

Not a Necessity—But

As one century gave way to another, retailers and manufacturers joined together in an effort to dispel the "erroneous idea that. . . jewelry is a luxury."[54] Simultaneously whetting and satisfying America's growing appetite for glittery things, the local jeweler drew heavily on the art and artifice of advertising "to make every man and woman in my town believe that some piece of ornamental jewelry was essential to their being well-dressed. It's just a matter of education."[55] "The folks in your town," explained Norman R. Williams, a Chicago "specialist in jewelry store advertising" addressing an audience of small-town jewelry store owners, "are human like you and I. Interested in things that are to their own advantage. Influenced by good advertising. Buying the things that are advertised well and continuously. If you didn't own the store, would your advertising interest your wife?"[56]

Buoyed by pleasing advertisements and a "sympathetic public," the jewelry store came to be as much a fixture of Main Street America as the general store.[57] Marion, Iowa, had its very own "first class jewelry store," as did Niles, California, whose establishment was "opposite the post office and next door to the only motion picture theatre in town."[58] In each locale, the jeweler came to feel that it was his "duty" to "see that the ladies in his community are supplied with jewelry correct for all occasions."[59] As often as not, local jewelers in Niles and Marion carried items made in Newark, a city which had already emerged by the late nineteenth century as one of the nation's leading manufacturing centers of consumer goods, from sturdy luggage to dainty earrings. "The trunk you travel with is, nine cases out of ten, of Newark manufacture," *The New York Times* reminded its readers as early as 1872. "The hat you wear was made there, the buttons on your coat, the shirt on your back, your brush, the tinware you use in your kitchen, the oil-cloth you walk on, the harness and bit you drive with, all owe to Newark their origin; and as to your wife's chain, bracelets, ear rings and pendants, they have been fashioned by some cunning Newark goldsmith."[60]

Newark jewelry was just as widely known for its variety, quality, and economy as its "cunning" craftsmanship. "Very fine jewelers recognize Shanley Belt Buckles as the most fitting gifts for men—gifts that reap affection as use increases their beauty," boasted the Newark manufacturer (Fig. 17).[61] Much the same could be said of the Blancard wedding ring whose "exquisite designs, careful workmanship and beautiful finish has no equal at so moderate a price," or of Krementz & Co.'s shirt stud (Fig. 18).[62] "Simplicity itself, it grips like an anchor"; this tiny item not only revolutionized the industry but brought domestic bliss to households throughout the nation.[63] So easy to use, the Krementz shirt stud, related one consumer, "has undoubtedly held millions of tempers in subjection."[64]

Shoppers, eyeing a Shanley belt buckle, a Krementz shirt stud, or a Blancard wedding ring nestled in a velvet-lined vitrine, eagerly took advantage of a growing number of "gift-giving opportunities" to purchase these items, especially for others. By the 1910s, such opportunities abounded: jewelers, as well as florists and greeting card manufacturers, diligently promoted them. "Here comes the bride," trilled jewelry

Where beauty grows with use—

IN fashioning platinum or gold or silver—or, perhaps, these precious metals in combination—the artist-craftsmen here put artistry and quality and usefulness into Shanley Belt Buckles.

Men who wear Shanley Belt Buckles find that their beauty grows with use; that they feel for them that subtle friendliness that used to go to pipes alone.

Fine jewelers show the name Shanley stamped on the back—the guarantee of the very, very finest in belt buckles that you can possibly give a man.

B. M. SHANLEY JR. COMPANY
Manufacturers of fine platinum and gold jewelry
NEWARK, N. J.

In platinum, green gold, sterling silver; hammered, engine-turned or striped designs—place for monogram. Hold the belt securely and release it instantly.

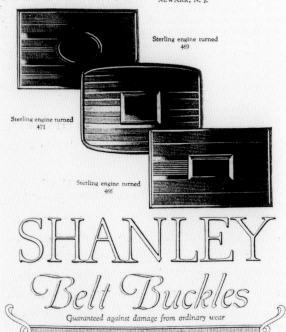

Sterling engine turned 469

Sterling engine turned 471

Sterling engine turned 466

SHANLEY
Belt Buckles
Guaranteed against damage from ordinary wear

Krementz
Evening Jewelry

YOU can distinguish Krementz studs and vest buttons with cuff links to match by the correctness of the designs and by the bodkin clutch back on the studs and vest buttons.

This practical bodkin clutch can be inserted as easily in the stiffest shirt front as in a soft shirt. It holds as securely as an anchor, yet a slight pressure of the finger is sufficient to release it.

Sold by better jewelers everywhere. Write for the names of those nearest who have a representative assortment of designs in stock

Krementz & Co.   **Newark, New Jersey**

Goes in like a needle

Holds like an anchor.

stores, readying their wares in preparation for the "bridal months" of May and June, while others, eager to become "*the* gift store of the community," cast their sights on the calendar as a whole.[65] "This is a gift-giving age . . . now we are insidiously tempted to give at Easter, Mother's Day, Father's Day, Thanksgiving, christenings, confirmation, graduations, weddings and anniversaries of all kinds," a critic sourly observed, underscoring the cyclical nature of gift-giving in the modern era.[66]

But many, perhaps most, potential gift buyers did not see things quite so darkly. Instead, they delighted in celebrating Christmas, the grand "festival of consumption," by purchasing tie pins and chain-link bags, sterling silver lorgnettes, pearl necklaces, and rosaries that came in as many as nine different styles and twelve different colors.[67] "Rings and pins, the art of the jeweler and the skill of the dress-maker . . . these with one great purpose are consecrated, and in the material lavishness of the season is seen the dreams of the world come true," mused a lyrical Theodore Dreiser.[68] A trade publication put it far more bluntly: "Santa Claus knows that a dollar goes farther at the jewelry store than it does anywhere else, in procuring usefulness and pleasure. . . . Ask Santa Claus. He Knows!"[69]

Over the years, Easter joined with Christmas to become a celebrated time for gift-giving, underscoring anew the ease with which so many Americans blurred the boundaries between the sacred and the secular. "A gift at Easter is becoming a Custom, as it should," observed the *National Jeweler*, the house publication of the American National Retail Jewelers Association, in 1925. "Easter is as appropriate a gift time as Christmas. Mr. Jeweler should avail himself of the opportunity to build up the custom."[70]

Some customers did exactly that, purchasing Day, Clark & Co.'s "distinctive and felicitous" Juliet Gift Set, a suite of hat and veil pins fashioned in the form of a miniature calla lily, just in time for the springtime festival (Figs. 19, 150).[71] Others got into the "Easter giving" mood by distributing crosses and 10-inch rosaries like those produced by the Vatti Rosary Company.[72] "Thousands are being sold as gifts to Catholics," the company boasted, proud of the popular appeal of its ecclesiastical jewelry. "A girl's gift to a man, to wear on a Waldemar chain; A man's gift to a girl, to carry by chain on the gloved finger" (see Fig. 181).[73]

Increasingly, Americans also took to marking personal rites of passage—birthdays, first communions, confirmations, graduations, engagements, and weddings—with gifts of jewelry. "Birthdays and the 21st in particular," when a young woman crosses "the line of demarcation between youth and ladyhood," are wonderful occasions for giving jewelry, proclaimed *Jewelry Fashions*, an "authoritative" guide, in 1917. "These days," it quickly added, the birthday girl "can't don a long skirt—even mother wears hers to her shoe tops—and her hair has been 'up' for a year or more, so what hallmark has she by which to announce to all the world her newly

acquired honors? The privilege of wearing 'real' jewelry."[74]

Pearls often topped the birthday girl's wish list. "Whether she is three or three-score, pearls are a fitting gift," related one manufacturer, noting that "people think of pearls when they think of birthdays."[75] "A necklace of real pearls adds just that touch to feminine attractiveness that makes a charming woman even more so," added another.[76] Prized for their versatility and practicality, pearls "clash with no color of dress,"

19. Advertisement for Day, Clark & Co., *Vogue*, vol. 45, March 15, 1915, p. 96.

"never look really out of place," and may "be worn at practically all times, except the most informal."[77]

Pearl-wearing brides, in turn, were encouraged to bestow a "V-shaped, jointed, gold pin" on their bridesmaids.[78] This item, its manufacturers, Thomas W. Adams & Co., related, "gives the necessary finishing touch to their costume, whether a morning or evening ceremony (Fig. 20)."[79] Grooms, too, were actively encouraged to bestow something tangible on their groomsmen. "Gifts to the ushers are mere man's nearest approach to jewelry," proclaimed *Vogue* in June

1914, highlighting the availability of cufflinks, cigarette cases, tie pins and gold cigar cutters.[80]

While gifts of jewelry tended to reinforce some of society's most firmly held and cherished notions of gender, from time to time an enterprising jeweler or an imaginative journalist might propose breaking the mold. Why not "equalize the sexes," suggested one writer who, bored by the American tradition of gendered gift-giving—of cigars on Father's Day and flowers on Mother's Day—proposed an alternative:

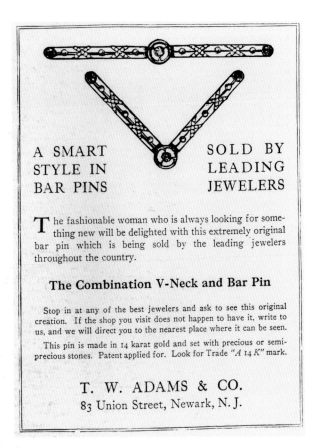

A SMART STYLE IN BAR PINS

SOLD BY LEADING JEWELERS

The fashionable woman who is always looking for something new will be delighted with this extremely original bar pin which is being sold by the leading jewelers throughout the country.

The Combination V-Neck and Bar Pin

Stop in at any of the best jewelers and ask to see this original creation. If the shop you visit does not happen to have it, write to us, and we will direct you to the nearest place where it can be seen.

This pin is made in 14 karat gold and set with precious or semi-precious stones. Patent applied for. Look for Trade "A 14 K" mark.

T. W. ADAMS & CO.
83 Union Street, Newark, N. J.

20. Advertisement for Thomas W. Adams & Co., *Vogue*, vol. 43, March 15, 1914, p. 98.

"Why not say it with jewelry on both days and thus put father and mother upon an equality basis?"[81]

Still, nothing more clearly underscored the extent to which gifts of jewelry had become inextricably bound up with the life cycle and the inequalities of gender than the prominence of the "all-important" engagement ring, the "conventional emblem" of a woman's impending nuptials (Fig. 21).[82] Usually a diamond solitaire (although, conceded some jewelers and even a few etiquette arbiters, "fashion rather prefers a large semi-precious [gemstone] to a microscopic diamond") (Fig. 22), the engagement ring tangibly and unambiguously proclaimed a woman's change in status.[83] A symbol whose meaning was shaped as much by consensus as convention, the engagement ring was reputed to be the one gift that "is purely spontaneous, called forth by affection only."[84]

Admittedly, an engagement ring was not "indispensable," or so conceded Mrs. Burton Kingsland, writing in the pages of the *Ladies Home Journal* of 1909 on "Good Manners and Good Form." The ring is "merely the outward and visible sign of an engagement and in no way affects the real fact. . . . [T]here are, doubtless, many persons who never receive any ring," she wrote reassuringly, "and the compact is none the less sacred."[85] Etiquette manuals, though, didn't quite see eye to eye with Mrs. Kingsland. As early as the 1890s, they held forth on "The Ring," describing in detail its placement ("on the fourth finger of the left hand, counting from the thumb"), its setting (the diamond is a "very appropriate stone for this purpose, either *solitaire* or incluster"), and when to present it. "Generally even the most impulsive girl can keep her secret until she has her ring, for until this accepted token of betrothal has been placed . . . she does not really feel properly engaged."[86]

As summer followed spring, the wedding ring—preferably a simple gold band—followed the diamond solitaire, generating additional goodwill as well as revenue for the jewelry trade. "The business revolving about the newlyweds is always worth having," jewelers were told. "Often it develops into regular family trade."[87] Fired by that possibility, retailers throughout the country decorated their windows with imaginatively wrought wedding scenes. In Chicago, C.D. Peacock's recreated the wedding of the "first American bride—Pocahontas," while Rank & Motteram in Milwaukee drew the attention of passersby with a "bridal group" of Kewpie dolls consisting of a minister, the bride, and her groom.[88]

Rank & Motteram could have just as easily introduced a jeweler into their "bridal group": like the minister, he too had become a respectable member of the community, with a highly burnished reputation to boot. "With his ear to the ground of the fashion world," the modern jeweler was no longer to be confused

21. Wedding and engagement rings, by Ferdinand Herpers, 1875-1885, gold, platinum, and imitation diamonds, The Newark Museum, Gift of Mrs. Henry F. Herpers, 1971 (71.304, 71.305)

22. Gold rings set with semiprecious stones, 1875–1950. Left row: F. & F. Felger, with carved jade, The Newark Museum, Purchase, 1996, The Members' Fund (96.72.3); Steeber-Kraus, with cabochon citrine, The Newark Museum, Purchase 1996 The Members' Fund (96.72.2); W.C. Edge & Co., woman's signet, private collection of a member of the Northern New Jersey Chapter of the Victorian Society. Middle row: Church & Co., with onyx, same owner; Jones & Woodland, with cherry amber, same owner; Durand & Co., with carved jade intaglio, private collection. Right row: Franklin Jewelry Co., with ruby, The Newark Museum, Gift of Vera and Sol Goodman, 1994 (94.141); Jabel, Inc., white gold with diamonds, The Newark Museum, Gift of Mrs. Mildred Baker, 1994 (94.64); Ferdinand Herpers, with cameo, The Newark Museum, Gift of Mrs. Henry F. Herpers, 1973 (73.314)

with the lowly repairman, suspect salesman or, worse still, the seedy pawnbroker of old.[89] Acutely attuned to both the economics of the marketplace and the vagaries of style, the modern jeweler was now to be seen as a paragon of probity and a pillar of rectitude. "The jeweler of today must be much more than a salesman. He is, indeed, an arbiter of taste . . . a man—almost an institution in the community—whose knowledge is accurate and whose judgement is to be relied upon with safety and satisfaction."[90] Every inch the businessman, from his three-piece suit to his tasteful gold cufflinks, the modern jeweler bespoke respectability. "The jeweler of today should be one of the best appareled and most popular men in his town [whose] most valuable asset . . . is his good name."[91]

Some jewelers, in fact, took this notion literally to heart. "The name Everts goes a long way in Dallas," the eponymous jeweler proclaimed. "Everts's name on the box adds much to the gift, but nothing to the cost." Hertzberg Jewelers was quick to agree. "The Hertzberg name on the box—how much it means." References like these spoke not only to the jewelers' probity and pedigree but to the customer's as well: after all, consumers hailed a gift from Hertzberg Jewelers as "proof incontestable of the giver's generosity and judgement."[92]

Not everyone, though, was quite so easily persuaded. In this instance, as in so many others bearing on modern life, ecclesiastical opposition ran high. As early as the 1870s, evangelical publications upbraided the otherwise devout for their devotion to "gilded trinkets" and "glittering . . . bridal presents.[93] Fervently maintaining that the "eternal fitness of all things" embraced plain dress as much as plain living, pious Protestants wholeheartedly embraced the tenets of austerity.

Some churchmen, to be sure, were not entirely opposed to material display, provided it was done tastefully. Horace Bushnell, the mid-nineteenth-century Congregationalist leader, for example, actually fashioned a "theology of taste," in which he affirmed the religious value of refinement.[94] Bushnell's belief that "taste is God's legacy" allowed believers "to pursue refinement in domestic life and taste and sensibility in personality as part of their salvation."[95] Though separated by decades and denomination, several early twentieth-century Reform rabbis,

such as Hyman Enelow, espoused a similar view. "I don't believe in robbing life of its little joys in the name of an all-compelling and all-saving sociology," explained the Kansas City cleric. "Gifts have their right and place in life."[96] Still, even the most materially aware clergy drew the line at overly jeweled and ornate crosses, a feeling shared by their cosmopolitan counterpart, the etiquette writer. "The sacred emblem of the cross set in shining jewels and worn at [a] ball or rout," chided one high priestess of good manners, "shows a most pitiable ignorance of the eternal fitness of things."[97]

Meanwhile, believers in the social gospel, like urban crusader and writer Washington Gladdens, also found it hard to square the love of glitter with the squalid realities of urban life. Take, for example, his well-known cautionary children's tale, "Santa Claus in the Pulpit."[98] In this 1890 fable, a young fellow named Mortimer encounters Santa Claus while dozing off during a Christmas-day sermon given by the minister of the "Minnesota Avenue Presbygational Church." Santa, armed with his very own "Grand Stereoscopic Moral Tester," is determined to teach young Mortimer and other equally gift-hungry children the true meaning of Christmas by laying bare the economic, human, and social costs of improvidence through a series of object lessons.

"A beautiful necklace, with links of solid gold" is flashed on the stereoscope screen, occasioning murmurs of delight, especially from the girls in the pews. "Isn't it a daisy," they say, whereupon Santa urges them to take a closer look. As the "ethical lens" of the Grand Stereoscopic Moral Tester shines its brilliant spotlight on the necklace, they come to see that "every link of that golden chain was transformed into an iron fetter." It is fastened tightly around the wrists of dozens of downtrodden, impoverished women workers, the employees of the gentleman who purchased the necklace. "It is out of their lifeblood that he is coining his gold," Santa says. "And to think that such a man should take the money that he makes in this way to buy a Christmas present. Ugh!"

In Jewish circles, the "red-letter day" of confirmation engendered similar, though slightly less dramatic, expressions of disapproval from both the clergy and children's book authors.

"Time to cry 'halt,'" warned Rochester rabbi Horace J. Wolf in the spring of 1915, inveighing against his congregants' confirmation-induced spending sprees. "All over the land jewelers and florists and booksellers and dressmakers and tailors are preparing for their annual harvest: Confirmation Day is at hand."[99] A decade later, novelist Elma Ehrlich Levinger returned to this theme in her 1925 tale, "Clothes: A Shabuoth Story."[100] In it, a group of female confirmands on the eve of their confirmation at Temple Emanuel avidly discuss "a most important problem": what to wear. In their discursive zeal for white kid slippers, silk stockings, lace dresses, and jewelry, the girls are completely oblivious to the growing alienation of one of their number, the smart but ever so poor Ida, whose struggling family simply can't afford such an elaborate display.

Rather than risk the disapproval of her chums and "spoil everything" by not making "a good appearance," Ida sells a cherished pair of gold bracelets "just to get clothes like the rest of us." But, as luck (and narrative convention) would have it, her beloved grandma, miles away in Canada, falls gravely ill and the money is spent on medical care. With no other resources and nothing to wear, Ida forgoes her very own confirmation. "But, why didn't you come anyhow, even if you didn't get a new dress," Irene, one of Ida's friends and the proud owner of a brand-new "exquisite gold chain," later demands to know. Ida, "her voice breaking into sobs," refuses to explain.

Later that evening, at the dinner table, a much chastened Irene tells her parents about Ida's plight and pleads with her father to take back the newly purchased necklace. "I know I couldn't wear it again without thinking how I dressed up like a peacock and kept Ida away," she tells him, seconds before bursting into tears and running from the room. "I'm glad she's unhappy over her unthoughtfulness," Irene's mother declares. "Perhaps it did her good to be confirmed after all. She needed this lesson."

Ultimately, despite lessons in morality, the insights of Grand Stereoscopic Moral Testers, or allusions to the Almighty, Americans found it awfully hard to resist the ornamental. Jewelry, they came to believe, was a "natural gift," an object whose meaning transcended its materiality and cost.[101] "There is no doubt that the giving of presents gives greater happiness to the human race than almost everything else, for it is by such presents that man gives expression to his love of family, of friends, of art." Jewelry, the *ne plus ultra* of presents, "is the affectionate expression of beautiful thought—it embraces sincerity and the desire to spread happiness," insisted one industry leader.[102] Firmly embedded in America's culture of celebration, jewelry came to be seen as the most munificent and transcendent of material objects: through some kind of alchemy, it affirmed the merchant's respectability, the giver's generosity, and the recipient's good fortune, binding all three together like links in a chain. Unlike other material objects, such as flowers which wilted or furs which molted, "the creations in the jeweler's shop," its devotees insisted, were enduring. They "do not die with the passing of a day or a season, but are to live perhaps for a lifetime."[103] In the end, jewelry was "imperishable—a gift that lasts, like the fidelity of a fine friendship, for as long as life itself!"[104]

Notes

1 Muriel MacFarlane, "Things That Are Selling and Salable," *NJO*, vol. 11, May 1915, p. 357.

2 "The Mode in Precious Jewels," *Vogue*, vol. 35, May 1, 1910, p. 21.

3 Mrs. Burton Harrison, *The Well-Bred Girl in Society* (New York: Doubleday & Co., 1898), p. 141.

4 William Leach, *Land of Desire: Merchants, Power, and the Rise of a New American Culture* (New York: Pantheon Books, 1993), p. 9. "Goods life" is an expression coined by Louis Mumford, as quoted in Thomas J. Schlereth, *Victorian America: Transformations in Everyday Life 1876-1915* (New York: Harper Collins, 1991), p. xv.

5 Samuel Chotzinoff, *A Lost Paradise: Early Reminiscences* (New York: Alfred A. Knopf, 1955), p. 63.

6 Ibid.

7 "An Early Easter," *NJO*, vol. 5, March 1910, p. 131.

8 *NJ*, vol. 21, April 1925, p. 21.

9 *NJ*, vol. 21, December 1925, p. 23. See also "The Limitless Possibilities of the Limited Purse," in *Jewelry Fashions* 1917, p. 13.

10 "Suiting Jewels to the Woman," *Vogue*, vol. 43, April 1, 1914, p. 90.

11 "Good Gifts for Men," *NJ*, vol. 26, December 1930, p. 30.

12 "Old Favorites in New Guises," in *Jewelry Fashions* 1917, p. 44.

13 W.J. Feeley Co., "Makers of the Rosary in Fine Jewels," *NJO*, vol. 11, January 1915, p. 37; Smith 1929, p. 5.

14 "Some Interesting Insect Jewelry," *NJO*, vol. 7, June 1911, p. 257.

15 "The Monocle: A Fad of the Moment," *Vogue*, vol. 37, January 15, 1911, p. 43; Muriel MacFarlane, "Appropriate Jewelry Never More Important," *NJ*, vol. 21, September 1925, p. 66.

16 John Kasson, *Rudeness and Civility: Manners in Nineteenth-Century Urban America* (New York: Hill and Wang, 1991), p. 62.

17 Hallie E. Rives, *The Complete Book of Etiquette—With Social Forms for All Ages and Occasions* (Philadelphia: John C. Winston, 1926), p. 131, emphasis added.

18 Kasson, *Rudeness and Civility*, p. 54.

19 Mary F. Armstrong, *Habits and Manners, Revised Edition, Adapted to General Use* (Hampton, Virginia.: Normal School Press, 1888), p. 80.

20 S.N. Behrman, "The Point of the Needle," in *The Worcester Account* (New York: Random House, 1954), p. 229.

21 Tashrak, *Etikete* (New York: Hebrew Publishing Co., 1912), p. 48.

22 Kasson, *Rudeness and Civility*, p. 93.

23 Cited in an advertisement for Krementz & Co., *Vogue*, vol. 47, February 1, 1916, p. 118; "Jeweled Chains, Collars, and Tiara," *Vogue*, vol. 8, November 1896, p. 406.

24 Armstrong, *Habits and Manners*, pp. 17, 29.

25 Rives, *The Complete Book of Etiquette*, pp. 134–139.

26 Emily Post, *Etiquette: The Blue Book of Social Usage*, new and enlarged edition (New York: Funk & Wagnalls, 1927), p. 583.

27 Taken from an advertisement for Krementz & Company, *Vogue*, vol. 45, March 15, 1915, p. 116.

28 Harrison, *The Well-Bred Girl*, p. 31.

29 Ibid.

30 "Suiting Jewels to the Woman," p. 90.

31 Rives, *The Complete Book of Etiquette*, p. 133.

32 *NJ*, vol. 16, December 1920, p. 90.

33 "Suit Your Ornaments to Your Style," *American Jewess*, vol. 8, January 1899, p. 45.

34 Cecil B. Hartley, *The Gentlemen's Book of Etiquette and Manual of Politeness* (Boston: DeWolfe, Fiske & Co., 1873), p. 138.

35 John H. Young, *Our Deportment or, The Manners, Conduct and Dress of the Most Refined Society* (Detroit: n. p., 1885), p. 325, emphasis added.

36 Walter B. Houghton, *American Etiquette and Rules of Politeness*, 7th ed. (New York: Standard Publishing House, 1883), p. 261.

37 Muriel MacFarlane, "Appropriate Jewelry Never More Important," p. 65.

38 Advertisement for the William B. Kerr Co., *Vogue*, vol. 43, June 14, 1914, p. 74.

39 Advertisement for Krementz & Co., *Vogue*, vol. 45, March 15, 1915, p. 116.

40 Advertisement for Krementz & Co., *Vogue*, vol. 45, February 15, 1915, p. 94.

41 Rives, *The Complete Book of Etiquette*, p. 134.

42 Charles Harcourt, *Good Form for Men: A Guide to Conduct and Dress on All Occasions* (Philadelphia: John C. Winston, 1905), p. 44.

43 Henry Lunettes (pseudonym for Margaret Conkling), *The American Gentleman's Guide to Politeness and Fashion* (Philadelphia: J.B. Lippincott & Co., 1866), p. 33.

44 Houghton, *American Etiquette and Rules of Politeness*, p. 257; Tashrak, *Etikete*, p. 47.

45 See, for example, Rives, *The Complete Book of Etiquette*, p. 39; "Too Much Jewelry Worn in Foreign Society," *Vogue*, vol. 8, November 1896, p. 406.

46 "The Limitless Possibilities of the Limited Purse," p. 13.

47 "Jewels No Longer Synonymous with Jewess," *American Jewess*, vol. 8, January 1899, p. 44.

48 Abraham Cahan, *The Rise of David Levinsky* (1917; ed. New York: Harper Torchbooks, 1960), p. 367.

49 "Issues Before Reform Jewesses in America," *American Hebrew*, January 2, 1925, p. 244.

50 "Suit Your Ornaments to Your Style," p. 45.

51 Ibid.

52 "Go on Conquering," *American Jewess*, vol. 8, January 1899, p. 45.

53 "Jewels No Longer Synonymous with Jewess," p. 45.

54 "Jobbers Hold Annual Convention," *NJO*, vol. 11, July 1915, p. 566.

55 "Not a Necessity—But," *NJ*, vol. 16, March 1920, p. 82.

56 "The Folks in Your Town," *NJ*, vol. 16, April 1920, p. 89.

57 "Trade Publicity—A Sound Investment," *NJ*, vol. 16, January 1920, p. 70.

58 See, for example, *NJ*, vol. 21, July 1925, p. 76; vol. 21, June 1925, p. 86.

59 *NJ*, vol. 16, November 1920, p. 48.

60 "Comments of the Press," in *Report and Catalogue of the First Exhibition of Newark Industries, Exclusively* (Newark: Holbrook's Steam Printery, 1882), p. 35.

61 Advertisement for Shanley Belt Buckles, *Vogue*, vol. 55, June 1, 1920, p. 136.

62 Advertisement for Blancard & Co., *NJ*, vol. 21, January 1925, p. 19.

63 Advertisement for Krementz & Co., *Vogue*, vol. 45, February 15, 1915, p. 94.

64 "Seed of Newark's Fame as Jewelry Center Sown More Than Century Ago," *Newark Evening News*, January 18, 1917, p. 14.

65 Virginia Caldwell, "Here Comes the Bride," *NJ*, vol. 21, June 1925, pp. 20-24; *NJO*, vol. 11, September 1915, p. 765.

66 Rives, *The Complete Book of Etiquette*, p. 68.

67 Leigh Eric Schmidt, *Consumer Rites: The Buying and Selling of American Holidays* (Princeton: Princeton University Press, 1995), p. 4.

68 Theodore Dreiser, *The Color of a Great City*, cited in Schmidt, *Consumer Rites*, p. 169.

69 *NJ*, vol. 21, December 1925, p. 23.

70 *NJ*, vol. 21, April 1925, p. 7.

71 Advertisement for the Juliet Gift Set by Day, Clark & Co., *Vogue*, vol. 45, March 15, 1915, p. 96.

72 Advertisement for Reed & Barton Co., *Vogue*, vol. 35, March 1910, p. 92.

73 "Rosary and Locket," *NJ*, vol. 16, April 1920, p. 93.

74 "Birthdays and the 21st in Particular," in *Jewelry Fashions 1917*, p. 24. See also "Cultivates Confirmation Business," *NJ*, vol. 16, May 1920, p. 84.

75 "Every Woman has a Birth-Day," *NJ*, vol. 21, April 1925, p. 33.

76 *NJ*, vol. 16, April 1920, p. 67.

77 *NJO*, vol. 11, March 1915, p. 247.

78 Brides should wear very little jewelry, *Vogue* recommended. "So much ornamentation is expended on the gown itself that jewels seem out of place, giving the effect of overloading."; "Vogue Points for Brides: Some of the Little Things of Peculiar Interest to the Prospective Bride," *Vogue*, vol. 38, May 1, 1911, p. 25.

79 Advertisement for Thomas W. Adams & Co., *Vogue*, vol. 43, May 15, 1914, p. 58.

80 "Gifts to the Ushers Are Mere Man's Nearest Approach to Jewelry," *Vogue*, vol. 43, June 15, 1914, p. 58.

81 "Equalizing the Sexes," *NJ*, vol. 21, July 1925, p. 18.

82 Post, *Etiquette*, p. 301; "The Wedding Question and Its Several Answers," in *Jewelry Fashions* 1917, p. 14.

83 Post, *Etiquette*, p. 302.

84 Rives, *The Complete Book of Etiquette*, p. 68.

85 Mrs. Burton Kingsland, "Good Manners and Good Form," *Ladies Home Journal*, March 1909, p. 44.

86 See, for example, "The Ring," in Maude C. Cooke, *Social Life, or The Manners and Customs of Polite Society* (Philadelphia: Co-operative Publishing Co., 1896), p. 160; Rives, *The Complete Book of Etiquette*, p. 64.

87 Caldwell, "Here Comes the Bride," p. 20.

88 See, for example, "Advertising Wedding Rings—and Gifts," *NJ*, vol. 21, May 1925, pp. 98-104, especially p. 100; William Bliss Stoddard, "Modern Brides Want Modern Rings," *NJ*, vol. 21, September 1925, p. 44.

89 "Dress Styles and Jewelry Fashions," in *Jewelry Fashions* 1917, p. 7.

90 "More Than a Salesman," *NJ*, vol. 21, July 1925, p. 32.

91 "Give the World Service," *NJ*, vol. 16, October 1920, pp. 75, 76.

92 "Your Name on the Box," *NJ*, vol. 21, July 1925, p. 45.

93 Mrs. C.A. Halpert, "Festivals and Presents," *Ladies Repository*, vol. 31, January-June 1871, cited in Schmidt, *Consumer Rites*, p. 182. See also Betty DeBerg, *Ungodly Women: Gender and the First Wave of American Fundamentalism* (Minneapolis: Fortress Press, 1990).

94 On Bushnell, see Richard Bushman, *The Refinement of America: Persons, Houses, Cities* (New York: Alfred A. Knopf, 1992), pp. 326–331.

95 Ibid., pp. 330, 331.

96 Rabbi Hyman Enelow, "Abuses of Confirmation—Prominent Rabbis Discuss Rabbi Wolf's Article on Modern Practices," *American Hebrew*, April 30, 1915, p. 742.

97 "When to Wear Jewels," in Cooke, *Social Life*, p. 413.

98 What follows is drawn from "Santa Claus in the Pulpit," in Washington Gladden's *Santa Claus on a Lark* (New York: The Century Company, 1890), pp. 163, 168, 169. I would like to thank Leigh Schmidt for bringing this reference to my attention.

99 Horace J. Wolf, "Time To Cry 'Halt,'" *American Hebrew*, April 23, 1915, p. 707.

100 What follows is drawn from Elma Ehrlich Levinger, "Clothes: A Shabuoth Story," in *Jewish Holyday Stories* (New York: Bloch Publishing Co., 1925), pp. 159-177.

101 "On the Look-Out for Inexpensive Gifts," *NJ*, vol. 21, August 1925, p. 83.

102 Colonel John L. Shepard, "Gifts That Last," *NJ*, vol. 16, December 1920, p. 72.

103 Editorial, *NJO*, vol. 11, October 1915, p. 785.

104 *NJ*, vol. 21, December 1925, p. 23.

Brooch, 1905–1910; see Fig. 50.

Producing What America Wanted: Jewelry from Newark's Workshops

ULYSSES GRANT DIETZ

Before a jeweler's window in St. Mark's Square, Venice, a Newarker of means listened to his wife. "Dear, please buy me that platinum ring—the one with the ruby in it. I do so want to take back home a typical souvenir of Venice; one that I may keep always and whenever I look at it be reminded of moonlight nights and gondoliers." The man succumbed, but being a jeweler himself, he examined the ring closely and learned that it was a product of Newark— the platinum had been refined and the setting made here, in one of the best of the city's some 200 jewelry factories. But he didn't tell his wife—he allowed her to keep on dreaming of her Venetian souvenir.

This charming story appeared on page 14 of the *Newark Evening News* for January 9, 1917, as the beginning of a two-part article titled "Newark Sparkles Among Cities as Home of Gold and Platinum Jewelry." It renders in romantic fashion two simple facts that have been virtually forgotten in the ensuing decades. Newark, New Jersey, was in its heyday the capital of the American fine jewelry industry; and the jewelry manufactured in Newark was of a style and quality that made it desirable to an enormous national and international market. A third, and crucial, fact is also vividly clear from the newspaper vignette: most people were unaware of the prevalence of Newark-made jewelry in the shops and department stores of America. This, along with the decline of America's fine jewelry industry after World War II, has allowed Newark's great history as a jewelry center to slip into obscurity.

What did Newark jewelry shops make? The simple answer is—everything, from gold collar buttons to diamond and platinum brooches. Where did this Newark-made jewelry sell? Again the answer is simple—everywhere, from Fifth Avenue to Fargo, in every jewelry store, large and small, all across America, and in Europe as well. On the eve of the stock market crash of 1929, when Newark's jewelry industry was at its peak in both output and prestige, the city was home to 144 manufacturing firms, who turned out an annual product worth $22,301,802. By 1929 Newark was one of the largest purchasers of gemstones in the world, and it was said that ninety percent of all solid-gold jewelry made in the United States came from Newark factories, including more than fifty percent of the 18- to 24-carat pieces.[1]

Newark established itself early on as the national center for the production of gold jewelry. In 1882, in a rare surviving promotional booklet published by Newark's Enos Richardson & Co., the four basic kinds of jewelry were laid out: a) jewelry in which precious stones dominate; b) jewelry in which gold dominates the design and stones are used as accents; c) silver jewelry; and d) gold-filled or gold-plated jewelry.[2] New York City was, by the 1880s, the national leader in the gem-dominated jewelry, spurred on by the brilliant marketing developed by Tiffany & Co. since its founding in 1837. Providence, Rhode Island, and the Attleboros in Massachusetts were the leaders in gold-plated and gold-filled jewelry.[3] Newark was left with the vast, genteel market of consumers who could not afford the "glamour jewelry" of New York City, and would not buy the "cheap jewelry" of New England, but were ready to lay down their money for the solid-gold goods that poured out of Newark's factories. It was also in Newark that Baker & Co., in 1891, first refined platinum in this country, thus giving the city an edge when platinum jewelry first came into vogue at the turn of the century.[4]

Documentation and Attribution

The documentation of Newark-made jewelry is difficult before 1906, when the Stamping Act required the denoting of carat quality on all American-made jewelry.[5] Moreover, maker's marks on jewelry were not required until 1961, and thus it was only voluntarily that Newark manufacturers put hallmarks of any sort on their products. For example, Krementz & Co., founded in 1866, only began using its characteristic touchmark—a profile view of its patented one-piece collar button—in 1896.[6] William Bagnall asserted that in the early 1800s the first Newark factory, that of Epaphras Hinsdale and John Taylor, produced "ear-rings, breast-pins, bracelets, necklaces and chains, all of solid gold, of a fineness not less than sixteen carats."[7] He similarly commented on the fineness of Enos Richardson & Co.'s products. However, unlike glamorous New York retailers such as Tiffany & Co. and Theodore B. Starr, very few Newark makers were known by name outside the trade, and trademarks were considered unnecessary. Thus many pieces have survived with no marks at all. Ultimately, it was the familiarity with Newark's quality, and confidence in that quality, that kept Newark at the center of the industry. As Bagnall noted in 1882, "while the retailer has not the guarantee of a bureau under the authority of the government, as in France; or of the Hall-mark, as in England, the well-earned reputation and high character of the firm are a sufficient guarantee."[8]

Thus is it speculation—albeit logical speculation—to attribute such things as a mid-nineteenth-century necklace and matching sleeve chains to a Newark maker (Fig. 23). This suite of three chains descended in the Ward family of Newark, and they were probably worn by the wife of New Jersey Governor Marcus L. Ward. The shorter chains were not bracelets, but were used to hold up and ornament the sleeves on mid-century dresses. The filigree ball clasps, apparently of a higher carat than the chains themselves, could also have been made in New York City, where such filigree work had been produced since the 1810s.[9] Likewise, the pair of baby bracelets—a common form of jewelry before the Civil War—made of thinly rolled engraved gold, can be attributed to a local producer because of descent in the same Newark family (Fig. 24). One would like to suppose that a Newark-owned mourning brooch, dated 1866, might have come from Durand & Co.'s shop (Fig. 25). The surrounding wreath of oak leaves, acorns, and lilies resembles in style and quality Durand's work for the testimonial medal given to Mayor Thomas Peddie in 1868 (see Fig. 7). However, without surviving documentation, such attributions can never be made with certainty.

Horace E. Baldwin, a great-grandson of Isaac Baldwin, founder of Baldwin & Co., was said by his descendants to have designed a gold and enamel brooch, set with a porcelain plaque enameled with a pharaoh's head, in the 1860s (Fig. 26). Family tradition says he designed it for Tiffany & Co. Two other pieces of jewelry, made of gold and human hair, also descended in the Baldwin family, and might well have been produced in the Baldwins' Newark shop (Fig. 27). A memento brooch from the Ogden family of Newark and a memento bracelet from the Ward family of Newark, both using elaborately woven human hair, were the sort of thing produced in

23. Necklace and sleeve chains, by an unknown maker, probably Newark, ca. 1850, gold, The Newark Museum, Bequest of Marcus L. Ward, 1921 (21.2029)

24. Pair of engraved baby bracelets, by an unknown maker, probably Newark, ca. 1860, gold, The Newark Museum, Bequest of Marcus L. Ward, 1921 (21.1955)

Newark shops (Fig. 28). Although there were manufacturers of hair jewelry in New York City, undoubtedly Newark jewelers produced such memento pieces for their clients as well. At least one reference for Alling Brother & Co. in 1860 shows that Charles Schuetz, one of their jewelers, mounted a "hair fob chain." Other entries in the Alling "hands ledger" (i.e., payroll account book) of 1859-1863 note that the firm worked with coral jewelry, as well as cameos, mosaic jewelry, and pearl and jet jewelry.[10]

25. Mourning brooch, by an unknown maker, probably Newark, dated 1866, gold with cameo, 1¼ × 1 in., The Newark Museum, Bequest of Sarah E. Eunson, 1941 (41.938)

26. Brooch in the Egyptian style, by Horace E. Baldwin, Newark, possibly for Tiffany & Co., 1860–1870, gold and enameled porcelain, 1⅜ in. (diam.), The Newark Museum, Gift of Mrs. Lathrop E. Baldwin, 1967 (67.155)

27. Memento necklace and watch chain, possibly by Baldwin & Co., Newark, 1850–1860, gold and human hair, The Newark Museum, Gift of Mrs. Lathrop E. Baldwin, 1945 (45.154, 45.163). These pieces descended in the family of Wickliffe Baldwin.

28. Memento brooch and bracelet, by unknown makers, probably Newark, 1850–1860, gold and human hair, The Newark Museum, Gift of Mr. and Mrs. Gordon Glenn, 1974 (74.237) and

Gift of Mrs. Joseph Ward, Jr., 1935 (35.288). The brooch descended in the Ogden and Breed families of Newark, and the bracelet was worn by Mrs. Joseph M. Ward, Jr., of Newark.

29. Ear drops and scroll brooch, by Ferdinand Herpers (ear drops) and Herpers Brothers (brooch), gold, enamel, and imitation diamonds. Ear drops, 1875–1885; brooch, 1880–1900. The Newark Museum, Gift of Henry F. Herpers, 1937 (37.635 b&c, 37.636). The ear drops were worn by Mrs. Ferdinand Herpers and use her husband's 1872 patent prong setting.

30. Brooch with multiple prong settings, by Ferdinand Herpers, 1875–1885, gold, enamel, and imitation diamonds, 1⅜ × 1⅞ in., The Newark Museum, Gift of Henry F. Herpers, 1937 (37.635a)

31. Brooch in the form of a wreath of grapes, probably by Herpers Brothers, 1880–1900, gold and pearls, 1 in. (diam.), The Newark Museum, Gift of Mrs. Henry F. Herpers, 1966 (66.622)

The earliest documented jewelry from Newark shops also underscores the complex interplay among different facets of the city's jewelry industry. Ferdinand Herpers patented his improved setting for diamonds in 1872 (see Fig. 8). A rare pair of ear drops and a splendid gem-set brooch survive to document his use of that patented setting to showcase diamonds (Figs. 29, 30). Although they were worn by Herpers' wife, these pieces were most likely intended as models to show specialists in diamond jewelry just what effects might be achieved with the new type of setting. The stones are held up high, by their mid-section (known as the girdle), on tiny set-back prongs. Thus the inherent fire of a well-cut diamond is given more play, creating a brilliant effect. Newark jewelry makers, with the probable exception of Durand & Co., did not typically use such large diamonds. Hence, it is likely that Herpers' major clients for his settings were in New York City. Herpers himself, although highly respected and successful as "one of Newark's most prominent German citizens,"[11] was probably not wealthy enough to have afforded such lavish pieces if they had been set with real diamonds. On the other hand, pieces with real diamonds would certainly have been broken up and lost long ago, as fashions changed and valuable stones were reset.

Two other unmarked brooches, probably from the 1880s or 1890s, show other kinds of settings that Herpers' workshop produced. One, a cluster of grape leaves using seed pearls as grapes, is typical of jewelry made in various Newark shops at the time (Fig. 31). Although Herpers specialized in galleries and settings, the firm clearly did other jewelry work as well as custom orders for family members. The second brooch, in a scrollwork setting, is also set with imitation diamonds, but uses a more standard form of prong setting (Fig. 29). The 1872 patent setting seems to disappear from the Herpers line by the 1880s, in favor of the more standard variety of open setting, produced in a wide range of sizes. By the end of the 1880s, Tiffany & Co. had co-opted the prong setting as the "Tiffany setting," and had established the nationwide standard for its production and use.[12]

The pervasiveness of Tiffany's influence is evident in a late nineteenth-century letter to Herpers' son Henry, from the W.J. Johnston Company of New York (whose factory was in Pittsburgh), stating that "we are using your settings for our Tiffany rings but they do not match our gold in color." Tiffany & Co. would certainly have been angered at this loose use of its name to identify a prong-set gem, but Henry Herpers was angered by the careless use of alloys that were sold as 14-carat gold. He notes on the letter in longhand, "there is no wonder why some people get rich when they sell this kind of gold for 14k."[13]

A bar pin and a locket, both from the Herpers family, suggest the ways in which Herpers' products could be used (Fig. 32). On the bar pin, gold wire galleries have been applied to a rectangular plate to mimic the elaborate wirework and granulation of Italian and French jewelry of the 1870s. Both of the galleries were part of Herpers' standard line, sample cards for which survive from different periods of the firm's history (Figs. 33, 34). All the elements decorating the surface of the locket were probably from the Herpers line of findings and decorative elements. A silver lace pin and ear drops from this same period also show the Herpers galleries applied to obtain a stylish effect (Fig. 35).

A surviving group of cameo-set jewelry was made over several decades in the Herpers shop. Having descended in the family, the pieces indicate the range of what Ferdinand Herpers, and then his sons, under the name Herpers Brothers, produced (Fig. 36). The earliest is a pendant and matching earrings. Set with small pearls and black stone cameos very much in the Neo-Grec style of the 1860s, they are the sort of things Ferdinand Herpers would have made both while he was employed by other Newark firms, and after he set up his own shop in 1865. A versatile craftsman, trained in a variety of skills, Ferdinand did casting, die-cutting, made rings and sleeve buttons, and set both stones and cameos.[14] Like many of his fellow German immigrants in the mid-nineteenth century, Herpers rose from journeyman to factory owner in the course of two decades. He combined business acumen with a hands-on understanding of the trade, carving out a successful niche in the jewelry industry.

A pair of large sleeve buttons from the 1880s (Fig. 36, lower row), set with pink stone cameos in a romantic Elizabethan style, amply demonstrates the uses for Herpers galleries throughout

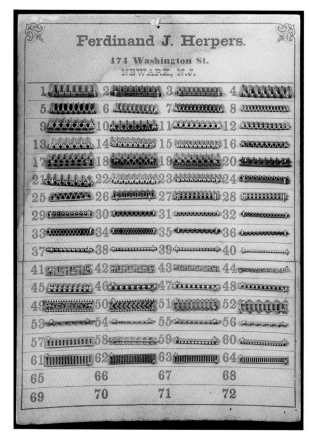

the trade. Two later brooches (Fig. 36, lower left, center right), these with pink stone cameos and a turn-of-the-century look, are typical of Herpers settings by 1900. The engraved brim on the circular brooch, as well as the pegged seed pearls on the oval one (which also has a pendant loop), would have been made in different parts of the Herpers' small factory.

32. Bar pin and locket, by Ferdinand Herpers, 1870-1880, gold and pearls. Bar pin, The Newark Museum, Gift of Henry F. Herpers, 1937 (37.630); locket, collection of Margarette Herpers Remington.

33. Sample card with galleries, by Ferdinand Herpers, 1865–1875, green cardboard and gold, 6½ × 4¾ in., The Newark Museum, Gift of Richard Herpers, 1958 (58.148a)

34. Sample card with galleries, by Herpers Brothers, 1900-1915, white cardboard and gold, 11½ × 7½ in., The Newark Museum archives. The gallery sample numbered 356 on this card appears on a bracelet made by Herpers (see Fig. 108).

35. Lace pin and ear drops, probably by Ferdinand Herpers, 1870–1880, silver, The Newark Museum (unaccessioned). The wirework galleries applied to these pieces of jewelry correspond to examples found on Herpers sample cards.

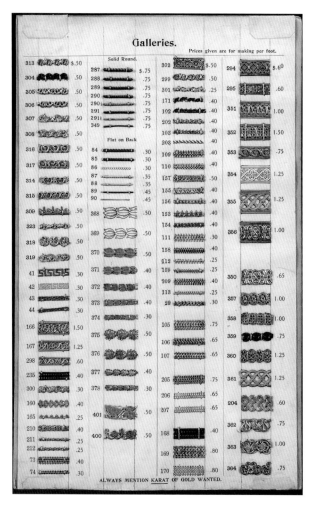

36. Cameo set jewelry. Clockwise from top: pendant and ear drops, by Ferdinand Herpers, 1865–1875, gold, stone cameos, and pearls, The Newark Museum, Gift of Mrs. Henry F. Herpers, 1973 (73.280); circular brooch with engraved setting, by Herpers Brothers, 1890–1900, gold and pink chaldedony cameo, The Newark Museum, same donor (73.301); pair of sleeve buttons, by Herpers Brothers, 1880–1890, gold and pink chalcedony cameos, The Newark Museum, same donor (73.286); pendant brooch, by William Link Co., Newark, using Herpers Brothers findings, 1900–1910, gold, pink chalcedony cameo, and pearls, collection of Margarette Herpers Remington.

It is of special note that both these brooches have the distinctive safety catch, invented by August Knaus of Philadelphia, but assigned by him for patent to Herpers Brothers on December 3, 1901 (Fig. 37). On the pearl-set brooch, this catch bears the trademark of the William Link Co. of Newark, although its elements were all from the Herpers line of findings. Herpers not only produced the findings and safety catches, but was happy to stamp the carat mark on the catches. Herpers also noted in its 1901 advertisements for the newly patented safety catch, "We stamp them with your trade mark." Thus they happily provided future jewelry historians with a good proportion of the surviving known jewelry marks. Bippart, Griscom & Osborn, another important Newark firm, also patented a safety catch in 1901, with a more complex mechanism.[15]

Herpers had no trademark of its own, but was one of the best-known manufacturers in the American jewelry industry. In the firm's surviving ledgers from 1874 through 1881, orders from no less than twenty-eight different Newark manufacturers provided a steady stream of business.[16] In addition, scores of jewelry makers from all over the country—New York, Philadelphia, Boston, Baltimore, Cincinnati, Chicago, Denver, Milwaukee, New Orleans, St. Louis, and San Francisco—looked to Herpers to supply gold elements for their jewelry. Herpers even sold findings to a jewelry maker in Providence, the other great center for jewelry making. In his handwritten notes on the business, Henry F. Herpers wrote that there were twenty-five jewelry manufacturers in San Francisco alone using Herpers findings, and that the firm's Pacific Coast clientele included jewelers as far north as Nome, Alaska, and as far south as San Diego.[17]

This sort of national operation was not unique to Herpers. Between 1865 and 1877, Newark's Alling Brother & Co. was selling to major retailers and manufacturers such as Tiffany & Co., Starr & Marcus, and Theodore B. Starr (New York), J.E. Caldwell, and Bailey, Banks & Biddle (Philadelphia), Bigelow & Kennard (Boston), Duhme & Co. (Cincinnati), Jaccard & Co. (St. Louis), M.W. Galt & Bros. (Washington, D.C.), and Samuel Kirk & Son (Baltimore).[18]

Production: Men, Women, and Machines

Since the professional standing of the Newark jewelry makers rested on a reputation for quality workmanship, some discussion of the processes within Newark's factories is in order. The best, and perhaps only, surviving account of a nineteenth-century Newark jewelry factory is in William Bagnall's 1882 booklet for Enos Richardson & Co., discovered by Martha G. Fales in the course of her research for *Jewelry in America*. (A copy of the booklet is now in The Newark Museum archives.) Apart from a surprisingly astute account of the history of jewelry-making in America, Bagnall takes the reader through a room-by-room tour of what was one of the largest jewelry factories in Newark, with a staff of about four hundred men and women (Fig. 38a). Each major step in the process of jewelry making was illustrated with woodcuts by R.T. Sperry, including plans of all four floors (Fig. 219) and an exterior view of the 70 x 100-foot building.

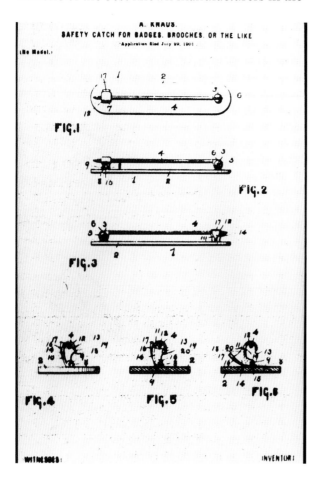

37. Letter of patent for a safety catch, assigned to Herpers Brothers, July 29, 1901, The Newark Museum archives.

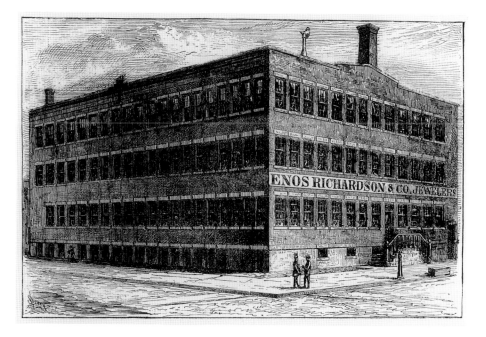

38a. Exterior view of factory of Enos Richardson & Co., Newark, woodcut from Bagnall 1882.

38b. Engine room of the Enos Richardson & Co. factory, Newark, woodcut from Bagnall 1882.

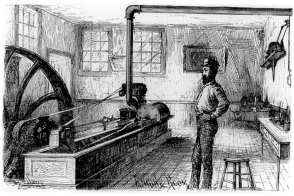

38c. Process for salvaging gold sweepings at the Enos Richardson & Co. factory, Newark, woodcut from Bagnall 1882.

38d. Work benches and belt-driven machinery on the first floor of the Enos Richardson & Co. factory, Newark, woodcut from Bagnall 1882.

38e. Drop-presses and work benches at the Enos Richardson & Co. factory, Newark, woodcut from Bagnall 1882.

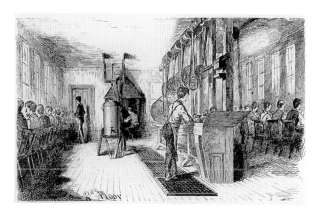

As one might expect, the hotter, heavier, and dirtier processes were done on the lower floors (Figs. 38b,c). Fuel to stoke the boilers, which turned the wheels that drove the belts of the various machines (Fig. 38d), took up a large part of the cellars. Here also was that very important suite of rooms, where all clothing and cloth used in the factory were carefully washed and where all wash-water was filtered to extract every particle of precious metal. Next to these washrooms were the amalgamator and grinder, used to perform the same task on all the sweepings of the factory. Bagnall reported that "several thousand dollars" worth of gold was saved in this way each year. This would represent hundreds of thousands of late twentieth-century dollars.[19] Joseph Krementz experimented with chemicals for amalgamating factory sweepings in the late 1890s, and the refining of jewelry factory sweepings would become a major Newark industry in its own right.[20]

Half the main floor of the factory was devoted to melting and alloying gold with other metals, to the production of steel dies and tools essential to the process, and to the coloring of gold (Figs. 38e-g). Pure gold was mixed with silver and copper in different quantities (the pure

38f. Melting gold, and jewelers getting their day's supply of gold, in the Enos Richardson & Co. factory, Newark, woodcut from Bagnall 1882.

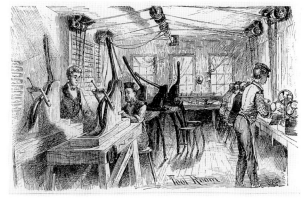

38g. Toolmaking and die-cutting in the Enos Richardson & Co. factory, Newark, woodcut from Bagnall 1882.

metal having been granulated by pouring it while molten into water) to produce 10-, 14-, and 18-carat metal for working (Fig. 39). Skilled die-cutters and engravers were important to a factory, because dies were extremely costly to make and would be used for many years. Lead strikes were made to test the precision of the dies, and to serve as models (Fig. 40). Because they are so valuable, dies are still kept in vaults by jewelry manufacturers today.

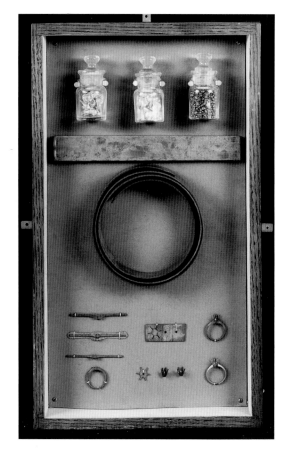

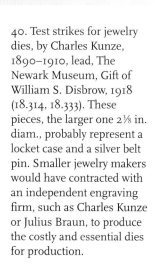

39. Steps in making a gold ring setting (granulated gold, silver, and copper samples; cast gold alloy bar; coil of gold alloy for stamping; ring in various stages of production), by Herpers Brothers, 1900–1920, The Newark Museum, Gift of Ferdinand and Henry F. Herpers, 1928 (28.152)

40. Test strikes for jewelry dies, by Charles Kunze, 1890–1910, lead, The Newark Museum, Gift of William S. Disbrow, 1918 (18.314, 18.333). These pieces, the larger one 2⅛ in. diam., probably represent a locket case and a silver belt pin. Smaller jewelry makers would have contracted with an independent engraving firm, such as Charles Kunze or Julius Braun, to produce the costly and essential dies for production.

Richardson & Co.'s method of coloring gold was to "boil" it in a solution of acid (Fig. 41). This eliminated all the alloy metals from the surface of the piece, leaving a matte, pure gold finish. Called "Roman color" in the nineteenth century, this effect is referred to as a "bloom" today. Electroplating pure gold onto the surface of a 14-carat piece was a less expensive way of coloring gold at the same period. Today, Victorian jewelry will often show a two-toned effect, created by the gradual wearing away of the Roman finish to reveal the paler, lower-carat gold beneath (Fig. 43).

The rest of the main floor was taken up with the many drop-presses, rolling machines, and the supply and finishing rooms. Rolling machines, first developed in the late eighteenth century for silversmiths, made the production of thin, uniform sheets of gold practical, and were highly important in making jewelry for a broad middle-class market (Fig. 42). Die-stamping, a one-person process aided by a powerful, heavy machine, allowed minutely detailed metalwork to be produced almost endlessly from a single die (Fig. 44). Die-struck metal had a hard, smooth finish, and was malleable, whereas cast metal tended to be porous and brittle (Fig. 45).[21] The finishing room was where final touches were put on each piece before inspection, after all the separate parts had been soldered together (Fig. 46). The supply room was where each employee picked up and returned the piece worked on that day. In this way, the precious materials were closely controlled, and the hon-

41. Coloring and galvanizing (electroplating) jewelry in the Enos Richardson & Co. factory, Newark, woodcut from Bagnall 1882.

42. Rolling out gold sheets, and drop-stamping gold in the Enos Richardson & Co. factory, Newark, woodcut from Bagnall 1882.

43. Chatelaine hook in the Egyptian style, by Sloan & Co., 1896–1900, gold, enamel, and turquoise scarab, 2⅞ × 1½ in., The Newark Museum, Purchase 1996 Friends of the Decorative Arts Fund (96.21b)

44. Steel dies for making animal charms, by Julius Braun, 1920–1930, collection of Buddy Braun.

45. Unfinished jewelry, by Enos Richardson & Co., 1900–1920, pink and yellow gold and silver, the largest piece 2⅛ in. (length), The Newark Museum, Gift of the Estate of Gertrude L. Grote, 1987, in memory of Herman E. Grote (87.59)

46. Finishing touches were put on completed jewelry before it was locked away in the vaults in the Enos Richardson & Co. factory, Newark, woodcut from Bagnall 1882.

esty of the workers was kept under constant scrutiny. Such practice still characterizes today's jewelry industry.

Ingots of gold were rolled out to appropriate thickness for particular kinds of jewelry, pieces were stamped on the drop-presses, the surfaces were given their Roman coloring, and then they were sent up to the higher floors for engraving, enameling, and polishing. Engraving was one of the most important handicrafts in a jewelry factory. Fine engraving increased the cost, but also the value, of a piece, and could dramatically alter its look (Fig. 47). Richardson had a staff of sixty engravers, most of them male (Fig. 48a, b). Enameling was usually done over an engraved surface, especially if the enamel was to be translucent (Fig. 48c). Powdered glass was applied to an engraved surface in a paste, and then fired in a small furnace to vitrify the paste without melting the gold (Fig. 49). Once fired, the rest of the piece was engraved, and then sent to the polishing room, where both the enamel and the metal were polished (Fig. 50). The polishing room at Richardson's was entirely staffed with women (Fig. 51), which was most likely the

case throughout the industry well into the twentieth century. Setting gemstones would be the last procedure before a piece was sent to the inspection and finishing room on the first floor. Richardson also appears to have made a large quantity of watch chains and necklace chains, for most of its third floor is devoted to chain production (Fig. 52). Here young men and women were segregated, certainly to avoid fraternization, but also so that women, with their small hands and greater manual dexterity, could work on the finest, most delicately linked chains.

By 1917, when the *Newark Evening News* ran a lengthy two-part article on the jewelry industry on successive Sundays, the processes had hardly changed at all from Bagnall's day. It is probable that workers in Richardson's factory were in the same building, working under the same, fairly high-quality conditions that prevailed in the industry in 1882. According to the article and accompanying photographs, workers still checked their material in and out each day; they still sat at long benches by windows; and they still received some of the highest wages of any industry in America.[22]

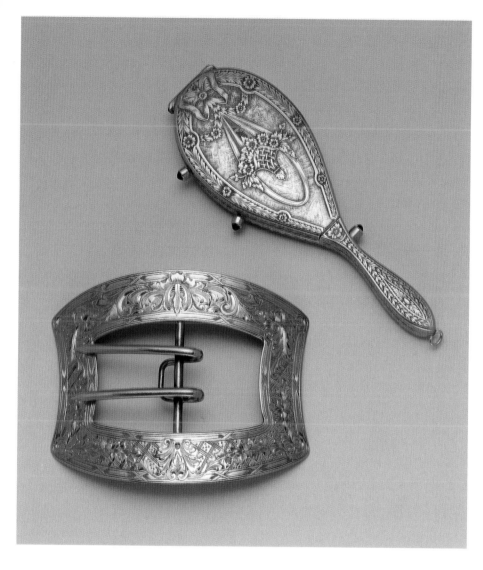

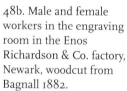

47. Compact and belt buckle engraved in the Louis XVI style, by Carrington & Co. (compact) and William B. Kerr Co. (buckle), 1900–1910, gold. Compact, 3⅞ × 1⅜ in., collection of Reuben Simantov, Inc., New York; buckle, private collection, New York.

48a. Soldering and engraving jewelry settings in the Enos Richardson & Co. factory, Newark, woodcut from Bagnall 1882.

48b. Male and female workers in the engraving room in the Enos Richardson & Co. factory, Newark, woodcut from Bagnall 1882.

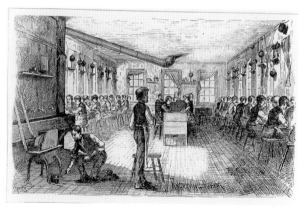

48c. Men enameling and women polishing fired enamels in the Enos Richardson & Co. factory, Newark, woodcut from Bagnall 1882.

49. Brooch in the form of a winged putto, by Krementz & Co., Newark, 1890-1900, gold, enamel, diamonds, and baroque pearl, 1⅛ × 1 in., The Newark Museum, Purchase 1992 Dr. and Mrs. Earl LeRoy Wood Bequest Fund (92.91). Powdered glass was applied to an engraved surface before a piece of jewelry was fired in the enamel kiln.

50. Brooch in the form of a woman with butterfly wings, by Whiteside & Blank, Newark, 1905–1910, gold, enamel, diamonds, 1⅜ × 1⅝ in., The Newark Museum, Purchase 1993 The Millicent Fenwick Fund (93.76). Final engraving and overall polishing were done after an enameled piece was fired.

51. Women polishing finished pieces of jewelry in the Enos Richardson & Co. factory, Newark, woodcut from Bagnall 1882.

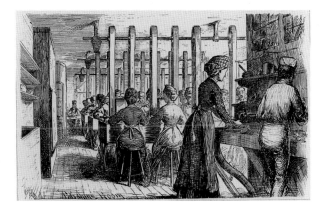

52. The main chain-making room in the Enos Richardson & Co. factory, Newark, woodcut from Bagnall 1882.

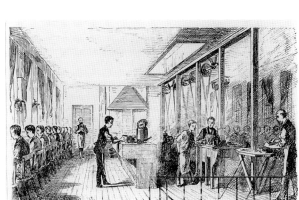

Today, over a century after Richardson published its booklet, Jabel Inc., first established to manufacture rings in Newark in 1916, maintains its factory very much in the way described above. The vault still holds the steel dies used for making jewelry, the toolmakers and die-cutters are still important and highly skilled, and handwork is still the essential element in the production of fine gold jewelry (Fig. 53). The major difference today is one of scale. Jabel was never as large a firm as Richardson was in its heyday, and today Jabel's engraving department consists of a single man, who learned the trade from his father. The market for gold jewelry has changed dramatically since 1882, but the method of production has remained unaltered.

53. Die and force for ring pattern numbers 224 and 206, and an unset ring, by Jabel Inc., 1929–1930, steel and white gold, collection of Jabel Inc., Irvington, New Jersey.

The forms of jewelry produced in Newark factories followed the patterns set throughout the Euro-American world. In the post-Colonial era and in the early nineteenth century, jewelry made in America was as limited in form as it was in quantity. This was not because there were no skilled goldsmiths in America; indeed there were very skilled goldsmiths working in all the major American cities before the Revolution. However, these men made primarily silver objects that served, at least nominally, some practical function in the Colonial home. Most of them, like Boston silversmith Zachariah Brigden, produced some gold jewelry. But jewelry was the exception, rather than the rule, even for the most affluent and prominent clientele before the nineteenth century.[23]

Beginning in the 1820s, however, and building momentum dramatically by the middle of the century, was a complete cultural revolution in America. A constantly increasing middle class of white-collar workers and professionals were transformed into consumers. The absence of an aristocracy in America gave middle-class people with salaries the chance to express themselves in ways once reserved only for the nobility. Simultaneously, the growth of an industrial infrastructure, based on machinery, transportation, and natural mineral and energy resources, made it possible for the first time in history to produce objects and process materials *en masse*, thereby making them affordable to people who were prosperous but not rich. This was as true for furniture, silver, ceramics, glass, clothing, and even houses as it was for jewelry.

Even as the ability to produce and to buy consumer goods grew, writers and self-styled tastemakers began to create a body of normative literature to guide Americans with disposable income, ensuring that they behaved the "right" way and owned the "right" things. Etiquette books, like jewelry itself, had once been useful only to aristocrats (or would-be aristocrats). George Washington owned an etiquette book and wore gold jewelry; the tenant farmers at Mount Vernon would have had no need for either.

By the mid-nineteenth century, etiquette books were a mainstay of middle-class American life. Americans of "old" wealth also looked to the

these books, because, as the middle class grew increasingly affluent, more complex rules were needed to maintain a distinct separation between various socioeconomic groups. Such regulations for consumption and behavior guaranteed that the classless American democracy was nonetheless clearly stratified. The major difference in American society was that America lacked an inherited aristocracy, so that *anyone* could learn the rules and climb upward in the hierarchy.

Jewelry played a distinct role in this consumer gentrification. As early as 1853, *Godey's Lady's Book* was advertising in every issue what amounted to a personal shopping service for ladies in any part of the country. Mr. Godey himself, having promised to make the most of a customer's check from the vantage of both economics and taste, noted:

Instructions to be as minute as is possible, accompanied by a note of the height, complexion, and general style of the person, on which *much depends* in choice. Dress goods from Levy's or Stewart's, ... jewelry from Bailey's, Warden's, Philadelphia, or Tiffany's, New York, if requested.[24]

This apparent hunger for the "right stuff" would work to benefit Newark's young jewelry industry in two ways. It created a constantly increasing national market for what once had been a restricted local product; and it offered the opportunity to expand that market still further by creating new forms and fashions in jewelry, thus feeding the hunger for novelty and the fear of being out of fashion. The desire for "fashionableness," which once had bankrupted only careless or profligate noblemen, was now able to work its influence on people whose hard-working yeoman ancestors wouldn't have cared less.

Although the Industrial Revolution in Victorian America produced a large number of very rich people, their ranks pale beside those of the comfortable, well-to-do Americans, who numbered in the millions by the end of the century. It was this particular middle-class market that the Newark jewelry makers tapped into; and it was these consumers who made Newark the virtual jewelry capital of the New World.

Already by the middle of the century, gift-giving, one of the major rationales for jewelry purchasing, had become prevalent enough to provoke a warning in *Godey's*. The plight of a young lady who overspends her budget on a bridal gift of a brooch in order to impress the bride's rich friends is seen as an example of the dangers of the new consumerism.[25] Jewelry, which had once borne only dynastic symbolism of wealth and power, was by the 1850s imbued with a range of romantic, sentimental meanings. It had become a symbol of affection, friendship, and kinship. When combined with social climbing and fashion consciousness, this generous instinct could, depending on whether you were a manufacturer or a customer, increase sales or lead down the road to ruin.

54. Four collar buttons in three different sizes, by Krementz & Co., 1900–1920, gold, The Newark Museum, Gift of Frank I. Liveright, 1971 (71.318)

Jewelry for Men

Men's jewelry changed surprisingly little between 1850 and 1950, because an accepted standard of decorum restricted what men could wear. Moreover, as Jenna Joselit discusses in these pages, worries about manliness magnified issues of good taste. As early as the 1870s, Cecil Hartley was warning men against sham in what little jewelry they did wear. "Let everything be real and good. False jewelry is not only a practical lie, but an absolute vulgarity . . . an attempt to appear richer or grander than its wearer is."[26] Such dicta were ideal for promoting the burgeoning market in solid-gold jewelry—and helping Newark's industry grow. The fact that Providence's gold-plated jewelry industry grew just as fast, if not faster, in the same period, might suggest that many people chose to ignore what the tastemakers advocated.

The rules set down by Charles Harcourt in his 1905 *Good Form for Men* sum up the restrictions: "It is a good rule to wear no jewelry—at any rate, none in sight—but what is evidently serving some purpose other than mere ornament."[27]

COLLAR BUTTONS

Given such principles of decorum, the ideal piece of men's jewelry was that which was most functional and least visible—the gold collar button (Fig. 54). The form of the collar button was well established by 1886, when Alling & Co.'s design books show a range of designs.[28] In the 1880s, J.H. Bentley & Co. also produced a range of collar buttons, as well as shirt studs and sleeve buttons.[29] George Krementz, who founded his Newark factory in 1866, achieved international success with the tiny collar button. Knowing that breakage was a problem, and that sturdy buttons

would give him a marketing edge, he developed a new machine for manufacturing collar buttons, inspired by a machine for making one-piece brass gun cartridges that he had seen at the Centennial Exposition in Philadelphia in 1876. By the 1880s, Krementz had perfected the same sort of machine for making collar buttons and was producing 10- and 14-carat gold buttons as well as rolled-gold-plate buttons. At one point, the Krementz product accounted for ninety-nine percent of all American-made collar buttons, and the firm sold as many as 1.5 million buttons annually.[30] The little gold button was so much a part of the firm's reputation that in 1896 the collar button became the company's trademark.

Collar buttons could be worn by men and by women, and were sold both singly and in sets. A typical man's evening set in the 1880s might include large sleeve buttons, shirt studs, vest buttons, and a collar button (Fig. 55). In the late nineteenth century, "white enamel buttons with a linen finish" made the gold of the jewelry completely invisible, so that only the wearer knew he had any precious metal on him.[31] Ladies' waist sets (referring to the blouse or shirtwaist) were virtually the same, except for the lack of vest buttons. In design, however, women were allowed far more elaboration, including the use of gemstones on their buttons.[32]

Mourning customs called for black jewelry, and a matte black enamel over gold button was the simple, elegant solution for men and for

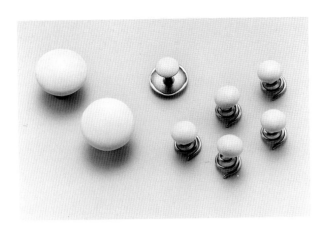

collection that matches this group was marked by Tiffany & Co., suggesting that Miss Bliss may well have made her purchase there. Even the grandest stores depended on such everyday jewelry for their bread-and-butter trade. The real phenomenon is not that elegant stores sold such items in quantity, but that jewelry had become an everyday affair; wearing gold somewhere on one's person was, for a vast number of Americans, as routine as eating breakfast or wearing a clean shirt.

SLEEVE BUTTONS AND SLEEVE LINKS

Sleeve buttons started out large in the third quarter of the nineteenth century, both for men and for women. J.H. Bentley & Co.'s hand-drawn design book for the late 1880s shows scores of different designs for sleeve buttons produced in gold and platina, an early form of platinum (Fig. 57). By February 1887, Bentley was producing link buttons, or sleeve links, featuring two matching buttons connected by loose links. Spiral-type shirt studs first appear in the firm's designs in November 1892.[34] Herpers

women. A.J. Hedges & Co. advertised a wide line of mourning jewelry to the trade early in the century.[33] A set of three pins by Hedges is included in a group of black mourning jewelry worn by Susan Dwight Bliss of New York in the early twentieth century (Fig. 56). Probably used as skirt pins, or to ornament the blouse, they were worn along with a pair of sleeve links by Riker Brothers, a set of shirt studs and a collar button by Carrington & Co., and a four-leaf clover brooch set with a small diamond by Krementz & Co. Miss Bliss probably purchased all these pieces—representing four different Newark firms—from the same New York retail store. A second collar button in The Newark Museum

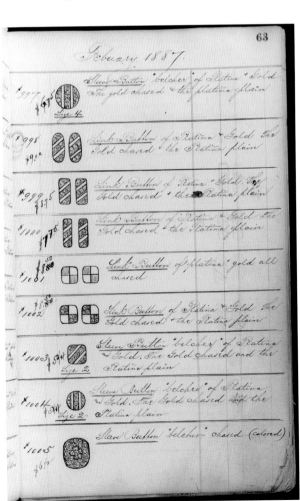

55. Man's white evening dress set, by Carter, Howkins & Sloan, 1880–1890, consisting of sleeve buttons, spiral-backed vest and shirt studs, and a collar button, gold and enamel, The Newark Museum, Bequest of Marcus L. Ward, 1921 (21.156-21.158)

56. Suite of mourning jewelry, 1900–1910, gold and enamel. A.J. Hedges & Co. (bar pins), Krementz & Co. (clover brooch), Carrington & Co. (studs and collar button), Riker Brothers (sleeve links), The Newark Museum, Gift of Susan Dwight Bliss, 1938 (38.566a-c, 38.565, 38.544, 38.545a-d, 38.557a,b)

57. Designs for sleeve buttons and sleeve links, from J.H. Bentley & Co. cost book, Newark, 1887, p. 63, The Newark Museum, Gift of Louis Waldman, 1939 (39.445)

58. Sleeve buttons. From top: in the Gothic style, by Herpers Brothers, 1880–1890, gold and platinum, The Newark Museum, Gift of Henry F. Herpers, 1937 (37.642); with griffins, by Carter, Howe & Co., 1900–1910, gold, collection of Donald R. Tharpe; with grotesque masks, by Carter, Howe & Co., 1900-1910, gold and diamonds, collection of Donald R. Tharpe; with scrollwork border by Larter & Sons, 1890–1900, gold and diamonds, collection of Gary N. Berger; in the Art Nouveau style by Krementz & Co., 1900–1910, gold, collection of Gary N. Berger; in the Beaux-Arts style, by Link & Angell, gold, collection of Gary N. Berger. Both men and women could have worn these sleeve buttons, although the former would have been ignoring the "rules" against men wearing diamonds.

59. Sleeve links. From top, left to right: in the Art Nouveau style, by Durand & Co., 1900–1910, gold, collection of Gary N. Berger; with engraved monogram, by Carrington & Co., 1910–1930, gold and enamel, The Newark Museum, Gift of Mrs. Keith L. McCoy, 1965 (65.207); in the Art Nouveau style, by Unger Brothers, 1900–1910, silver, The Newark Museum, Purchase 1993 The Millicent Fenwick Fund (93.180); in the Art Deco style by Strobell & Crane, 1920–1930, platinum and gold, private collection; with carved "man in the moon" faces, by Sansbury & Nellis, retailed by Tiffany & Co., 1900–1910, gold and tiger eye, collection of Gary N. Berger; with hammered finish by Carrington & Co., 1910–1920, platinum, gold, enamel, and cabochon sapphires, The Newark Museum, Purchase 1993 The Millicent Fenwick Fund (93.184)

Brothers was producing platinum and gold sleeve buttons at this same period (Fig. 58, top). The dumbbell-shaped sleeve buttons, known also as stiff-bar buttons (Fig. 58, middle and bottom rows), appear in the late nineteenth century, and were worn contemporaneously with the loose link buttons (Fig. 59), although the large one-sided sleeve buttons seem to have died out by about 1900. Sleeve buttons and links were worn by both men and women on blouses and shirts in the daytime, and neither advertisements nor design records indicate any clear gender division based on design. Strictures on what men "could" wear, intended to avoid perceived vulgarity or effeminacy, probably created some sort of self-censorship, but undoubtedly there were almost as many jewel-studded sleeve buttons worn by men as by women.

Sleeve buttons and links were offered at all price levels and in a dizzying array of designs. Unger Brothers, in its 1901 holiday retail catalogue, promised "500 different styles" of both link and stiff-bar buttons in silver.[35] Both Larter & Sons and Alling & Co. were offering numerous, if smaller numbers of designs in gold links and bar-type buttons in 1910.[36]

STUDS

Studs were the third important element in the jewelry associated with the shirt or blouse, and were made for children as well as for adults (Fig. 60). The button-type stud, having a flat gold back and a small ornamented button at the front, was the basic form for years. Children's studs came in sets of three, and they were connected by thin chains to prevent loss.[37] Larter, Elcox & Co., later Larter & Sons, revolutionized the stud with its patent in 1898 of the spring-back stud (Fig. 61).[38]

man's white tie in place for evening wear. Such clips were being advertised in *Vogue* in 1914 as appropriate gifts for ushers at a wedding,[41] but they don't survive in nearly the quantity of their more useful cohorts. Vest buttons, which varied in number from two to four, depending on the style of the vest that season, were produced by all the major makers, and followed the same styles as links and studs (Fig. 63).

The coordinated shirt and vest set for men, packaged and marketed as such, seems to have

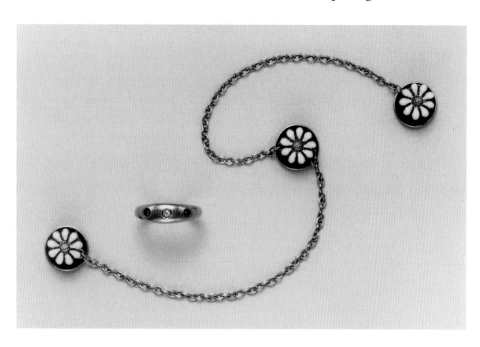

60. Child's stud set and ring, by Carter, Howe & Co. (studs) and Larter & Sons (ring). Studs, 1890–1900, gold and enamel, The Newark Museum, Purchase 1994 Stella Goldstein Purchase Fund (94.159); ring, by Larter & Sons, 1900–1920, gold, diamond, and citrines, collection of Simonette Hakim.

61. Shirt studs and tie holders. Clockwise from top: set of spring-back studs in the Art Deco style, by Larter & Sons, 1920–1930, gold, platinum, onyx, and diamond chips; button-type studs, by Carrington & Co., 1900–1920, gold, platinum, and enamel; pair of white-tie holders, patented by Bippart, Griscom & Osborn in 1899, gold and pearls; set of spring-back studs by Larter & Sons, 1900–1920. The Newark Museum, Gift of Frank I. Liveright, 1971 (71.315, 71.317, 71.316)

Inserting the stud into the starched shirt-front was made easier by the use of a spring plunger. When the spring was released, it anchored the stud firmly into the shirt. Simple pearl studs were typical early on, but the Larter stud, which would also have been sold to other manufacturers to be topped with their designs, became standard parts of the man's dress set and appeared in nearly as many design varieties as sleeve links. Spurred on by the success of its whimsical trade ads (Fig. 62), Larter adopted the spring-back stud as its trademark, much as Krementz had adopted the collar button trademark; in 1902, Larter reported sales of 300,000 spring-back studs.[39] Krementz & Co. patented its own shirt stud mechanism, advertising the bodkin-type stud in *Vogue* throughout 1916 (see Fig. 18).[40] Other shirt-related accessories were attempted, but appear to have had more limited success. In 1899, Bippart, Griscom & Osborn patented odd little stirrup-shaped devices intended to clip a

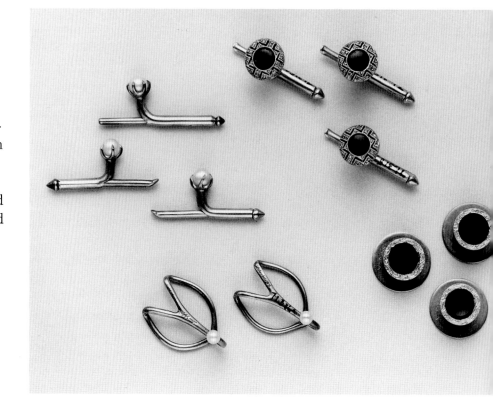

This Is An Exaggerated Case.

We have never seen a gentleman's shirt in quite this condition—but a broad illustration may emphasize our point; we are the Pioneer Manufacturers of the Spring-Back Studs...

WHEN making them this way (which is the way many manufacturers now make them), we received numerous complaints that they would not stay in a buttonhole, often causing—in a modified form—an annoyance like in the above picture.

AFTER many months of experimenting we overcame this great objection and produced the new Larter Shirt Stud made thus: with twice the length pin or piston as the old style, making it impossible to work out of buttonhole.

NOW we receive strong indorsements from manufacturers, retailers and consumers who have used them.

Are You Selling the Right Kind?

...MADE BY...

LARTER, ELCOX & CO.

21 & 23 MAIDEN LANE,
NEW YORK.

62. Advertisement for Larter, Elcox & Co., *The Jewelers' Circular—Weekly*, vol. 40, February 28, 1900, p. 41.

63. Vest buttons in the Art Nouveau style, by Krementz & Co., 1900–1910, gold, The Newark Museum, Purchase 1995 Membership Endowment Fund (95.105.6)

64. Advertisement for men's jeweled dress sets, by Larter & Sons, from the Larter *Gold Book,* 1925–1926, collection of Larter & Sons, Laurence Harbor, New Jersey.

Fine Diamond Complete Sets

While we illustrate only one Larter Automatic Stud and Vest Button, also a half pair of Links, each set consists of three Studs, four Vest Buttons and a pair of Links.

Larter & Sons

come to the fore in the early twentieth century. Krementz, in its 1914 *Vogue* advertisements, set the tone with rather ominous copy: "Social convention permits so little latitude in choosing a man's formal apparel, that his jewelry, though seemingly but a detail, requires more than ordinary consideration. *Correctness is paramount;* then quality, design and finish" (emphasis original).[42] Larter & Sons, whose trade ads mimicked such high-tone verbiage,[43] offered both high-end and inexpensive versions of the shirt and vest set (Figs. 64, 65), as did Krementz (see Fig. 14). Carrington & Co. was probably Newark's largest producer of high-end dress sets, offering a wide variety of gem-set designs that were probably retailed by the most elegant shops nationwide (Fig. 66). This firm, like many Newark firms, seems to have focused on dress sets and accessory objects (see Fig. 47), rather than produce a broad line of jewelry, such as Krementz did.

Despite the limitations in type, man's jewelry seems always to have been an important part of Newark's industry.

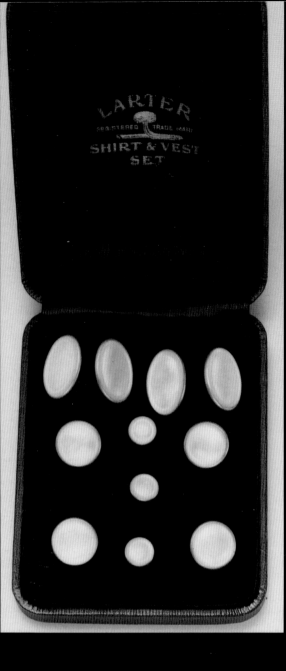

65. Shirt and vest set in original sales case, by Larter & Sons, 1900–1920, plated metal and mother-of-pearl, The Newark Museum, Gift of Joseph W. Hammond, 1993 (93.134)

66. Man's dress set, by Carrington & Co., 1920–1930, consisting of cuf-flinks, vest buttons, and shirt studs, gold, cabochon sapphires, and mother-of-pearl, collection of Gary N. Berger.

67. Two-part belt clasp (top) and suspender buckles (bottom) in the Renaissance style, by William B. Kerr Co., 1900–1910, silver, enamel, and red stones, private collection.

68. Tie clasps. From top: in the form of a coiled snake, by Riker Brothers, 1890–1900, gold, diamonds, and demantoid garnet, The Newark Museum, Gift of Gary N. Berger and Ulysses Grant Dietz, 1995 (95.105.1); with a nude woman in waves, by Unger Brothers, 1900-1910, silver and garnet, collection of Gladys and Robert Koch; in the Arts and Crafts style, by Day, Clark & Co., 1900–1915, gold and enamel, The Newark Museum, Gift of Mr. and Mrs. Irving J. Soloway, 1996 (96.3)

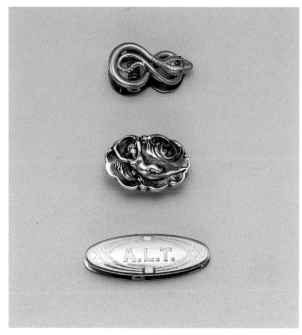

WATCH CHAINS AND BUCKLES

Suspender buckles were produced in gold and in silver by several Newark firms (Fig. 67), and tie clasps for daytime wear, by Larter and other firms, were available in a profusion of styles, coordinated with sleeve links (Fig. 68).[44] "Mannish" clasp belt buckles were patented by B.M. Shanley, Jr. Co. in 1915 and advertised in *Vogue* (see Figs. 9, 17). Newark competitor William B. Kerr also advertised a line of men's gold and silver belt buckles in *Vogue*.[45]

Although Newark was a major center for making watch chains, virtually no marked examples have come to light, making attribution nearly impossible. Watch cases were produced by a number of Newark firms, almost always for retailers, who used them with imported or American-made movements (Fig. 69). The largest watch case company was the Crescent Watch Case Company, which moved to Newark in 1891. The Essex Watch Case Company, the Newark Watch Case Company, and Thomas Benfield were the other firms that together produced some hundreds of thousands of watch cases each year.[46]

The greatest degree of elaboration permitted in man's jewelry was in the watch chain, but

even then there needed to be some pretense to function. Seals, lockets, and spherical ornaments known as Queen's balls were typical Newark-made pendants to a man's watch chain in the 1880s.[47] Ornate and stylish watch fobs came into vogue at the turn of the century and held their popularity until the 1910s. Carter, Howe & Co., one of the Newark firms that produced a wide range of jewelry for men and women, produced heavy, glamorous fobs with "functional" seals (Fig. 70). They also made fobs for women, which were worn at the waist with a chatelaine hook, while men's fobs hung from their vest pockets.[48] Unger Brothers offered a range of stylish silver fobs, for men and for women, at a far lower cost than their solid-gold counterparts.[49] Cigar cutters and pocket knives were two other functional additions to the man's watch chain, and were made by various firms, including Enos Richardson, Thomas W. Adams (see Fig. 13), Larter & Sons,[50] and Unger Brothers.

69. Man's pocket watch, by Henry Blank & Co. for Tiffany & Co., 1945, gold, The Newark Museum, Gift of Ulysses Grant Dietz, 1996, in honor of his parents' fiftieth wedding anniversary (96.40.1); man's patent belt buckle, by B.M. Shanley, Jr. Co., 1915–1925, white and yellow gold, collection of Kevin Shanley. The pocket watch was a wedding gift in 1945 to a bridegroom from his mother-in-law.

70. Two men's watch fobs and a woman's fob pin, by Carter, Howe & Co., 1900–1910. Left to right: fob in the Beaux-Arts style, yellow gold, The Newark Museum, Purchase 1993 The Millicent Fenwick Fund (93.183); woman's fob pin, yellow gold and amethyst, private collection; fob in the Egyptian style, green gold, The Newark Museum, Purchase 1993 The Millicent Fenwick Fund (93.44).

Aside from the wedding ring, rings for men were traditionally restricted to signet rings of gold, or those with a single semiprecious stone, either plain or carved with an intaglio seal. Although surviving documents make it clear that diamond rings for men were produced, purchased, and worn by the thousands, this was "officially" frowned upon throughout the period covered by this study.[51]

Interestingly, Newark manufacturers seem to have stuck largely to the rules, and the men's rings found in trade advertisements are almost exclusively of the acceptable signet or stone variety. Durand & Co., by the turn of the century, was producing a well-known line of men's and women's signet rings (see the woman's signet with a jade intaglio in Fig. 22, middle row). Alling & Co. was producing a range of men's and women's rings in the 1880s, following models established earlier in the century.[52] Ferdinand Herpers was making gold and platinum rings, using his 1872 patent diamond setting, in the 1880s. As these all would have been retailed elsewhere, only a few documented examples have descended in the Herpers family (see Fig. 21). Larter & Sons showed just how much variety could be packed into the design of a signet, with and without stones, for men or for women, in its 1925 line.[53] Larter, which is still producing rings today, made signets for Cartier well into the present century (see Fig. 13). Larter trade advertisements of 1925 made it clear which gender was being targeted (Figs. 71a, 71b, 72), and the firm produced rings for babies and children as well (see Fig. 60). In the 1930s, Henry Blank & Co., formerly Whiteside & Blank, specialized in exotic and costly novelties such as ring watches, set with rubies and sapphires (Fig. 73). Jabel Inc., established in 1916, not only produced a wide line of lacy filigree rings in white gold and platinum (see Fig. 22, right row), but also specialized in putting old stones in up-to-date settings. The firm's 1925 publication *Ring Transformations* shows vividly how Jabel's designers could give new life to old gems (Fig. 74).

Tiffany & Co. turned to the firm of Jones & Woodland in Newark to produce most of its high-end class rings (Fig. 75). Tiffany also produced some rings in its own Newark factory. For the United States Military Academy at West

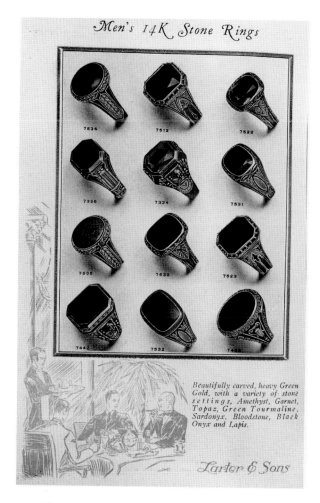

71a. Advertisement for men's rings, by Larter & Sons, from the Larter *Gold Book,* 1925–1926, collection of Larter & Sons, Laurence Harbor, New Jersey.

The Gothic-style ring in 71b appears in this advertisement, no. 7326.

Point and the United States Naval Academy at Annapolis, Jones & Woodland produced graduation rings for Tiffany's as well as smaller rings, sometimes lushly gem-set, called "sweetheart" rings. These were given to officers' wives as engagement rings (Fig. 76). Jones & Woodland, who began specializing in rings in the 1890s, advertised its line of men's and women's rings in *Jewelry Fashions,* a trade publication of 1917. As noted there, "the ring is to the jewelry trade, the same as sugar to the grocer." To keep up with fashion and create new demand in the marketplace, the firm changed ring designs and stone colors annually, and also produced rings within a broad price range in order to "be within the means of the general public."[54] Larter & Sons advertised in this same publication, offering dress sets, pocket knives, and signet rings.[55]

71b. Gold rings set with semiprecious stones, 1880-1930. Left row: Strauss & Strauss, in the Egyptian style with opal matrix, The Newark Museum, Purchase 1994 Stella Goldstein Purchase Fund (94.156); M. Bryant & Co., with tiger eye cameo, private collection of a member of the Northern New Jersey Chapter of the Victorian Society; W.C. Edge & Co., with pearl, collection of Nancy N. Kattermann. Middle row: Allsopp Bros., large amethyst, private collection; Larter & Sons, in the Gothic style with amethyst, private collection; M. Bryant & Co., with amethyst and opals, private collection of a member of the Northern New Jersey Chapter of the Victorian Society. Right row: Church & Co., with moonstone, same owner; Allsopp Bros., with amethyst, The Newark Museum, Purchase 1994 Stella Goldstein Purchase Fund (94.155); Allsopp Bros., with amethysts and pearls, private collection of a member of the Northern New Jersey Chapter of the Victorian Society.

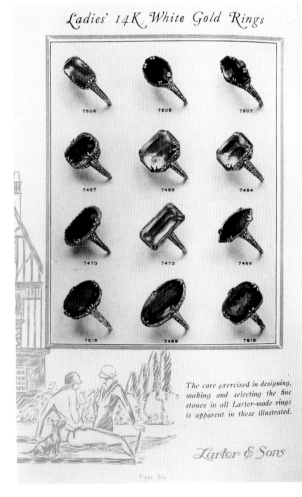

72. Advertisement for women's rings, by Larter & Sons, from the Larter *Gold Book*, 1925–1926, collection of Larter & Sons, Laurence Harbor, New Jersey.

73. Design drawing for three ring watches, by Henry Blank & Co., 1930–1940, gouache on paper, Henry Blank & Co. papers, New Jersey Historical Society, Newark.

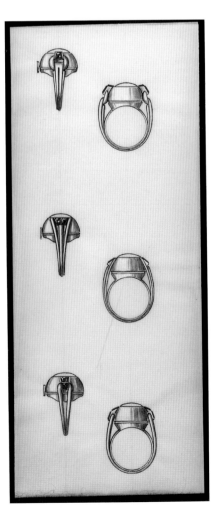

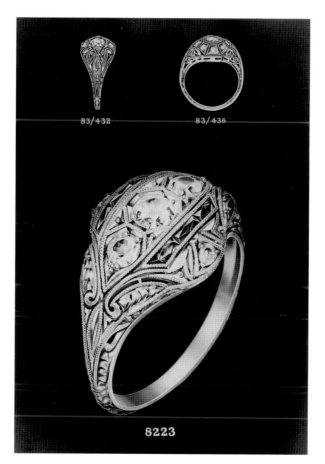

74. Plate from *Ring Transformations*, by Jabel Inc., 1925, collection of Jabel Inc., Irvington, New Jersey.

75. Class ring for Hunter College, New York City, by Jones & Woodland for Tiffany & Co., 1900–1925, gold, amethyst, Tiffany & Co. Permanent Collection.

76. Boxed set of sweetheart rings for the United States Naval Academy, by Jones & Woodland for Tiffany & Co., 1931–1944, gold, diamonds, sapphires, and semiprecious stones, Tiffany & Co. Permanent Collection.

Scarf Pins

Scarf pins were another jewelry form in which gentlemen could indulge. While it does not seem that particular designs were restricted to men, the rules for avoiding effeminacy or vulgarity applied, and the more sober designs that survive, set with cabochon stones, were most likely aimed at a male consumer. Scarf pins were often produced with the same motifs found on other pieces of jewelry, but on a smaller scale. This made variety and novelty easily attainable. As an 1893 trade commentary noted, "it would be impossible to enumerate the designs of scarf pins. They are up in the thousands (Fig. 77)."[56] Men and women could and did use scarf pins, also called tie pins, of essentially the same form, but women used them in greater profusion and in a wider variety of ways. Men were restricted to a single pin in their cravat or necktie, and even this was not considered to be in good taste by the 1940s.[57]

77. Scarf pins, 1890–1920. Top row: Crane & Theurer, gold and garnet, private collection; Brassler Co., gold and lapis lazuli, private collection; Krementz & Co., gold and amethyst, private collection; A.J. Hedges & Co., gold, lapis lazuli, enamel, and pearls, private collection. Middle row: Moore & Son, gold and pink chalcedony cameo, The Newark Museum, Gift of Mrs. Henry F. Herpers, 1973 (73.283); Krementz & Co., gold and diamond, collection of Louis Scholz; Unger Brothers, silver, collection of Louis Scholz; Irving Manufacturing Co., gold, diamond, and sapphire, private collection; W.F. Cory & Brother, gold and cabochon garnet, private collection; Whiteside & Blank, gold and diamonds, collection of Nelson Rarities, Portland, Maine. Bottom row: Link & Angell, gold and carnelian, collection of Louis Scholz; Day, Clark & Co., gold and ruby, collection of Nelson Rarities, Portland, Maine; Heiser Manufacturing Co., gold, cabochon amethyst, and enamel, The Newark Museum, Gift of Ulysses Grant Dietz, 1993, in memory of Robert E. Dietz II (93.164); Carter, Howe & Co., gold, enamel, and pearls, collection of Louis Scholz; Alling & Co., gold, enamel, and diamonds, collection of Nelson Rarities, Portland, Maine.

COMMEMORATIVE JEWELRY

The only other sort of jewelry seen as appropriate for men was related to civic, academic, or military service. Masonic jewelry, both costly and costume, was made by Newark houses, although much of it is not marked. Whitehead & Hoag, producers of political and military pin-badges, offered a line of Masonic jewelry in gilt base metal, sometimes with enamel (Fig. 78). Frank Holt & Co. made gold and silver sports badges, as did Herpers Brothers, along with other commemorative jewelry (Fig. 79). The higher-end producers would have made Masonic jewels, the most elaborate of which were the past-masters' jewels, presented annually to past Masonic leaders. One particularly splendid surviving example, with a Newark history, shows all the earmarks of Newark jewelry makers of the 1890s—fine engraving, applied beading, enameled lettering, small diamonds and sapphires, and a carved moonstone (Fig. 80).

Tiffany & Co. produced large quantities of commemorative jewelry in its Newark facility, ranging from thirty-seven different pieces for

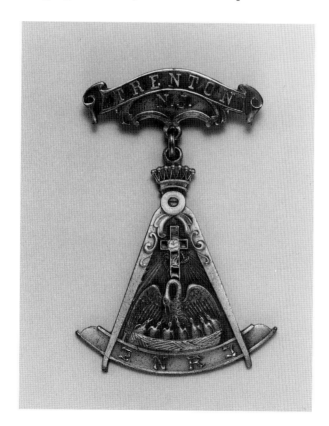

78. Masonic badge, by Whitehead & Hoag, 1890–1910, gilt base metal and enamel, The Newark Museum, Purchase 1995 Alice W. Kendall Bequest Fund (95.27)

79. Commemorative jewelry, by Frank Holt & Co. Gymnastics badge, 1900–1910, gold, The Newark Museum, Purchase 1994 Alice W. Kendall Bequest Fund (94.80); Montclair Victory Reunion pendant, 1919, silver, private collection of a member of the Northern New Jersey Chapter of the Victorian Society.

various Princeton organizations and prizes to splendid medallions marking historic events. Corporate jewelry, including service pins and pieces marking membership in every sort of secular and religious organization, was part of an extensive line made in Newark and sold through Tiffany's New York store. Smaller pieces were often subcontracted to other Newark firms, including Bennett & Long, Bippart & Co. (later Bippart, Griscom & Osborn), Brassler Co., Dalzell & Co., Day, Clark & Co., Dreher & Son, Durand & Co., Riker Brothers, and Sloan & Co.[58] However, Tiffany produced its grandest commemoratives in-house, the designs marked "SS" (for silver shop), referring to the Newark factory (Figs. 81–83). This sort of object has its most obvious roots in European military decorations of the eighteenth and nineteenth centuries. Its grandest Newark ancestor is the Peddie testimonial medallion, made by Durand & Co. in 1868 (see Fig. 7). Tiffany's commissions in this line included the order worn by the Society of the

80. Masonic past-master's jewel, by an unknown maker, probably Newark, 1896, gold, carved moonstone, diamonds, sapphires, and enamel, 4 in. (length), The Newark Museum, Bequest of Marcus L. Ward, 1921 (21.1926)

81. Utah Semi-Centennial Pioneer Jubilee medal, 1897, by Tiffany & Co., gold and enamel, Tiffany & Co. Permanent Collection.

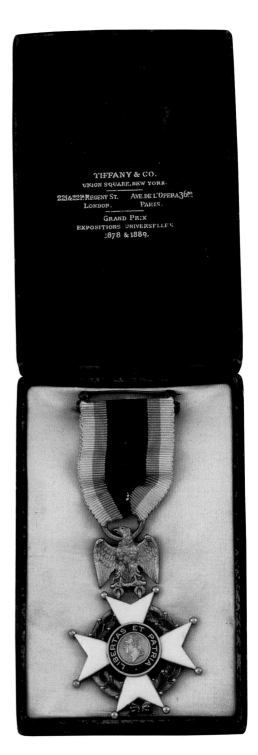

82. Sons of the American Revolution medal, 1890–1900, by Tiffany & Co., gold, enamel, and silk, Tiffany & Co. Permanent Collection.

83 Society of Colonial Wars medal, 1890–1900, by Tiffany & Co., gold, enamel, and silk, Tiffany & Co. Permanent Collection.

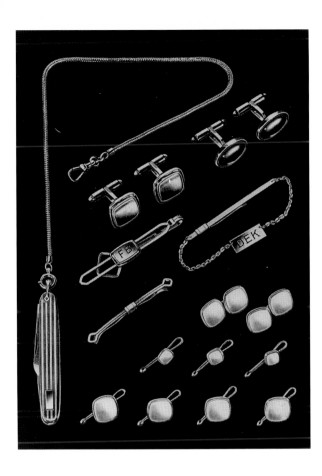

Cincinnati, first designed by Charles L'Enfant for George Washington in the eighteenth century, and the badges still worn today by the Regent and Vice Regents of the Mount Vernon Ladies' Association of the Union.[59]

Even after World War II, the basics for a man's jewelry wardrobe did not change much. A Krementz & Co. promotional booklet of 1946 features cufflinks, vest buttons, and studs, as well as tie clasps and a pocket knife on a chain—the same equipment allowed men in the 1880s (Fig. 84). However, while Krementz speaks of "correct styling and rich appearance" in its jewelry, the pieces were all being made of rolled-gold plate. Krementz & Co. clearly saw the realities of the postwar world: as Newark's fine jewelry industry was slowly fading away, survival meant turning to the medium that had kept Providence the costume jewelry capital for over a century.

Jewelry for Women

Numerically, man's jewelry might have dominated Newark's jewelry factories, but aesthetically woman's jewelry dominated the Newark industry. In the Gilded Age following the Civil War, factory production of jewelry made a higher output feasible, mining and transportation developments made precious raw materials available more cheaply than ever before, and a growing standard of living encouraged higher consumption all across the economic spectrum, from the wildly rich to the merely comfortable. In jewelry, as in all household furnishings, producers began to think up new ways to expand their consumer base. Tastemakers and arbiters of fashion were ready to report on novelties to the trade and to the public, instilling in consumers' minds the need for types of jewelry that had not existed a generation or two earlier. Just as George Washington would have been bewildered by the complex array of silver flatware used on American tabletops in the 1880s and 1890s, so his wife, Martha, would have puzzled over the endless variety of jewelry that poured out of Newark's factories at the same period.

Central to Newark's "mission" as a producer of jewelry was the mandate to gear its products to the "average" American woman. A 1904 article on the "Past, Present and Future of the Jewelry Industry," by W. Augustus Steward, chronicled the rise of René Lalique as the master jeweler of the world. Steward compared Lalique's art—for it was seen as just that—with the fine but lesser jewels of other European Art Nouveau artists. He then followed the modification and simplification of the Parisian styles to Germany, and in particular to Pforzheim, showing how production jewelers were able to "place upon the world's market neat, dainty, and remarkably cheap artistic productions, such as the masses of people can buy." With no derision, Steward acknowledged that Lalique produced jewelry for "my lady," and that "there are a great number of men whose mission it is to produce jewelry for the middle class women, artisans and peasants' wives...."[60] Pforzheim was Newark's counterpart in Germany, producing modestly priced solid-gold jewelry. The same sort of jewelry, often designed by German-born workers trained in Pforzheim (as was Ferdinand Herpers), was the mainstay of the Newark industry; and it was this sort of jewelry that American women looked for in jewelry shops from Alaska to Florida. Newark manufacturers tamed European designs for the American consumer.

Chains, Necklaces, and Lockets

Gold chains with pendants or lockets had been standard articles of jewelry from the second quarter of the nineteenth century (see Figs. 23, 32, 52). W.C. Edge in Newark was a leading producer of woven gold-wire chains of various forms. Edge, one of the few English-trained jewelers to emigrate to Newark, arrived there in 1865, and eventually succeeded in reducing the cost of producing braided gold-wire chains (known as foxtail chains) from $1 per foot to 2¢ per foot.[61] In 1896 it was reported that "a popular necklace is of gold chain punctuated at intervals with enameled beads, pearls or opals." Edge chains of this type, as well as braided chains or those with slides and swivels used to attach pendants, were staples for most retail jewelers by the late 1880s (Fig. 85).[62]

By the end of the century, a range of necklace forms had become specialties of Newark's factories. Newark did not produce the glittering arrays of diamonds that Tiffany's offered or displayed at international exhibitions, but city manufacturers also knew that most women didn't buy that sort of thing anyway. For the minority of very wealthy American women, diamond and pearl chokers, called dog collars, had become standard parts of the jewelry repertoire. This vogue was popularized by Alexandra, Princess of

Wales, who loaded herself with lavishly jeweled dog collars, as did her grandest American imitators, such as Consuelo Vanderbilt, who became the Duchess of Marlborough in the 1890s. For the less grand lady of fashion, an elegantly scaled-down version of this form was produced by Bippart, Griscom & Osborn in Newark at the end of the century (Figs. 86, 87). Instead of diamonds, vivid orange citrines are used; baroque pearls, interesting and relatively inexpensive, are set in Renaissance-style leaves enameled with pale translucent colors. The gold chains that link the segments of the piece all have the characteristic Roman finish, which has a satiny, rich color. A similar necklace, of Roman gold set with amethysts, was featured in a 1906 article by Ella H. Benedict, entitled "Design and Fashion in the Jewelry of To-day." She speaks of "appropriateness of design," and praises the variety of American jewelry design, noting that "fashions in jewelry here and abroad are very similar in style and design."[63] This was jewelry being considered primarily for its aesthetic rather than its inherent value.

The festoon necklace was another late nineteenth-century innovation that met with huge success in the middle-class marketplace. For Christmas 1907, *Vogue* reported that J.E. Caldwell was offering "a pretty amethyst necklace, with baroque pearls and festoons of fine gold chain" for $30.[64] Elsie Bee, in her weekly column for the trade, noted the popularity of the

86. Dog collar necklace in the Renaissance style, by Bippart, Griscom & Osborn, 1890–1900, gold, enamel, citrines, and baroque pearls, The Newark Museum, Purchase 1993 The Millicent Fenwick Fund (93.45)

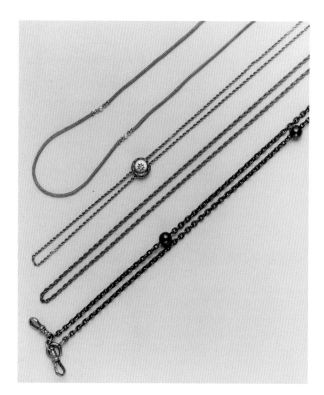

85. Chains were a mainstay of Newark's jewelry industry. From top: three braided-wire necklace chains, by W.C. Edge & Co., 1890–1910, gold, pearls, and diamond, collection of Nancy N. Kattermann; mourning sautoir, by Krementz & Co., gold and steel, The Newark Museum, Gift of Susan Dwight Bliss, 1938 (38.552b)

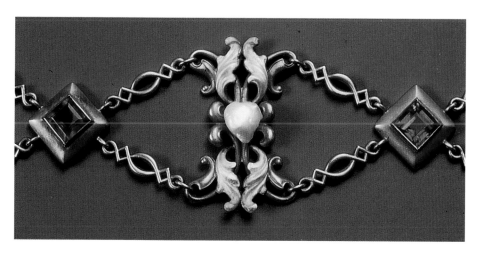

87. Detail of Fig. 86.

festoon or "draped" necklace that was a favorite for 1904.[65] Dreher & Son, a Newark firm specializing in colored gemstones, produced its own version, pairing bright blue Montana sapphires with spectacle-set yellow citrines (Fig. 88). The glitter and the glamour of the great aristocratic bibs of diamonds and pearls were invoked, but at a price affordable to a vastly wider audience.

The pendant necklace and its longer version, the lavaliere, were probably the most common and popular forms, adapting themselves to fash-

ions and varying pocketbooks from the 1890s well into the Depression of the 1930s. Elsie Bee, the indefatigable chronicler of jewelry fashions for the trade, writes of the lavaliere as being inspired by the unhappy mistress of Louis XV, Louise de la Vallière, and also of the simultaneous popularity of pendants on slender neck chains.[66] Just such a lavaliere is the one made about 1910-1920 by Wordley, Allsopp & Bliss (Fig. 89). Set with a large aquamarine in green gold—both newly fashionable early in the century—this pendant is highlighted with white enamel and seed pearls, which were hallmarks of Newark jewelry from various factories. Chic, but not too expensive, the lavaliere would have been ideal as a daytime piece for a grand lady, or as an evening necklace for a woman of more modest income.

Mourning sautoirs in black would have been a necessary adjunct to a jewelry wardrobe. The black color could be produced either by enameling or by giving jewelry a dark gray gunmetal finish. Joseph Krementz, who experimented with chemically obtained finishes for his

88. Festoon necklace and two brooches with colored stones, by E.A. Dreher & Son, 1890–1910. Necklace, gold, citrines, and Montana sapphires, The Newark Museum, Gift of Neil Lane in memory of Robert Rehnert, 1996 (96.35); floral brooch, gold and Montana sapphires, The Newark Museum, Purchase 1993 The Millicent Fenwick Fund (93.181); brooch in the Renaissance style, gold, garnets, and peridots, private collection.

89. Three necklaces with original chains. From top: pendant necklace with patent brooch mechanism, by Bippart, Griscom & Osborn, 1900–1910, gold and turquoise, collection of Simonette Hakim; lavaliere necklace, by Wordley, Allsopp & Bliss, 1910–1920, green gold, aquamarine, enamel and pearls, The Newark Museum, Purchase 1994 Stella Goldstein Purchase Fund (94.152); pendant necklace by Thomas W. Adams & Co., 1900–1910, gold, garnets, and pearls, The Newark Museum, Purchase 1994 Franklin Conklin, Jr. Bequest Fund (94.58)

90. Two design drawings for sautoir watches for Tiffany & Co., by Henry Blank & Co., 1925–1930, gouache on paper, New Jersey Historical Society, Newark.

family's jewelry firm in the 1890s, worked on several different gunmetal finishes, for base metal, gold, and silver (Fig. 85, bottom).[67] At the top of the line, Whiteside & Blank produced diamond-encrusted sautoir watches—worn as pendants on long chains interspersed with gemstones—for Tiffany & Co. One sautoir and its matching watch had a factory price of $5,957.48 in 1918, which would represent perhaps half its retail cost on Fifth Avenue (Fig. 90).[68]

All three of the necklaces in Fig. 89 show the variety of slender chains that accompanied pendants. Bippart, Griscom & Osborn supplied its French-derived Art Nouveau pendant with a removable mechanism to convert it to a brooch. Thomas W. Adams & Co., working in a drier, Arts and Crafts style, used tiny articulated joints to allow its small but beautifully crafted pendant to move freely. The combination of semiprecious stones and seed pearls, like that of opaque enamel lines and seed pearls, is also typical of Newark jewelry of the turn of the century. The same combination, and yet with very different looks, is seen in two pendant necklaces by Brassler Co. (Fig. 91) and a third by Krementz & Co. (Fig. 92, bottom). One of the Brassler necklaces is in an architectonic Louis XVI mode, while the other is of a lighter Arts and Crafts style. Both combine popular semiprecious

stones with small diamonds, another typical Newark feature. Brassler seems to have taken great care with its jewelry, for the backs show detailed hand engraving of a high quality. The firm's vice president and chief designer, Hans Brassler, was recognized for his artistry in 1909, the year he opened his own firm in Newark, with a commission to design jewelry for a full-color cover for *The Jewelers' Circular—Weekly*. The editors, who had never before attempted such an ambitious color cover, praised Brassler's jewelry designs, saying that they represented "the distinct advance that has been made in art jewelry in this country in the past few years."[69]

Stones were chosen for their color, and also for their sentimental value. Beginning in the early 1890s, birthstone jewelry became increasingly popular. Both retailers and consumers were quite aware of the associations between gemstones and months, and the particular meanings of the gems.[70] In 1909, Tiffany & Co. went so far as to have its gem expert, George F. Kunz, produce a little book called *Natal Stones: Birth Stones, Sentiments and Superstitions Associated with Precious Stones*. Kunz's national reputation as a gem expert, and the scholarly tone of this thirty-four-page booklet, lent the weight of history to gemstone fashions. Garnets were the birthstone for January, amethysts for February,

91. Two pendant necklaces by Brassler Co., 1909–1915. From top: gold, amethysts, and diamond; gold, moonstones, demantoid garnets, and diamonds. Collection of Nelson Rarities, Portland, Maine.

92. Three pendant necklaces. From top: by Frank Krementz & Co., 1900–1910, gold, amethysts, and pearls, collection of Krementz & Co., Newark; by Krementz & Co. 1920–1930, white gold, teardrop amethyst, and diamonds, collection of Nelson Rarities, Portland, Maine; by Krementz & Co., 1900–1910, gold, garnets, and pearls, collection of Krementz & Co., Newark.

July was turquoise, and aquamarine was the stone for October. Kunz also described the talismanic and sentimental meanings of stones, including stones that were not associated with a given month. The book went into at least twenty-three editions.

Riker Brothers capitalized on its skill with unbacked transparent enamels, called today *plique à jour*, to produce a pendant necklace in the Renaissance style (see Fig. 174), while Sloan & Co., in its variation on the pendant, combined a citrine and seed pearls with Louis XVI wreaths of laurel to evoke France's *ancien régime* (see Fig. 16). In the 1910s, Alling & Co. offered a line of pendants in a variety of shapes and sizes, set

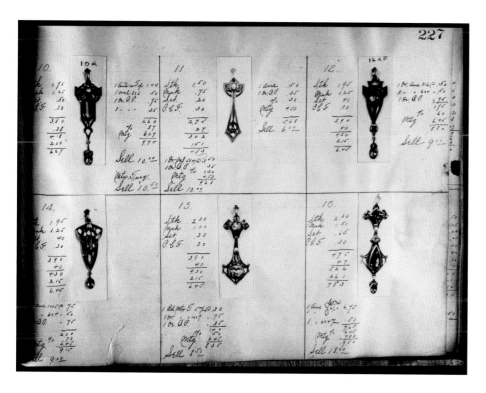

93. Pendant designs, from
the Alling & Co. cost book,
ca. 1910, p. 227, photo-
graphs on paper, collection
of Larter & Sons, Laurence
Harbor, New Jersey.

with the same sorts of stones its competitors
offered. The factory costs ranged from $4.25 to
$18 (Fig. 93).[71] By World War I, the pendant
necklace had been modified to follow fashion.
Day, Clark & Co. offered faceted amethyst balls
as pendants in 1917, and Krementz & Co. offered
large teardrop-form amethysts set in white gold
on elaborate Art Deco chains a few years later
(see Fig. 92).[72]

Lockets had served as necklace pendants since
the mid-nineteenth century. In 1886, Alling &
Co. designers were drawing swivel lockets with
elaborately engraved surfaces (Fig. 94). J.H.
Bentley & Co.'s 1890 designs featured both
round and square lockets of gold and platinum,
set with seed pearls or small diamonds (Fig. 95).
The Jewelers' Circular and Horological Review
reported that square lockets of just this type
were worn by men on their watch chains in the
mid-1890s.[73] Women could wear lockets on
chains, on chatelaines hooked to their belts, or
suspended from brooches (which were then
called chatelaine pins). The most glamorous
were those "new enameled lockets enriched with
gems ... worn ... sometimes from a long
chain."[74] Surviving examples by Whiteside &
Blank and Carter, Howe & Co., exemplify the elegant, Louis XVI style that effectively mimicked
French and Russian jewelry of the same period.
The chains have enameled beads to match the
lockets (Fig. 96).

Alling & Co.'s 1910 locket line showed a
strong Neoclassical style (Fig. 97), while Larter,
Elcox & Co. (later Larter & Sons) advertised a new
line in 1903 that included Art Nouveau designs
as well as Japanese motifs harking back to the
1870s and 1880s.[75] One of Larter's 1903 lockets,
featuring a crane and a frog, with a diamond set

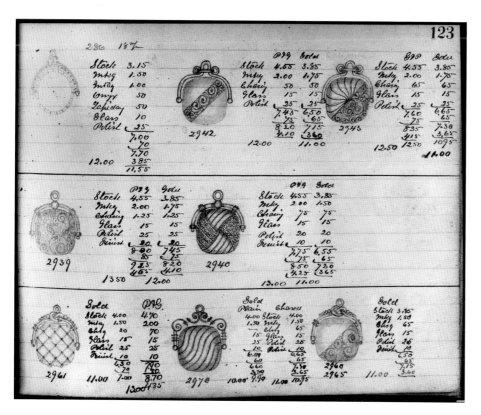

94. Locket designs, from
the Alling & Co. cost book,
1886–1887, p. 123, ink on
paper, collection of Larter
& Sons, Laurence Harbor,
New Jersey.

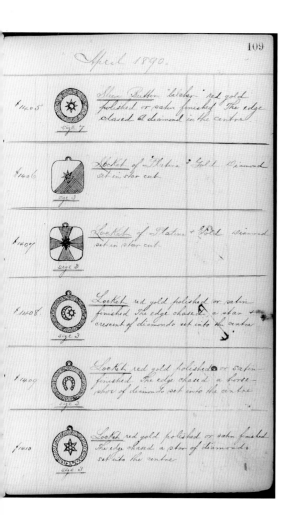

95. Locket designs, 1890, from the J.H. Bentley & Co. cost book, 1883–1891, p. 109, ink on paper, The Newark Museum, Gift of Louis Waldman, 1939 (39.445)

96. Enameled locket necklaces, 1900–1910. Left to right: Whiteside & Blank, gold, enamel, and diamond, collection of Barbara Neiman; Carter, Howe & Co., gold and enamel, private collection, New York.

97. Locket designs, from the Alling & Co. cost book, ca. 1910, p. 152, photographs on paper, collection of Larter & Sons, Laurence Harbor, New Jersey.

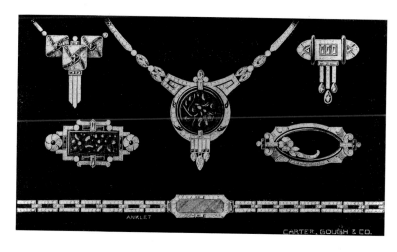

98. Three lockets, 1900–1910. Counterclockwise from top: with a lion, by Charles Keller & Co., gold and diamond, The Newark Museum, Purchase 1994 Stella Goldstein Purchase Fund (94.154); with a crane, by Larter & Sons, gold and diamond, private collection; with a snake, by Alling & Co., gold and diamond, The Newark Museum, Purchase 1995 Membership Endowment Fund (95.105.8)

99. Yachting locket commemorating the *Atalanta*, by Tiffany & Co., 1890–1900, gold and enamel, Tiffany & Co. Permanent Collection.

100. Designs for jewelry in the modern style, 1927, by Carter, Gough & Co., from "A Review of the Styles in Fine Jewelry of the Year 1927," in *The Jewelers' Circular*, vol. 96, February 23, 1928, p. 171.

into an engraved sunrise, demonstrates the ongoing Japanese influences on the Art Nouveau style (Fig. 98). As early as 1869, French jeweler Alexis Falize had depicted Japanese cranes on his enameled jewelry, and in the early twentieth century the crane's role as a symbol of long life continued to make it a popular design motif.[76] Charles Keller & Co.'s locket in Fig. 98 may have been intended as a zodiac sign. If the flower can be read as a water lily, it was the flower for July—which at the turn of the century was Leo's month, according to popular lore.[77]

The serpent coiling around both sides of the Alling & Co. locket in Fig. 98 ultimately owed its popularity both to Japanese *netsuke* and to Sarah Bernhardt's celebrated portrayal of Cleopatra in 1890 (see p. 76), and in 1901 were apparently just as popular in jewelry as ever.[78] One must allow that the image of the serpent, with its overtones of temptation and Paradise Lost, could also have been an evocative motif on a locket intended to hold the picture of a loved one. There seems also to have been a seasonal flurry of yachting motifs on daytime jewelry, highlighted with little enameled pennants. Tiffany & Co.'s Newark factory produced a grand example

of this kind of locket—probably worn by the skipper's wife—to commemorate the yacht *Atalanta* (Fig. 99).

Newark-made necklaces continued to follow trends in materials and in styles right up through World War II. Carter, Gough & Co., the final incarnation of the Carter firm before it was purchased by Krementz & Co. during the Depression, offered some surprisingly glamorous diamond jewelry in the French Art Deco manner (Fig. 100), while Charles Keller & Co. offered more modest, yet still stylish, versions in lacy white gold.[79]

The Depression seriously hurt the jewelry market. To quote J.B. Bishop, of Newark manufacturer Bishop & Bishop, in 1937: "after the business crash in 1929 there was a different story to tell in our factory. The demand for quality merchandise ceased."[80] Many Newark jewelry makers would not survive the Depression, or would be swallowed up through merger by other, stronger firms. Moreover, as the jewelry market began to recover during the late 1930s and early 1940s, less formal, sportier modern styles came to dominate new Newark designs (see Fig. 201).

BRACELETS

Bracelets from Newark makers follow the same progression through the nineteenth century as all other jewelry forms. Typically worn in pairs, they were designed in one of the historical revival styles that dominated the first three quarters of the century. Although no documented examples have yet come to light, Italian micromosaics and *pietra dura*, or hardstone, plaques were set into Neo-Grec bracelets by Newark jewelers, and cameos were also mounted in

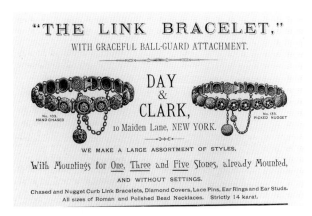

bracelets in Newark shops. By the 1880s, however, novelty and marketing—those great creators of jewelry buyers—had crept in, and the variety of bracelet forms was expanding rapidly. About 1887, Day & Clark (later Day, Clark & Co.) offered an early version of the link bracelet, both with and without the small gems that would become a trademark of Newark bracelets (Fig. 101). Alling & Co. also advertised its "lock bangles," to the trade, and its 1886 cost books show both bangles and link bracelets.[81] The factory costs for the basic bangles were $8.50 or $9.50, depending on the amount of engraving. The link bracelets, with all their additional gold and handwork, could cost up to $42 from the factory, making them expensive items once they entered the retail world (Figs. 102, 103). W.C. Edge had perfected a bracelet using a fabric woven of gold wire, for which the firm had received a patent in 1880.[82] Edge advertised this specialty, and another link bracelet variant, in 1887 (Fig. 104). A pair of these woven gold-wire bracelets survives in the Edge family (Fig. 105).

A.J. Hedges produced a unique link bracelet that seems to have been popular in the late 1880s and 1890s. Using an 1879 patent for making jewelry of mottled multicolored gold, the Hedges

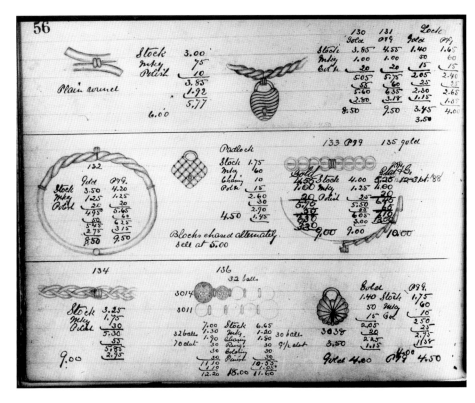

101. Advertisement for Day & Clark, including a bracelet design, ca. 1887, in *Alphabets, Monograms, Initials, Crests, Etc.* (New York: E.W. Bullinger, ca. 1887).

102. Designs for bracelets, from the Alling & Co. cost book, 1886–1887, p. 56, ink on paper, collection of Larter & Sons, Laurence Harbor, New Jersey.

103. Designs for link bracelets, from the Alling & Co. cost book, 1886–1887, p. 54, ink on paper, collection of Larter & Sons, Laurence Harbor, New Jersey.

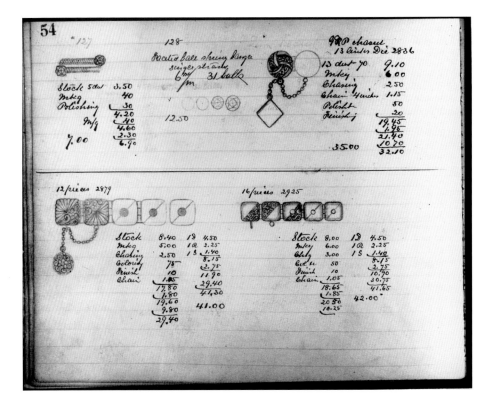

105. Woven-wire bracelet, by W.C. Edge & Sons, 1880–1890, gold and pearls, collection of Nancy N. Kattermann.

104. Advertisement for W.C. Edge & Sons, ca. 1887, in *Alphabets, Monograms, Initials, Crests, Etc.* (New York: E.W. Bullinger, ca. 1887).

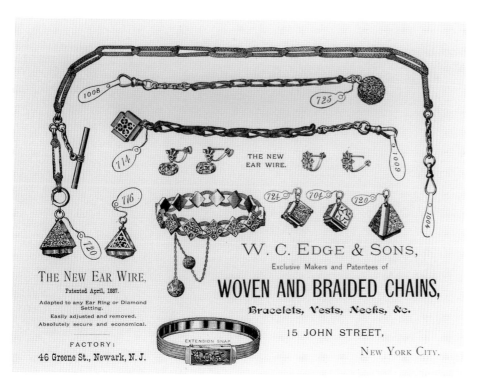

bracelet mimics small squares of checked cloth, pinned together at the edges (Fig. 106). This technique of combining yellow, white, red, and green gold in a single object was used in a variety of forms in Hedges' line (see Fig. 213).

Elsie Bee noted in her weekly commentary on jewelry fashions in 1891 that "bracelets in the form of serpents have come to the fore again. This may or may not be due to Sarah Bernhardt's introduction of serpents natural and serpents that are masterpieces of the goldsmith's art in her personification of Cleopatra."[83] Alphonse Mucha had designed a celebrated serpent armlet for Bernhardt, made by Georges Fouquet in Paris. Carter, Howe & Co. produced a more mundane, but nonetheless chic, coiled snake bracelet, with ruby-colored eyes, in silver or gold, for a less theatrical audience (Fig. 107).

The bangle and the link bracelet seem to have carried on a genteel fashion battle throughout the nineteenth century, with one or the other form taking precedence in any given season. The wide, hinged bangles and link bracelets of the mid-nineteenth century were worn in pairs, but the slender, lighter weight *fin-de-siècle* bangles, like their flexible, link competitors, could be worn in multiples, depending on the time of day, the materials used, and the wealth of the consumer. In early 1897, it was noted in the trade that "flexible gold bracelets, with jeweled enrichment, have returned to stay." Just as the Christmas season was gearing up that same year, the analysis was that "flexible bracelets divide favor with the more formal bands and bangles."[84]

Alling & Co. updated its 1880s tubular lock bangles with the addition of an enameled plaque—essentially a locket panel—depicting a woman with an ornate diadem set with diamonds (Fig. 108). Such headdresses echo Sarah Bernhardt's costumes on the stage as Cleopatra and Theodora in the 1890s. A third famous Bernhardt role, that of the title character in Edmond Rostand's *La Princesse Lointaine*, also involved an elaborate headdress, but with large flower blossoms behind the ears.[85] This image, too, popularized by Mucha's posters, made its way into American jewelry (see Fig. 77, the Alling & Co. scarf pin, as well as Fig. 40). More typical are the one-piece hollow bangles by Bishop & Bishop and Riker Brothers, with die-rolled or hand-engraved decoration, sometimes set with stones (Figs. 108, 109). Reed & Barton's New York store placed a holiday season ad in 1906 in *Vogue*, offering gold bracelets like this for $50. A couple of diamonds or sapphires might raise the retail cost to $110.[86] Fritzsche & Co. produced a hinged bangle in the form of a bent horseshoe nail as its entry in the popular

106. Jewelry of multicolored gold, by A.J. Hedges & Co., 1879–1890. Bracelet, gold, ruby, diamond, and sapphire, collection of Christopher English Walling; ring, private collection, New York.

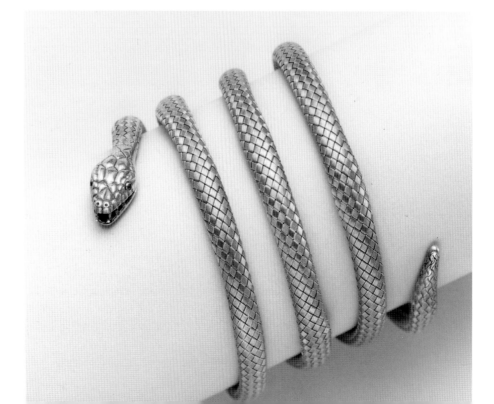

107. Woven-wire bracelet in the form of a coiled serpent, by Carter, Howe & Co., 1890–1900, silver and red stones, The Newark Museum, Gift of Gary N. Berger and Ulysses Grant Dietz, 1995 (95.58.1).

109. Dated bangle bracelets. From top: with design of dragons, by Riker Brothers, engraved date of 1908, gold and sapphires, collection of Doris Weinstein; in the form of a coiled horseshoe nail, by Fritzsche & Co., gold and diamonds, patent date of January 28, 1908, collection of Stephen Fishbach; with hand-engraved foliate decoration, by Riker Brothers, dated Christmas 1906, gold, collection of Joyce Chapman.

108. Bangle bracelets, 1890–1910. From top: with a profile of a "Byzantine" woman, by Alling & Co., gold, enamel, and diamonds, The Newark Museum, Purchase 1994 The Millicent Fenwick Fund (94.45); by Herpers Brothers, gold, collection of Margarette Herpers Remington; by Alling & Co., gold, peridots, and pearls, collection of Ruth Caccavale; by Bishop & Bishop, gold and cabochon garnets, The Newark Museum, Purchase 1993 The Millicent Fenwick Fund (93.175)

realm of "horsey jewelry." Such bangles (Fig. 109) were "the newest thing out" in 1907, and were made by other jewelers as well.[87] Unger Brothers, in the 1890s, produced silver tubular bangles mimicking ancient gold jewelry, although in addition to the classical lions' heads, they also included bulldogs (Fig. 110). By the turn of the century, delicate openwork bangles became more popular, a line of them appearing in Alling & Co.'s 1910 factory cost book.[88] Herpers Brothers made a bangle using one of its more elaborate gold gallery designs. Tiffany & Co.'s Newark plant also produced pierced silver bracelets in a Celtic style, set with amethysts, at the turn of the century (Fig. 111). Silver jewelry, although less expensive, was not necessarily relegated to less wealthy buyers. It was considered chic for summer wear with the all-white costumes that prevailed in hot weather. A certain Arts and Crafts élan probably gave silver jewelry cachet as well, something that would later work to the advantage of silversmiths such as Georg Jensen.

A rare link bracelet, of small gold knots, probably represents Unger's early years, before

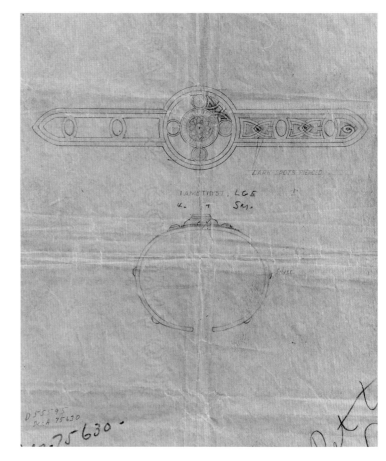

110. Bangle bracelets inspired by ancient examples, by Unger Brothers, 1890–1900, silver and red stones, private collection.

silver jewelry occupied the firm's full attention (Fig. 112, bottom). One other link bracelet by Unger, of interlocking gold and platinum links, is known and may also be of this early period.[89] Bippart, Griscom & Osborn's chrysoprase and pearl bracelet, with "art links," exemplifies Newark flexible link bracelets of the early twentieth century, while the same firm's platinum and diamond link bracelet, descended in the Bippart family, reveals the change in style by the end of World War I. Brassler's sapphire and pearl link bracelet (Fig. 113) shows the attention to detail typical of that firm's jewelry, while the elaborate bracelet by Riker Brothers, made of Art Nouveau plaques and replete with diamonds and a large pink kunzite (see Fig. 10), probably represents the grandest type of link bracelet from Newark's factories at the turn of the century.

The link bracelet with lapis lazuli cabochons and carved moonstones, by Theberath & Co., made about 1920 (Fig. 112, top), may demonstrate the middle-market version of the lavish "fruit salad" bracelets being produced in the 1920s by New York firms such as Cartier. Carved Asian stones, especially jade, were extremely popular by the end of World War I,[90] and

111. Design for silver bangle bracelets in the Celtic style set with amethysts, by Tiffany & Co., 1890–1900, Tiffany & Co. Archives.

112. Link bracelets, 1890–1920. From top: by Theberath & Co., ca. 1920, gold, platinum, carved moonstones, and lapis lazuli, private collection; by Bippart, Griscom & Osborn, 1915–1920, platinum and diamonds, collection of H. Jack Hunkele; by Bippart, Griscom & Osborn, 1900–1910, gold, chrysoprase, and pearls, The Newark Museum, Purchase 1995 Membership Endowment Fund (95.105.4); by Unger Brothers, 1890–1900, gold, diamond, ruby, and sapphire, collection of Gladys and Robert Koch.

113. Link bracelet, by
Brassler Co., 1900–1910,
gold, sapphires, and
pearls, collection of Doris
Weinstein.

114. Designs for three Art
Deco bracelets, by Henry
Blank & Co., 1920–1930,
gouache on paper, Henry

Blank & Co. papers, New
Jersey Historical Society,
Newark.

Cartier's introduction of carved ruby, emerald, and sapphire beads fueled a strong fashion throughout that decade. Henry Blank & Co. in Newark produced at least a few versions of the costly "fruit salad" bracelet, along with the luxurious Art Deco link bracelets that are so identified with New York jewelers in the 1920s and 1930s (Fig. 114). These would undoubtedly have been sold, without the firm's trademark, under other names, such as Raymond Yard; Shreve, Crump & Low; Black, Starr & Frost; Oscar Heyman & Co.; or Tiffany & Co.—all firm names that appear in the Blank archives.[91]

Henry Blank & Co. specialized, however, in watches and especially wristwatches—which in their most glamorous forms were bracelet watches. Long before men began to wear watches on their wrists, around World War I, women sported watches with jeweled bands. Elsie Bee noted in 1901 that "watch bracelets are an established style and all sorts of serpent and adjustable or 'expanding' bracelets are very much in evidence."[92] Whiteside & Blank, as the firm was known before 1915, purchased the rights to a 1905 patent on an expanding metal watch bracelet, which it produced in gold and

enamel for firms such as Tiffany & Co. and Patek Philippe (Fig. 115).[93] But even more glamorous are the bracelet watches the firm produced in the 1930s and 1940s, in two-color gold, with large semiprecious gemstones used both as decoration and as transparent crystals for the tiny watch faces (Fig. 116). No examples with the firm's "Cressarrow" trademark (a crescent pierced by an arrow) have yet come to light, but they must have been sold by high-end retailers all over the country.

Between 1937 and 1942, Tiffany & Co.'s Newark factory produced a line of modern gold and silver bracelets clearly influenced by the success of the modern silver jewelry that Georg Jensen's Manhattan shop had been selling since 1922 (Fig. 117).[94] One bracelet, designed about 1938, featured an airplane and an eagle (Fig. 118) and seemed to be aimed at the patriotic consumer as war loomed ever larger in Europe. Others were designed to be made *en suite* with matching earrings, brooches, and necklaces, and relate in design to a centerpiece and candelabra produced for Tiffany's display in 1940 at the New York World's Fair (Figs. 119, 120).[95] Tiffany also retailed sporty modern bracelets made by

115. Lady's bracelet watch, by Whiteside & Blank for Tiffany & Co., 1905–1910, gold, enamel, and sapphire, collection of Louis Scholz.

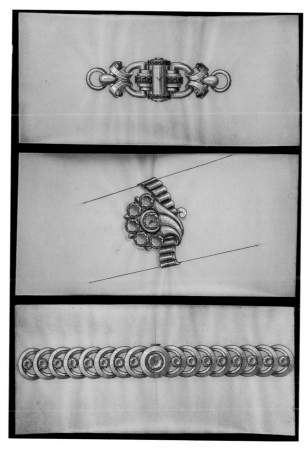

116. Three designs for bracelet watches in the modern style, 1930–1940, by Henry Blank & Co., gouache on paper, Henry Blank & Co. papers, New Jersey Historical Society, Newark.

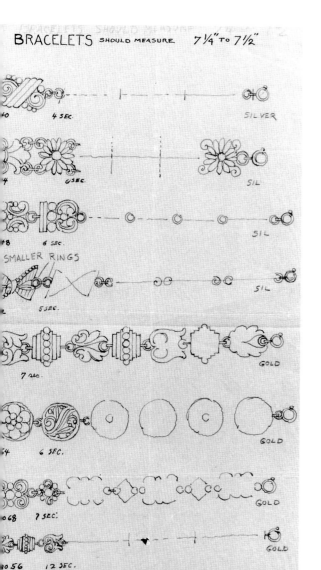

117. Designs for eight silver and gold bracelets, by Tiffany & Co., ca. 1941, ink on paper, Tiffany & Co. Archives.

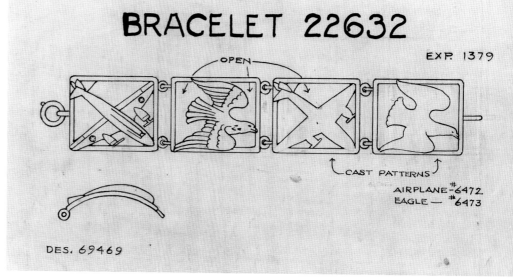

118. Design for a silver bracelet, number 22632, by Tiffany & Co., ca. 1938, ink on paper, Tiffany & Co. Archives.

other firms in Newark, such as Allsopp-Steller, that combined yellow and pink gold with semi-precious stones (see Fig. 207).

After World War II, Krementz & Co. began producing its celebrated line of rolled-gold-plate jewelry. This included both bangle and link bracelets in modern designs of two-color gold plate (Fig. 121). Krementz was the first Newark jewelry manufacturer—whose ranks had already been much thinned by Depression, war, and corporate merger—to acknowledge the fact that Newark's days as the center of the solid-gold jewelry industry were numbered.

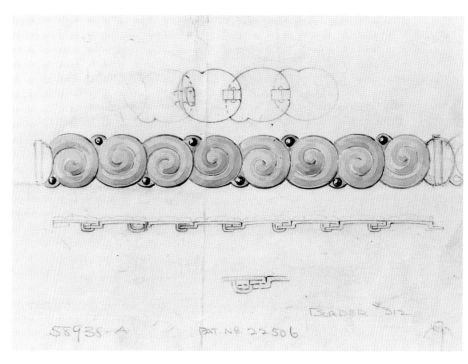

119. Design for a two-color gold bracelet, number 22506, by Tiffany & Co., ca. 1937, gouache on paper, Tiffany & Co. Archives.

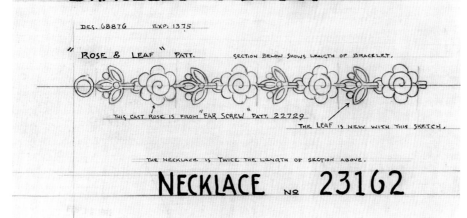

120. Design for a silver bracelet, number 23161, by Tiffany & Co., ca. 1942, ink on paper, Tiffany & Co. Archives.

121. Women's rolled-gold-plate jewelry, 1946, from Krementz & Co., *The Story of Gold in Modern Jewelry*, 1946, p. 9.

ACCESSORIES: LUXURIOUS TRIFLES FOR A GILDED AGE

Perhaps the most remarkable phenomenon related to the rise of jewelry in America was the vast array of accessories that the jewelry firms of Newark produced in gold and silver. The availability of raw materials, and the assistance of machinery, made it possible for skilled workers to create a range of products the likes of which had never been seen in the Western world. The influence of fashion arbiters and dictators of manners had produced a hunger for precious metal objects that expanded the possibilities for marking one's social status.

Buckles, for shoes and for belts, have perhaps the longest tradition among jewelry accessories, both in gold and in silver (see Fig. 47). Silver and even gold shoe buckles had been a small part of the output of Colonial silversmiths in America,[96] for such objects were traditionally made of base metals. By the end of the nineteenth century, buckles were being produced in precious metals, in unprecedented quantity, by a large number of firms in Newark (Fig. 122).

122. Engraved silver shoe buckles, 1900–1910. From top: rectangular, by Link & Angell; oval, by William B. Kerr Co., The Newark Museum, Gift of Mrs. William L. Dempsey, 1979 (79.613a-c)

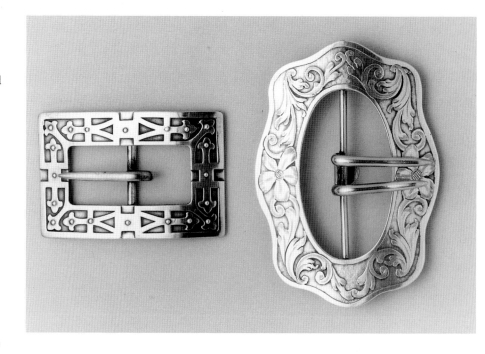

By the second decade of the twentieth century, the B.M. Shanley, Jr. Co. was specializing in silver, gold, and platinum men's belt buckles (see Figs. 9, 17), while William B. Kerr and Unger Brothers seem to have dominated the silver buckle market from the 1890s onward (Fig. 123). As Elsie Bee reported in 1896, "The belt has come to stay, and belt clasps and buckles are in greater demand than ever."[97]

Smaller firms, such as Pryor Manufacturing (absorbed by Shanley in the late 1910s[98]) and John W. Reddall & Co. also produced stylish and novel buckles and clasps. A particularly grand silver-gilt clasp in the form of paired wings by Reddall follows closely the mode of 1900 (Fig. 124): "Wings or wing-like forms figure largely in the new departure: and of them all the most novel shape is the angel's wing, long and sharply pointed, as in the pictures of old Italian masters."[99] Kerr produced some spectacular Renaissance-style belt clasps in gilded silver, set with semiprecious stones, which would have been dazzling accompaniments to a lady's costume (Fig. 125). As styles grew more restrained in the 1910s, Kerr's elegant buckles followed suit, with pastel enamels on engraved silver echoing the most costly products of European jewelers (Fig. 126).

A rare surviving black silk belt by Unger Brothers has both a large front clasp and an ornamental slide to place at the small of the back (Fig. 127). A consumer could probably have purchased belts complete at a retail store, for it was noted in 1896 that "jewelers now supply their patrons with belts as well as buckles."[100] The girdle was a form of belt that was uniquely popular around the turn of the century. It consisted of a series of plaques connected by chains, fastened at the front by a double clasp. The backs of the

124. Belt clasp in the form of wings, by John W. Reddall & Co., 1900–1910, gilt silver, private collection.

125. Belt clasp in the Renaissance style, by William B. Kerr Co., 1890–1910, gilt silver and amethysts, private collection.

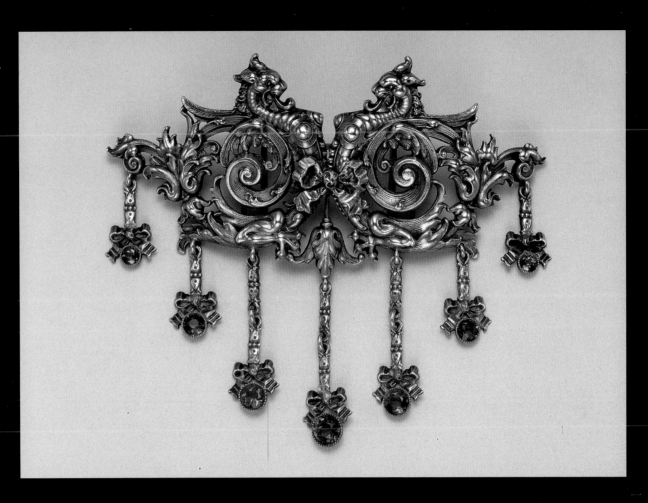

126. Belt buckle in the Neoclassical style, by William B. Kerr Co., 1910–1920, silver and enamel, private collection.

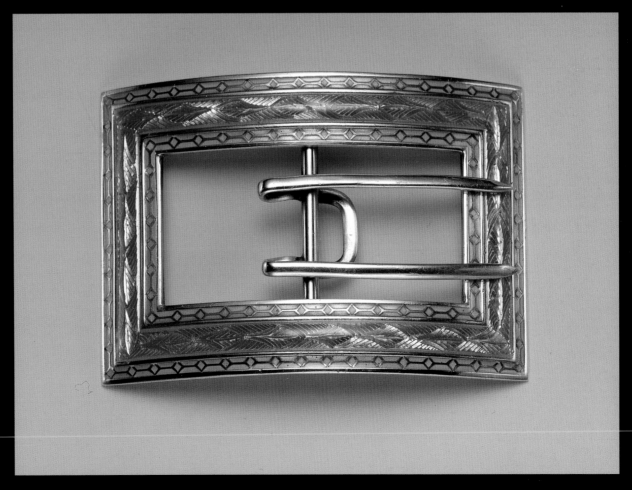

127. Black silk belt with silver clasp and slide, by Unger Brothers, 1900–1910, private collection.

plaques had bars, through which could be threaded ruched ribbons or strips of silk. The ends were stitched in place, thus creating a belt to match any outfit. Unger Bothers offered one such girdle (Fig. 128) with plaques showing a woman's head in profile surrounded by swirling irises. Unger listed this in its massive 1904 wholesale catalogue as design number 0410, (0410½ if gilded), and also showed girdles using various fabrics.[101]

Motifs such as the irises were adapted directly from French designs of the same period. Jewelry style columns in *The Jewelers' Circular—Weekly* were a means of immediate transmission of French motifs of this sort to the American manufacturers.[102] A girdle by Kerr of the same time uses the water lily, a prime floral motif in Art Nouveau jewelry. A 1901 jewelry fashion column notes: "A water lily—stems and leaves and bloom—furnishes the *motif* of a charming silver belt clasp in the new art fashion of light and graceful intertwining curves."[103] The most massive and sculptural of girdle designs by Kerr features a series of large plaques depicting water

nymphs—probably representing Wagner's Rhine Maidens from his epic *Gotterdäm-merung*.[104] Although of silver rather than gold, the inherent sculptural qualities of this piece—and even more modest examples—created a daring artistic quality attractive even to wealthy consumers. In less monumental conceptions, entire suites of matching silver jewelry were produced to create an ensemble. Kerr manufactured a girdle of Art Nouveau daisies, for which one could also buy coordinated necklaces, bracelets, and even earrings (Figs. 129, 130).

128. Silver girdles in the Art Nouveau style, 1900–1910. From top: in a design of "Rhine Maidens," by William B. Kerr Co., private collection; in a design of water lilies, by William B. Kerr Co., The Newark Museum, Purchase 1991 Carrie B.F. Fuld Bequest Fund (91.61); in a design of a woman's head surrounded by irises, by Unger Brothers, The Newark Museum, Purchase 1994 The Millicent Fenwick Fund (94.35)

129. Suite of silver jewelry with a motif of daisies, consisting of bracelet, necklace and girdle, by William B. Kerr Co., 1900–1910, private collections.

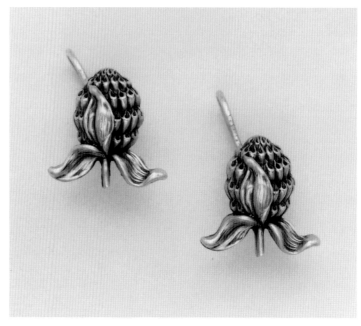

130. Silver earrings in the form of clover blossoms, by William B. Kerr Co., 1900–1910, private collection.

Associated with the belt was, inevitably, the chatelaine. Such devices were commonplace from the middle of the nineteenth century, but by the end of the century had become a significant product line for jewelry manufacturers. Silver or gold chatelaine hooks were suspended from a woman's sash or belt (Fig. 131) and from this could then be hung any number of useful articles. Of particular importance at the end of the century was the chatelaine bag which, in the hands of the Newark jewelers, became a fine chain-mail mesh bag of precious metal. Unger Brothers offered retail customers "chain purses" with matching chatelaine hooks in "all sizes, all styles, very large variety" (Fig. 132).[105] It is astonishing today that such complex and large objects were routine accessories, even for middle-class women. Retailers advertising in *Vogue* in 1902 could sell plated or base-metal chain bags for as little as $7, or sterling silver ones for $18 to $25. Gold-filled mesh bags were available the same year for $7 to $11, while a solid-gold mesh bag in 1906 could sell for as much as $485.[106]

131. Chatelaine hook in the Renaissance style, by William B. Kerr Co., 1900–1910, silver, 1⅞ × 1⅝ in., The Newark Museum, Purchase 1979 Carrie B.F. Fuld Bequest Fund (79.52)

132. Chain purse in the "Tulip" pattern, by Unger Brothers, 1900–1910, silver, collection of Barbara, Neal, and Stephen Schatz.

Small chain bags could in fact be worn as if they were large pendants. It was said in 1896 that "gold purses are still worn hung from a long neck chain."[107] When enriched with a large, faceted semiprecious stone, such a small bag did indeed become a massive lavaliere. "A yellow topaz in the top of a gold purse, pleases a desirable class of patrons."[108] Another column noted that the special expandable purse tops, made of crisscrossed metal bars, did not allow for the use of splendid topazes on these "luxurious trifles."[109] A rare surviving example of this sort of small bag with a huge stone was made by Carter, Howe, & Co. (Fig. 133). Although the stone here is a citrine, most consumers would have seen no difference between this and a topaz.

The most lavish surviving chatelaine bag from a Newark firm is an Egyptian-style example by Sloan & Co. (Fig. 134). Accompanied by its original chatelaine hook (see Fig. 42), the bag is of matte Roman-finish gold, decorated with applied wirework and beading, and ornamented with enamels. Following the celebrity of Sarah Bernhardt and her stage version of Cleopatra in 1890, the scarab was widely used as a decorative motif in jewelry. Elsie Bee noted that "a large turquoise or amethyst scarab may form the top

133. Mesh bag in the Renaissance style, by Carter, Howe & Co., 1900–1910, gold and citrine, collection of Sandy Adams.

jewel of a chain purse . . . ," and that "the scarab has become almost as ubiquitous as the serpent . . . and is by no means confined, as at first, to seals and rings, but is found in sleeve links, pendants, brooches, purse tops, umbrella handles and various other situations."[110] By 1909 it was noted by Lillian E. Purdy that "the gold mesh bag has now become a staple article, and the sales in this department of jewelry continue with steadiness."[111]

As late as World War I, mesh bags continued to be chic accessories; yet they were not, perhaps surprisingly, intended solely for evening wear. According to Newark's Durand & Co., which specialized in mesh bags, precious-metal chain purses could be used at different times of day. Green-gold mesh bags were appropriate for day-time shopping, although by this period the chatelaine hook had disappeared in favor of the gold-mesh wrist strap. Platinum and gold could be mixed for afternoon events where jewelry would be worn, such as a tea or a concert; while bags of jewel-encrusted platinum mesh were "considered in good form for evening affairs." Given that platinum was selling for $110 per ounce in 1917, "good form" might have been an understatement.[112]

134. Mesh bag and chatelaine hook in the Egyptian style, by Sloan & Co., 1896–1910, gold, enamel, and turquoise scarabs, The Newark Museum, Purchase 1996 Friends of the Decorative Arts Fund (96.21)

Vanity cases, card cases, spectacle cases, cigarette boxes, and match safes were all made of precious metal in Newark shops. Various firms offered gold and silver match safes, before the days of safety matches, to protect sulfur matches from getting damp or accidentally catching fire in one's pocket (Figs. 135, 136). In 1895 it was noted that "match safes of dull silver and covered with repoussé ornament in which goddesses and loves [cupids] are conspicuous, have made a sudden and prominent appearance."[113] These containers were used by men and by women, as were the matching cigarette cases. Tiffany & Co.'s Newark factory produced a matching lady's cigarette case and match safe (Figs. 137, 138) for its display at the 1901 Pan American Exposition in Buffalo. Such jeweled accessories were "made expressly for the fair sex," for whom smoking was as chic to some as it was scandalous to others.[114]

135. Match safes, 1890–1910. Counterclockwise from top: in the Rococo style, by Unger Brothers, silver, The Newark Museum, Gift of Miss Hannah Wimpleberg, 1933 (33.237); in the Art Nouveau style, by William B. Kerr Co., silver, The Newark Museum, Purchase 1995 Charles Edison Bequest Fund (95.103); plain with script monogram, by Battin & Co., gold, collection of Gary N. Berger.

136. Match safe in the Renaissance style, 1890–1900, by Unger Brothers, gold and ruby, collection of Barnett Rarities, Birmingham, Michigan.

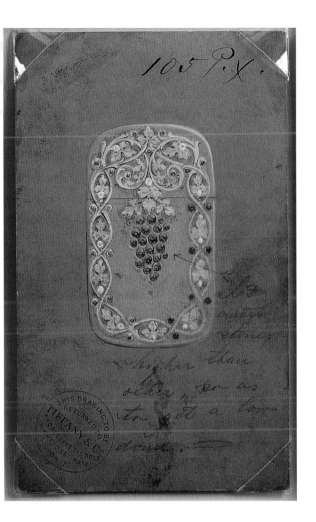

137. Design for a match safe with a motif of grapevines, designed by Paulding Farnham for Tiffany & Co., ca. 1900, gouache on paper, Tiffany & Co. Archives.

138. Cigarette case with a motif of grapevines, designed by Paulding Farnham for Tiffany & Co., 1901, gold, diamonds, Montana sapphires, and amethysts, Tiffany & Co. Permanent Collection.

Tiffany's also made other exquisitely enameled and engraved accessories in the Newark plant, early in the century (Figs. 139, 140) and well into World War II (Fig. 141), but the firm was by no means alone. Carrington & Co. made miniature Louis XVI-style powder compacts to be worn on chains (see Fig. 47), as well as gold cigarette cases for men and women.[115] B.M. Shanley advertised gold and jeweled vanity cases, and also made luxurious spectacle cases with cabochon jewels for clasps (Fig. 142).[116]

William B. Kerr Co., purchased by Gorham in 1906,[117] continued to make silver card and vanity cases well into the 1910s and 1920s (Fig. 143), and Henry Blank & Co. produced a line of Art Deco accessories with lavishly enameled cases in the 1920s that rivaled the best of the French competition (Figs. 144, 145). Allsopp-Steller, which was purchased by Krementz & Co. about 1950, produced silver woman's accessories in the 1940s that were enriched with gold and precious stones. These were sold largely to Tiffany & Co. for retail in its Fifth Avenue store (Fig. 146).[118]

139. Vanity case in the Louis XVI style, by Tiffany & Co., 1910–1920, gold, Tiffany & Co. Permanent Collection.

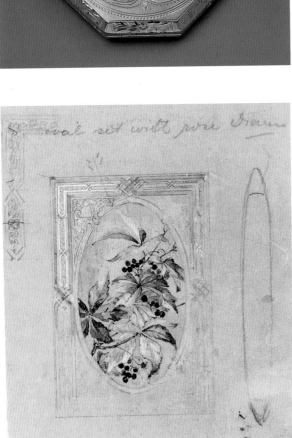

140. Design for an enameled cigarette case with a design of bittersweet, by Tiffany & Co., 1890–1900, gouache on cardboard, Tiffany & Co. Archives.

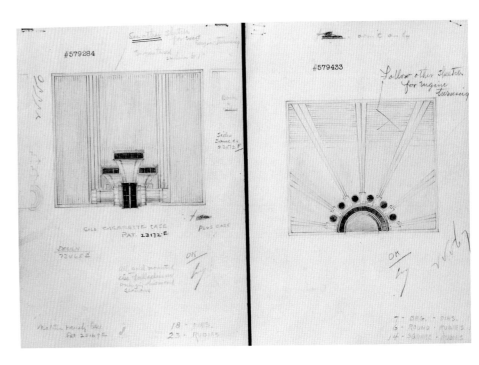

141. Two designs for cigarette cases in the modern style, by Tiffany & Co., early 1940s, ink and gouache on paper, Tiffany & Co. Archives.

142. Spectacle case in the Renaissance style, by B.M. Shanley, Jr. Co., 1908, gold and ruby cabochon, The Newark Museum, Gift of Mrs. William L. Dempsey, 1980 (80.42). This case was given to Bernard Michael Shanley, Jr., by his wife as a tenth wedding anniversary gift in 1908, the year the firm was founded.

143. Purse and powder box in the modern style, by William B. Kerr Co. (purse), 1910–1930, silver and gold, The Newark Museum, Gift of Mrs. Clifford Gould, 1990 (90.236). The powder box was manufactured by a different firm, although the two pieces were clearly retailed together.

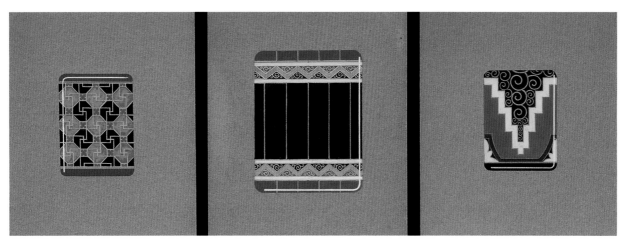

144. Three designs for enameled gold cases for purse watches in the Art Deco style, by Henry Blank & Co., 1920–1930, gouache on paper, Henry Blank & Co. papers, New Jersey Historical Society, Newark.

145. Design for enameled gold case for a purse watch or card case in the Art Deco style, by Henry Blank & Co., 1920–1930, gouache on paper, Henry Blank & Co. papers, New Jersey Historical Society, Newark.

146. Silver accessories with jeweled enrichment in the modern style, by All-sopp-Steller, 1940–1950, collection of Krementz & Co., Newark.

Lorgnettes—folding spectacles—were an accessory that appealed as much to the sense of vanity as to that of luxury. Although the numerous designs possible with die-stamping made lorgnette cases "veritable works of art" in the eyes of the consumer, the spectacles themselves were probably popular because they were "decorative, easy to wear, and dispense[d] with eye glasses for the nonce (Fig. 147)."[119] Krementz, which specialized in gold lorgnettes in an array of styles, from plain to Egyptian to Art Nouveau, capitalized on this idea in its trade ads. Quoting at length from a *Harper's Bazaar* article from July 1895, Krementz was quick to point out in its advertising that women's objections to wearing eyeglasses could easily be overcome by the lorgnette. It was not only quick to raise to the eyes, and easy to open with the press of a button, but was "graceful, and capable of being used as effectively as a fan.... It suggests no creeping invasion of age, since youth and roses, equally with wrinkles and gray hairs, find it a satisfactory possession."[120] Unger Brothers offered both silver and silver-gilt lorgnettes in its lush Art Nouveau patterns. Both Durand and Frank Krementz (of the same family, but a different firm from Krementz & Co.) offered "shopping lorgnons" in yellow or white gold for daytime, as did Carter, Gough & Co. Frank Krementz's version had nose clasps, enabling it to be worn like a pince-nez, thus saving the lady's arm from "the strain of holding the lorgnons to the eyes sometimes for hours at a time."[121]

147. Lorgnettes with spring mechanisms, 1890–1910. From top: in the Egyptian style, by Krementz & Co., gold, steel, and glass, The Newark Museum, Purchase 1994 Franklin Conklin Memorial Fund (94.59); in the Art Nouveau style, by Unger Brothers, gilt silver, collection of Gladys and Robert Koch.

Opera glasses, most typically sold in mother-of-pearl cases, were also produced in jeweled gold. A rare surviving example made at Tiffany's Newark works acknowledges the truth to the trade report that, among the opera glasses brought out for the season, "gold and precious stones are not disdained (Fig. 148)."[122]

It is hard to conceive how relatively commonplace such "luxurious trifles" were as recently as the 1930s. All these accessory items in gold or platinum, and even in silver, have become relatively scarce today simply by virtue of their material value. Most have been—and are daily still being—melted down for scrap, victims as much of their inherent value as of changes in fashion.

148. Opera glasses in the Louis XVI style, by Tiffany & Co., 1900–1910. gold and diamonds, Tiffany & Co. Permanent Collection.

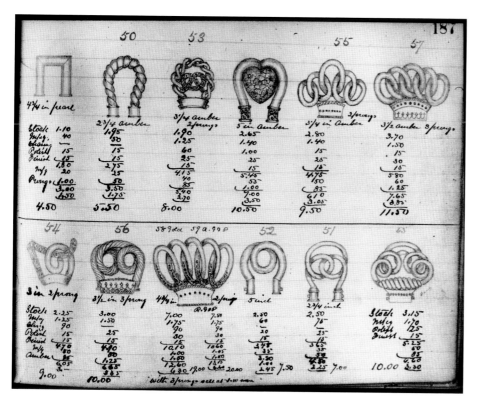

149. Designs for hairpins and ornaments, from the Alling & Co. cost book, 1886–1887, p. 187, ink on paper, collection of Larter & Sons, Laurence Harbor, New Jersey.

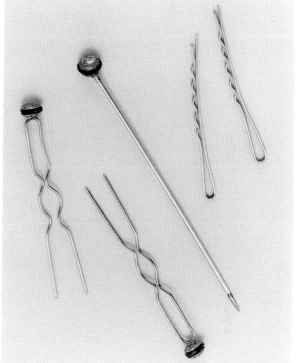

150. Gold hair accessories, 1900–1910. Bobby pins, by Enos Richardson & Co., The Newark Museum, Gift of the Estate of Gertrude L. Grote, 1987, in memory of Herman E. Grote (87.59g-h); veil pins and hatpin with faceted amethyst and onyx beads, by Day, Clark & Co., from its Juliet Gift Set, collection of Simon-ette Hakim.

Hair-related accessories were ubiquitous in the late nineteenth and early twentieth century. Alling & Co. was making a variety of elaborate gold ornamental hairpins in 1887 (Fig. 149); even bobby pins, that most mundane of hair accessory, were made in solid gold by Enos Richardson (Fig. 150). Day, Clark, & Co. specialized in "rondelle" jewelry, which featured applied vermicelli wire-work and faceted onyx or amethyst beads. One popular Day, Clark item was the Juliet Gift Set, consisting of gold pins for fastening both the hat and the veil to the hair (Fig. 150). These were marketed in *Vogue*, in different patterns, for Easter, for Christmas, and as suitable for teenage girls (see Fig. 19).[123] Side and back hair combs, used to sculpt and secure the coiffures of the period, were made in gold, silver, and tortoise-shell. John W. Reddall & Co. advertised solid-gold side combs in 1895,[124] while the stock in trade for firms like Herpers, Krementz, and Day, Clark & Co. was tortoiseshell trimmed with gold and semiprecious stones (Figs. 151, 152). Hatpins loomed large, because of the size and popularity of hats. Huge numbers of hatpins were made of non-precious materials, but they were produced in gold and silver by Newark firms such as Unger, Kerr, and Carter, Sloan & Co. (Figs. 153-155). As in all jewelry of the period, we find Renaissance, Art Nouveau, and Egyptian motifs.

During the great age of jewelry manufacturing in Newark, there was virtually no accessory that could not be made in precious metal. From intimate items such as men's suspender buckles (see Fig. 67) and garter side-elastics (used to hold up the socks, Fig. 156), to mustache combs, glove-button hooks, and folding fans (Figs. 157, 158), everything was fair game for the jeweler's imagination. "Silver bib holders [were] among the conveniences provided for children," and napkin clips (on longer chains) were available for unsure adults, in Art Nouveau, Rococo, or Neo-Classical styles (Fig. 159).[125] "Violet holders" (see Fig. 157), being "convex enough to confine the stems of the orthodox bunch of violets," were touted in the trade journals. Unger Brothers made hand-held posy vases, to hold a scented nosegay on a hot, crowded city street (Fig. 160). Even gold and silver spurs, in pairs for men and singly for ladies riding sidesaddle, were not unheard of in the age of novelties (Fig. 161).[126]

152. Advertisement for back hair combs, by Day, Clark & Co., *The Jewelers' Circular—Weekly*, vol. 50, February 1, 1905, p. 94.

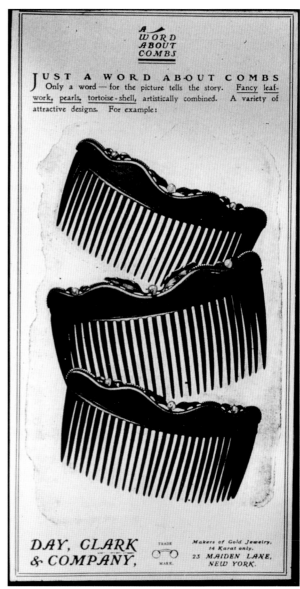

153. Three hatpins, 1890–1910. Left to right: in the Art Nouveau style, by Whitehead & Hoag, silver plate, collection of Marguerite Fairbrothers; in the form of a lotus bud, by Carter, Howe & Co., gold and green onyx, The Newark Museum, Gift of Janet and Ricardo Zapata, 1995 (95.18.2); in the form of a lion's head, by Unger Brothers, silver and red stones, collection of Marguerite Fairbrothers.

154. Silver hatpins, 1890–1900. Clockwise from top: in the form of a winged putto, by William B. Kerr Co.; in the form of a sweet-pea blossom, by William B. Kerr Co.; in the form of a bulldog's head with red stone eyes, by Unger Brothers, collection of Marguerite Fairbrothers.

155. Hatpins in a silver hatpin holder, 4¼ in. (height), by Unger Brothers, collection of Marguerite Fairbrothers.

156. Pair of man's garter side-elastics in the Renaissance style, by William B. Kerr Co., 1890–1900, silver and rubberized silk, private collection.

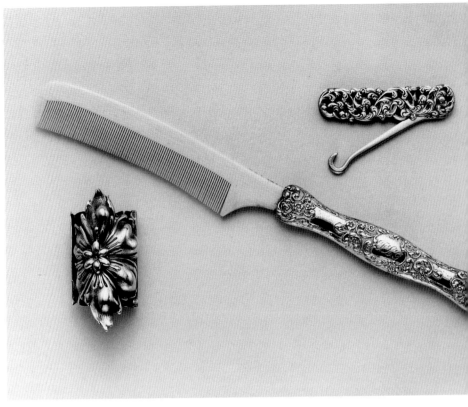

157. Silver accessories by Unger Brothers, 1900–1910. Left to right: violet holder, private collection; mustache comb, The Newark Museum, Gift of Miss Jewel Zelder, 1974 (74.285); folding glove-button hook, The Newark Museum, Gift of Mrs. Clinton C. Gilbert, 1942 (42.195)

158. Folding fan by Battin & Co., 1890–1910, silver and silk, private collection.

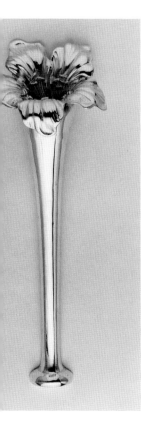

159. Pairs of bib and napkin clips on chains,
1900–1910. Left to right:
bib clips in the form of
poppies, by Pryor Manu
facturing Co., silver, The
Newark Museum, Gift of
Janet and Ricardo Zapata,
1995 (95.18.1); napkin or
bib clips in the Neoclassical style, by Unger Brothers, silver and enamel, The
Newark Museum, Pur-
chase 1994 The Millicent
Fenwick Fund (94.34);
napkin clips in the Rococo
style, by Unger Brothers,
silver. The Newark
Museum, Purchase 1994
The Millicent Fenwick
Fund (94.33)

160. Silver hand-held posy
vase, by Unger Brothers,
1890–1900, private collection.

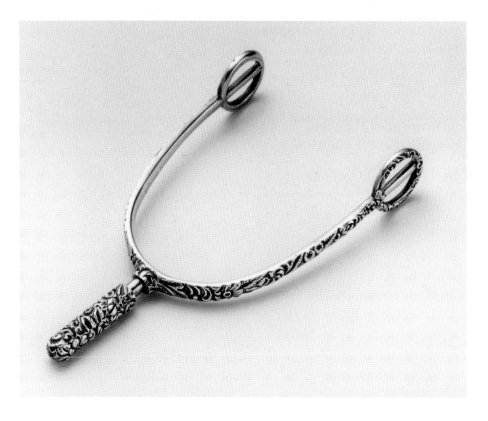

161. Silver sidesaddle spur,
by William B. Kerr Co.,
1890–1900, collection of
Louis Scholz.

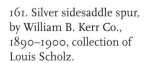

Of all the forms of jewelry produced during the past 150 years, the brooch seems to have survived in the greatest numbers. This is, quite simply, because the function of the brooch has remained virtually unchanged since its rise in popularity during the second quarter of the nineteenth century. Regardless of styles and fashions, brooches can always be worn, especially if there is sentiment attached. Despite attempts to make the brooch functional, it remained an object of decoration. Moreover, unlike most expensive and grand pieces of jewelry made in this period, brooches—small in scale, well-made, and visually charming—are still around. Great gemstones rarely make it through a century without being reset in updated settings or even recut. Pocket watches and fobs, and all the accoutrements of lifestyles past, have ceased to be meaningful to many people. However, to quote the inevitable Elsie Bee: "No manifestations in the way of jewelry are so dainty and poetical as those of the brooch."[127] The possibilities of brooch design were almost endless in Newark's jewelry

heyday; and the appeal of the brooch was almost universal.

The essential brooch in the Victorian prime of Newark jewelry-making was the lace pin, so called because it was used to fasten—or just decorate—the lace fichus, tippets, and collars that made up part of every lady's costume. The cameo brooch has its roots in the early nineteenth century, as part of the Neoclassical fashion that dominated American taste from the post-Revolutionary years until the 1840s. Brooches set with imported cameos were made in Newark in the 1860s and in the 1890s, during two of the periodic revivals of the form (see Fig. 36).

J.H. Bentley & Co. and Alling & Co. were both designing and producing gem-set gold lace pins in the latest style by the middle of the 1880s (Figs. 162, 163). Typically, a lace pin would have matching ear drops, and these survive with enough frequency to confirm their popularity (Fig. 164), although few can be attributed to specific Newark makers due to the lack of marking of any kind before the 1890s. Terminology seems to have been fairly fluid, and Alling's use

163. Designs for lace pins and ear drops, from the J.H. Bentley & Co. cost book, 1885–1893, p. 45, ink on paper, The Newark Museum, Gift of Louis Waldman, 1939 (39.445)

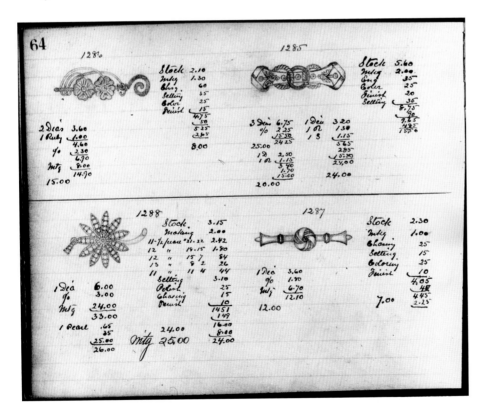

162. Designs for lace pins, from the Alling & Co. cost book, 1886–1887, p. 64, ink on paper, collection of Larter & Sons, Laurence Harbor, New Jersey.

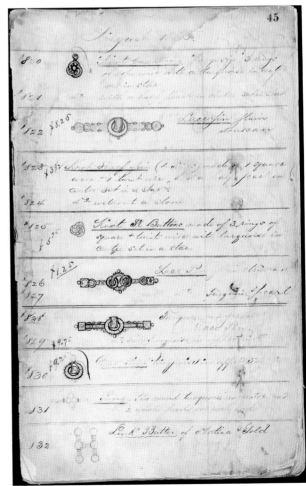

of the term "lace pin" refers equally to forms that somewhat later are called bar pins. Both bar pins and lace pins were, however, used for the same purpose. Early in the twentieth century, *Vogue* published articles on the latest fashions in embroidered muslin and lace neckwear for women, showing them decorated with jeweled pins of various shapes and sizes.[128]

The bar pin, usually long and narrow (Fig. 165), was by the end of the nineteenth century often accompanied by a pair of smaller versions known as handy pins (Fig. 166). These were used for a variety of functions, from holding shoulder straps in place to fastening cuffs in lieu of sleeve buttons. In 1887, Alling & Co. made cuff pins, which were simply short bar pins, while in 1917 Bippart, Griscom & Osborn was offering "spot pins" to match its "bar brooches." While sold as sets, various publications hailed the versatility of bar pins, both to the retailer and the consumer, suggesting that the pieces in the sets were sold separately as well (Fig. 167).[129] Day, Clark & Co. advertised engine-turned bar pin and handy pin sets with rich translucent enamels, much like the

Carter, Howe & Co. version shown in Fig. 165. Kohn & Co. produced a less expensive line in 10-carat gold.[130] Sets of handy pins, in pink or blue enamel, were also marketed for babies, with the additional function of holding the bib. In a 1914 issue of *Vogue*, Thomas W. Adams promoted a novelty bar pin that was hinged at the center, and thus could be worn with V-neck dresses or as a straight bar pin (see Fig. 20). A.J. Hedges made a complete line of handy pins, in seven different sizes.[131] In 1909, the same firm also packaged four bar pins in three different sizes (veil, sash, and handy pins) with a matching bangle bracelet "in a variety of stones" as "a handsome gift for a Spring Bride."[132]

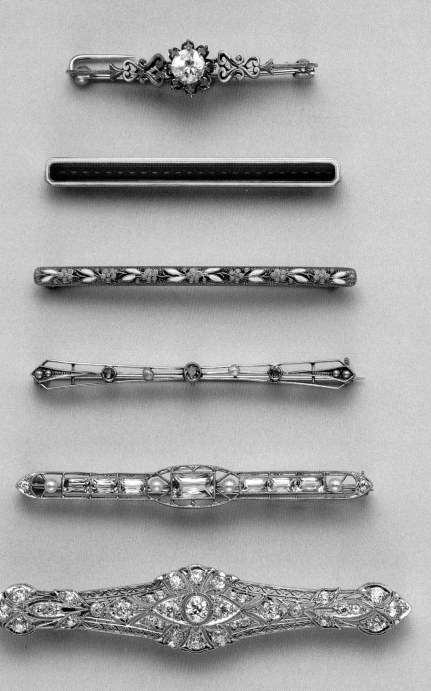

165. Bar pins. From top: in the Neo-Grec style, by Ferdinand Herpers, 1875–1880, gold and imitation diamond, 2 in. (length), The Newark Museum, Gift of Henry F. Herpers, 1937 (37.641); with guilloché enameling, by Carter, Howe & Co., 1900–1910, gold and enamel, The Newark Museum, Purchase 1995 Membership Endowment Fund (95.105.7); with floral motif, by Frank Krementz & Co., 1915–1920, gold and enamel, The Newark Museum, Gift of Mrs. Leo di Rebaylio, 1925 (25.1086); with open filigree, by Keller Jewelry Manufacturing Co., 1910–1920, gold, sapphires and pearls, The Newark Museum, Gift of Gary N. Berger and Ulysses Grant Dietz, 1996 (96.40.3); filigree in the Arts and Crafts style, by Carter, Gough & Co., 1915–1925, platinum, gold, aquamarines, pearls, and diamonds, The Newark Museum, Purchase 1993 The Millicent Fenwick Fund (93.176); filigree in the Art Deco style, by Bippart, Griscom & Osborn, 1920–1930, platinum and diamonds, collection of H. Jack Hunkele.

166. Two pairs of handy pins. From top: by Krementz & Co., 1900–1920, gold, pearls, and pink enamel, collection of Louis Scholz; by Wordley, Allsopp & Bliss or Allsopp-Bliss, 1915–1925, platinum, gold, and sapphires, private collection.

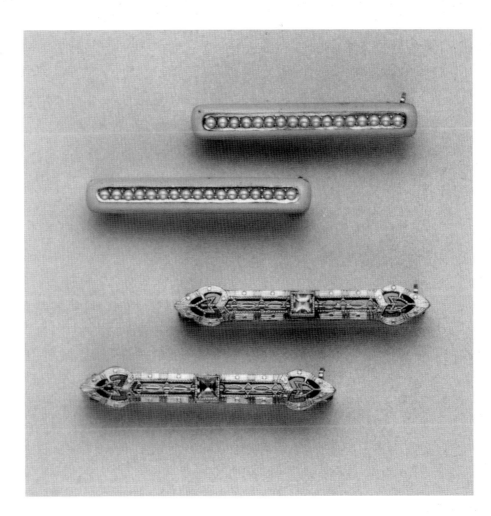

167. Matching bar pin and two handy pins, by Krementz & Co., 1900–1910, gold and enamel, collection of Krementz & Co., Newark.

The brooch blossomed as a decorative form by the end of the century as women began to wear more than one, and wanted different brooches to accompany different outfits and seasons. In the 1860s, the large Neo-Grec cameo could serve any and all brooch "needs" for the Victorian matron, but by the 1890s the etiquette as well as the variety of brooch-wearing possibilities had expanded to accommodate both the manufacturer and the consumer. Maud Cooke outlined a detailed protocol for brooch-wearing in her 1896 *Social Life, or,*

Novelty in brooches was a major selling point, and the trade noted in 1898 that "Brooches of unique design are in request. These ornaments are no longer worn with old time precision directly in the center of the collar; but a little to left side. In some instances, two brooches appear, one to the right side and one to the left side of the collar."[134] The variety of brooches in the late nineteenth and early twentieth century was as broad and eclectic as the contemporaneous styles for interior decoration.

168. Three crescent brooches. From top: with alternating gems, by Bippart, Griscom & Osborn, 1890–1910, gold, pearls, and sapphires, 2 in. (length), collection of Kathleen Bennett; with serpent, by Riker Brothers, gold, pearls, enamel, demantoid garnet, and rubies, private collection, Pennsylvania; with blossom, by Thiery & Co., gold, enamel, pearls, and diamond, collection of Helene P. Konkus.

169. Designs for lace pins, including one in the form of a bee, from the Alling & Co. cost book, 1886–1887, ink on paper, p. 68, collection of Larter & Sons, Laurence Harbor, New Jersey.

The Manners and Customs of Polite Society. A single brooch, with some apparent useful function—such as holding a lace collar or a pendant watch—was all that a lady should wear during the morning or on the street. For visiting, something slightly grander would be possible. Enameling was acceptable, but not even a tiny diamond in a flower pin was correct during daylight hours. Glittering gems were only appropriate in the evening, and even here the grandeur of the occasion dictated quantity and quality. Full-dress evening clothes allowed for "any number of well-chosen jewels," so long as they harmonized.[133] One should not believe, however, that these rules were adhered to with any strictness. Miss Cooke was most likely reacting to popular jewelry-wearing habits, trying to correct bad ones as well as to instill good ones in her readers.

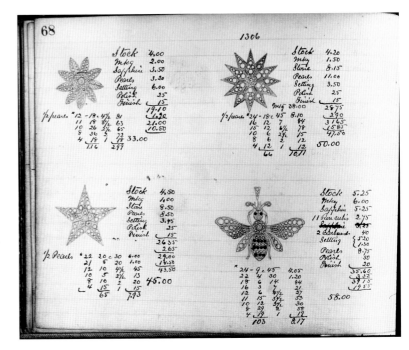

170. Lizard brooch, by Riker Brothers, 1890–1900, gold, enamel, demantoid garnets, and diamond, 1½ in. (length), private collection.

Crescents afforded many decorative possibilities, partly because the designs could be enlivened with applied snakes, flowers, or insects. Newark's crescent pins were inspired by the great diamond crescents worn by European aristocrats and American socialites (Fig. 168).[135] Even though Maud Cooke disapproved of wearing beasts or reptiles as jewelry, the practice seems to have been extensive in America by 1889, and Alling & Co. was making a jeweled bee lace pin as early as 1886 (Fig. 169).[136] Elsie Bee noted in 1895 that "The English are commenting on the American's love for insects, snakes and grotesque animals in jewelry," and reported on enameled lizard pins the same year (Fig. 170).[137]

Insects had a special place in this glittering menagerie (see Fig. 10). Enameled butterflies and bees were a specialty of A.J. Hedges & Co., while Crane & Theurer produced a jeweled and enameled spider of daunting scale (Fig. 171). Both spiders and dragonflies had their roots as motifs in the Japanism of the 1870s, and both made the aesthetic transition into the Art Nouveau period, which itself borrowed heavily from Japanese naturalistic motifs. Spider pins were noted in the 1894 *Jewelers' Circular and Horological Review*, while the new dragonfly and butterfly craze was noted in 1895, on the same page as an ad from Hedges featuring its new dragonfly veil

171. Insect jewelry. Counterclockwise from top: spider, by Crane & Theurer, gold, enamel, and diamonds, private collection; dragonfly, by Riker Brothers, 1900–1910, gold, enamel, and diamonds, collection of Christie Cavanaugh; dragonfly, by A.J. Hedges & Co., 1890–1900, gold, demantoid garnets, and diamonds, 1¼ × 1⅛ in., The Newark Museum, Purchase 1992 The Dr. and Mrs. Earl LeRoy Wood Bequest Fund (92.92)

pin (Fig. 172).[138] The dragonfly in particular was taken up by the leaders of the Art Nouveau movement and became a trademark of that style.

One of the most sophisticated insect designs that came from a Newark factory was Whiteside & Blank's brooch showing a woman's body with butterfly wings (see Fig. 50). Although somewhat tamer and smaller than similar designs produced by French jeweler Gaston Lafitte in 1903 and 1904, this brooch comes as close to embodying the French Art Nouveau aesthetic as any from a Newark shop. First advertised to the trade

173. Three swallow brooches, 1895–1905. Counterclockwise from top: by Carter, Howe & Co., gold and enamel, 2⅜ in. (length), private collection, Pennsylvania; by Carter, Howe & Co., gold and enamel, private collection; by Riker Brothers, gold, enamel, and diamonds, The Newark Museum, Purchase 1993 The Millicent Fenwick Fund (93.178)

in 1905, it was offered in a number of different versions. The Museum's version of this pin probably retailed at about $80, while two additional small diamonds would have added another $15 to the cost.[139] Riker also produced a variation on the woman with wings (Fig. 174), this time slipping an angel's wings onto a Renaissance-type caryatid emerging from a flower. On the whole, such motifs probably interested American adapters and consumers for their style and novelty, rather than for the high-flown symbolism implicit in the conceptions of René Lalique and his fellow European designers.

Enameled birds were reported as entering the American jewelry repertoire in 1893 (Fig. 173).[140] Swallows were favorites at the end of the century, although they had appeared in Japanese-inspired decoration in the 1870s. It is easy to

174. *Plique à jour* enameling, by Riker Brothers, 1890–1900. Clockwise from top: necklace pendant in the Renaissance style, gold, enamel, and diamond, 1⅛ × 1 in., collection of Nelson Rarities, Portland, Maine; brooch in an Art Nouveau/Renaissance style, gold, enamel, and turquoise, private collection, Pennsylvania; brooch in the Japanese style, gold, enamel, and ruby, collection of Reuben Simantov, Inc., New York; brooch in the Japanese/Art Nouveau style, gold, enamel, and diamonds, collection of Reuben Simantov, Inc., New York.

imagine a little flock of blue enameled swallows of varying sizes adorning a woman's bodice or bonnet. Other Japanesque water birds were used in Art Nouveau brooches with transparent enameling by Riker Brothers, one of the few Newark firms that produced the backless *plique à jour* technique (Fig. 174). These *plique à jour* brooches parallel designs found in the 1909 *Modern Design in Jewellery and Fans*, published in English, French, and German, a copy of which was owned by Herpers Brothers (Fig. 175).[141]

Other beasts appeared with the same sort of variety. Ram's head jewelry was capturing the imagination late in the nineteenth century. A ram's head brooch by Riker Brothers (Fig. 176) might have been a reference to classical antiquity. Italian jewelers had been using this motif in their neo-antique jewelry since the 1860s, as had English and Austrian makers. Tiffany & Co. produced a celebrated copy of an ancient double lion's head bracelet in the late 1870s, and ram's head versions appeared at the same time.[142] On the other hand, the ram's head could also have alluded to the zodiac. In 1909, Tiffany's book on birthstones by George F. Kunz cited Aries the ram as the symbol for March, and the stone for that month as the ruby.[143] Perhaps the ruby eye on the Riker Brothers ram was chosen for that reason as well.

Elsie Bee reported in 1892 that "a new watch chatelaine pin is a griffin or other medieval bird with wings outspread . . . [I]t holds a sword with a jeweled head." Another source a year later commented that "mythological animals furnish excellent models for unique jewelry. The Griffon [*sic*] . . . is one of those which is deserving of a

175. Plate of designs from *Modern Design in Jewellery and Fans,* book purchased by Herpers Brothers in 1909, The Newark Museum, Gift of Ferdinand J. Herpers, 1952 (52.265)

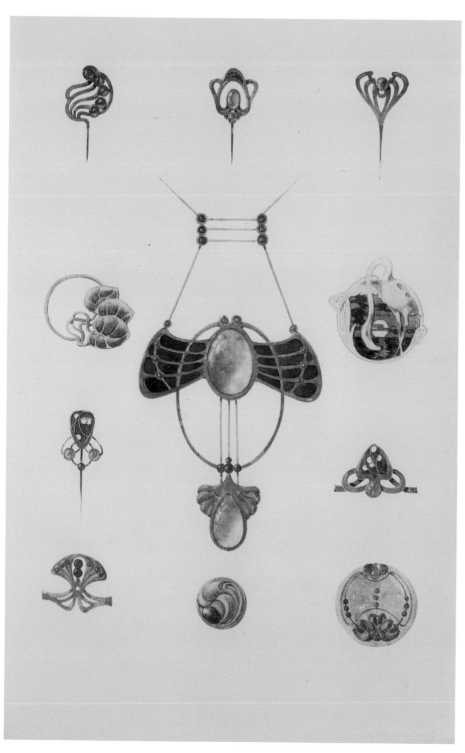

176. Brooch in the form of a ram's head, by Riker Brothers, 1890–1900, gold and ruby, ⅞ × ⅞ in., The Newark Museum, Gift of Gary N. Berger and Ulysses Grant Dietz, 1995 (95.105.2)

177. Griffin brooches, 1890–1900. Clockwise from top: by Riker Brothers, gold and ruby, 1⅝ × 1⅜ in., The Newark Museum, Purchase 1993 The Millicent Fenwick Fund (93.183); by Riker Brothers, gold, enamel, and diamonds, collection of Christie Cavanaugh; by Krementz & Co., gold and pearl, collection of Christie Cavanaugh; by Alling & Co., gold and diamond, private collection, Pennsylvania.

178. Plate of designs from *Die Perle (The Pearl)*, a jewelry design book published in Austria, in German, French and English, in 1879, and purchased by Herpers Brothers in New York City. The Newark Museum, Gift of Ferdinand J. Herpers, 1952 (52.259)

place in gold ornaments."[144] A large griffin brooch by Riker Brothers has a curved prong on the back, suitable for hanging a watch (Fig. 177). The smaller enameled version also has one of these chatelaine fixtures and closely matches Elsie Bee's description. Krementz and Alling both offered their versions of the griffin chatelaine pin. This Renaissance creature seems to have been produced in brooch form by the French firm of Plisson & Hartz between 1898 and 1904, but its roots go back to the neo-Renaissance-style *broches chimères*, or chimera brooches, designed by Parisian jeweler Alphonse Fouquet in the 1870s and 1880s.[145] Newark jewelers could also have found inspiration for griffin brooches in the designs of Carl Winkler that appeared in *Die Perle*, a massive compendium of jewelry design published in Vienna and sold in

New York City (Fig. 178). Ferdinand Herpers purchased the book, published in German, English, and French, for use in his Newark workshop.[146]

Still other flying creatures, less easy to categorize, appeared in the 1890s to slake the thirst for novelty. Bat-winged creatures with demonic heads must have added a dash of daring to a lady's corsage, while the owl was a popular symbol of wisdom, with references to the Greek goddess Athena (Fig. 179).

Not all brooches were figural. Stylized wreath forms were long popular. Some, such as the little pearl and ruby wreath by W.C. Edge (Fig. 180), were merely conventional designs, while others, such as the emblematic brooch adopted by the Church of Christ, Scientist (Fig. 181), used the wreath as a religious symbol, encircling the cross and crown of the Knights Templar. This brooch,

La Perle.

Bijouteries
composées de motifs ornementés par
Carl Winkler, estampeur à Hanau s/M.
(Texte voir Table des matières.)

Die Perle.

Schmuckgegenstände
zusammengesetzt aus Ornamentmotiven von
Carl Winkler, Estampeur in Hanau a/M.
(Text siehe im Inhaltsverzeichniss.)

The Pearl.

Jewelry
composed of ornamented motives by
Carl Winkler, estampeur, Hanau o/M.
(Text see index.)

Herausgegeben von Martin Gerlach.   II. Jahrgang. Blatt 23.   Xylographie u. Verlag von M. Gerlach & Co. Wien.
déposé.

179. Brooches with wings. From top: bat-winged demon's head, by Alling & Co., 1890–1900, gold and pearl, ⅝ × 2¼ in., private collection, Pennsylvania; brooch in the form of an owl, by A.J. Hedges & Co., gold, enamel, pearls, and amethyst, private collection, New York.

180. Brooch in the form of a wreath, by W.C. Edge & Co., 1890–1900, gold, pearls, and rubies, 1⅛ × 1⅛ in., collection of Nancy N. Kattermann.

181. Christian Science Church brooch in the form of a wreath, by Riker Brothers, 1900–1910, gold and pearls, The Newark Museum, Purchase 1994, Stella Goldstein Purchase Fund (94.158); cross in the Gothic style, by Sloan & Co., gold and amethysts, The Newark Museum, The Mrs. Roger Young Collection, Bequest of Mrs. Roger Young, 1960 (60.224)

113

produced in different sizes, was made for the Christian Science Church by Riker Brothers, although the design was patented in 1900 by a Concord, New Hampshire jeweler, James C. Derby.[147] The cross was a popular piece of jewelry, and not only among Catholics, from the middle of the Victorian era onward. John A. Riley & Sloan Co. (later Sloan & Co.) advertised both crucifixes and crosses in 1895, and Kohn & Co. included crosses in its 1909 line.[148] The amethyst-set cross by Sloan & Co. in Fig. 181 might have been worn during a period of semi-mourning, when purple stones were considered correct.

Colored semiprecious stones were a major focus of Newark jewelry makers. American turquoise and sapphires from Montana appear frequently in Newark jewelry, partly because of the color, but also because availability tended to create fashions.[149] Dreher & Son seems to have specialized in using bright blue Montana sapphires and other high-quality colored stones (see Fig. 88). Amethysts became extremely popular late in the century, in part no doubt because they were said to be the favorite stone of Alexandra, Princess of Wales.[150] Krementz & Co. even went so far as to produce a pair of amethyst hearts, edged in pearls, under a pearl-set coronet, to commemorate Edward, Prince of Wales, and his consort (Fig. 182). This piece might have been made in 1902, when other American jewelers were advertising pieces made to honor the coronation of Edward VII, but in 1897 it was being noted that "colored stones, cut in heart shape and mounted as brooches, are exceedingly pretty, especially

183. Oval gold brooch with a large faceted amethyst surrounded by pearls, by Krementz & Co., 1910–1920, 1⅛ × 1¼ in., collection of Krementz & Co., Newark.

182. Brooch of paired hearts under a coronet, by Krementz & Co., 1895–1905, gold, amethysts, and pearls, ¾ × 1 in., collection of Nelson Rarities, Portland, Maine.

when surmounted by a crown of pearls." Heart-shaped amethysts are cited as early as 1891.[151]

Large semiprecious stones, which were glamorous but affordable, became the centerpiece of other brooches, "of round or oblong shape in a setting of brilliants, small pearls or a framework of gold."[152] A Krementz amethyst brooch and a W.F. Cory & Brother cabochon moonstone show the use of seed pearls with this format (Figs. 183, 184). Alling & Co. offered the same kind of brooch in its 1910 line.[153] Kerr mixed Renaissance and Egyptian allusions in its silver frame-brooch set with a large jade scarab (Fig. 185), while Bippart, Griscom & Osborn placed a stylish Art Nouveau frame around a large cabochon of American turquoise, creating a lavish look at a moderate cost (Fig. 186). In the popular "fashion mythology" of the day—which was documented and encouraged by trade journals to promote sales—scarabs were symbols of fidelity, amethyst hearts signified loyalty and deep love, sapphires were tokens of truth, and turquoise foretold prosperity (Fig. 187).[154]

184. Oval gold brooch with a large cabochon moonstone surrounded by pearls, by W.F. Cory & Brother, 1910–1920, $1\frac{1}{8} \times 1\frac{1}{4}$ in., collection of Mr. and Mrs. Dean A. Fales, Jr.

186. Brooch in the Art Nouveau style set with a large cabochon, by Bippart, Griscom & Osborn, 1900–1910, gold, turquoise, and pearl, $1\frac{1}{2} \times 1\frac{1}{4}$ in., private collection.

185. Brooch in the Renaissance style set with a scarab, by William B. Kerr Co., 1890–1900, gilt silver and jade, $2\frac{1}{2} \times 1\frac{3}{8}$ in., private collection.

187. Oval brooch in the Egyptian style set with a scarab, by Unger & Christl, 1900–1908, gold, enamel, and green chalcedony scarab, $\frac{3}{4} \times 1$ in., The Newark Museum, Purchase 1996 The Members' Fund (96.72.1)

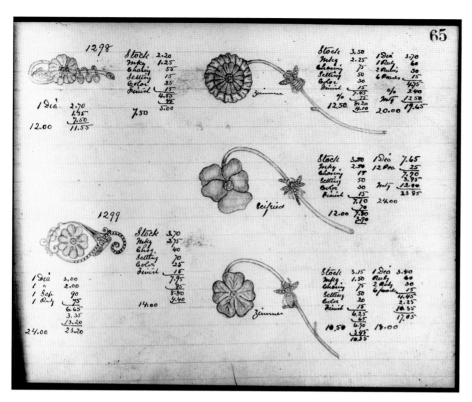

188. Designs for lace pins of flower form, from the Alling & Co. cost book, 1886–1887, p. 65, ink on paper, collection of Larter & Sons, Laurence Harbor, New Jersey.

189. Flower jewelry. Clockwise from top: spray of pansies, by A.J. Hedges & Co., 1930–1940, gold, enamel, and pearls, 2¾ × 1½ in., private collection, New York; pansy ring, by Larter & Sons, 1925–1950, gold, enamel, and pearl, collection of Helene P. Konkus; brooch in the form of a violet, by Krementz & Co., 1900–1920, gold, pearls, and diamond, The Newark Museum, Gift of Mrs. Mildred Baker, 1994 (94.65); brooch with a woman smelling a poppy, by Krementz & Co., 1900–1910, gold, enamel, and diamond, private collection, New York; chatelaine pin in the form of a sweet-pea blossom, by Bippart, Griscom & Osborn, 1890–1900, gold and enamel, The Newark Museum, Purchase 1993, The Millicent Fenwick Fund (93.46); brooch with lilies, by Whiteside & Blank, 1890–1910, gold, enamel, and pearl, private collection.

The flower also became a ubiquitous form for brooches, making a strong appearance in the Alling design books of 1886 and 1887 (Fig. 188). Newark jewelers became particularly adept at designing and producing enameled flowers. Apparently the vogue for enameled blossoms surged after the 1889 Paris Exposition, probably due to Tiffany & Co.'s remarkable display of life-sized enameled gold orchids, designed by Paulding Farnham. However, Elsie Bee included the whole fraternity of American jewelers when she recalled that the quality of the American enameling quickly overshadowed that of imported floral brooches.[155]

By the mid-nineteenth century, age-old meanings attributed to flowering plants had been codified into a complex "language of flowers." This network of meanings was enshrined in numerous publications devoted to documenting and deciphering the romantic floral vocabulary.[156] It is hard to know whether this mid-century arcana was still popular at the end of the century, but the more obvious meanings had most likely slipped into common parlance. The child's stud set of daisies probably used that flower because it signified innocence (see Fig. 60), and the suite of silver daisy jewelry by Kerr would have had the same intent (see Fig. 129), especially if worn by a teenage girl. The ever-popular pansy was a symbol of modesty (see Fig. 213), the violet meant

love or faithfulness, and the sweet-pea blossom signaled departure or delicate pleasure. Perhaps these meanings were all understood when Krementz, Bippart, Griscom & Osborn, and A.J. Hedges were marketing their flower brooches (Fig. 189). Krementz's Art Nouveau poppy brooch, a faithful transcription of a French design, could well have included the poppy's meaning of consolation or evanescent pleasure in its iconography. Even associations of the poppy with opium maintain such allusions, for opium-based laudanum was a widely used sedative in the nineteenth century, not merely a drug of the demimonde. Few women would have failed to appreciate the symbolism in such a brooch.

In the early 1890s, silver jewelry, and brooches in particular, were "having a great vogue."

Designs for silver jewelry, style spotters were quick to note, were not mimicking gold jewelry, but were being created specifically for silver pieces.[157] Silver, because it was relatively inexpensive, could be readily fashioned into large-scale sculptural brooches that added a dramatic flair to daytime clothes. American silver jewelry seems generally to have been not only larger in scale, but also more daring in design than gold jewelry. This might be because consumers were willing to take a larger fashion risk on a modestly priced silver brooch than on a far more costly gold one. In particular, the silver sash pin or belt brooch, worn at the waist, was, according to an advertisement in *Vogue* in 1902, "the latest Parisian fad."[158] These large sterling pins sold for $5 each and came in a variety of finishes, including "French gray," oxidized silver, gold-plated, and mourning black.

Unger Brothers made both sash pins, which mimicked buckles in form (Fig. 190), and belt

190. Sash pin in the form of a buckle, by Unger Brothers, 1900–1910, silver, 1⅝ × 2⅜ in., The Newark Museum, Gift of Mrs. Mildred Baker, 1966 (66.364)

191. Three silver belt brooches and a match safe, by Unger Brothers, 1900–1910, collection of Drucker Antiques, Mt. Kisco, New York.

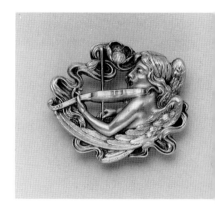

192. Silver belt brooch in the Art Nouveau style, by William Link Co., 1900–1910, 1½ × 1¼ in., collection of Kathleen Bennett.

brooches, in high relief (Fig. 191). The pin designed like a woman's head with butterfly wings (Fig. 191, top left) makes an interesting comparison with the Whiteside & Blank butterfly-woman brooch in gold and enamel (see Fig. 50). The silver pin is twice the size of its gold counterpart, and less sweet—more bizarre—in design. It was definitely a bigger "risk" to wear this piece of jewelry than the gold one and yet, at $5, an affordable risk. William Link also produced lush French-style belt brooches (Fig. 192) and even paid homage to Sarah Bernhardt's Cleopatra in a patented 1902 design (Fig. 193). In the former piece, the eroticism of the violin-playing angel, wreathed in swirls of smoke, must have been daring indeed for a nice American lady to wear in 1902. Even more unusual is the three-dimensional Indian's head produced

193. Silver belt brooch in the Egyptian style, by William Link Co., ca. 1902, 2 × 2 in., The Newark Museum, Gift of Gary N. Berger and Ulysses Grant Dietz, 1993 (93.177)

194. Silver belt brooch in the form of an Indian's head, by LaPierre Manufacturing Co., 1900–1910, 2⅜ × 1¼ in., private collection.

by LaPierre in Newark (Fig. 194). LaPierre specialized in toilet articles and silver-overlay on glass and china, but must have jumped onto the belt brooch bandwagon during its short run. Tiffany & Co. seems not to have embraced the belt pin vogue in the same way, but at the Newark factory it did produce large-scale silver brooches in the Celtic style set with big faceted amethysts (Fig. 195). By World War I, the belt brooch had all but disappeared; yet it left a remarkable legacy from Newark's silver jewelers.

Newark firms produced brooches in all modern styles and materials right through the first decades of this century. Carter, Gough & Co. showed some splashy Art Deco brooch designs in its 1927 and 1928 lines (see Fig. 100 and p. 130 n. 79), although no examples with the firm's mark

195. Designs for silver and amethyst brooches in the Celtic style, by Tiffany & Co., ca. 1900, ink on paper, Tiffany & Co. Archives.

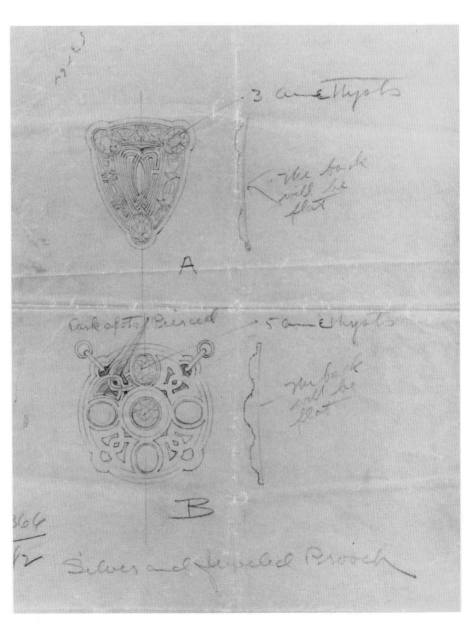

196. Bouquet brooch in the modern style, by Krementz & Co., 1935–1945, gold, morganites, rubies, and diamonds, 3 × 1⅜ in., collection of Nelson Rarities, Portland, Maine.

197. Spray brooch in the modern style, by Lester & Co., 1935–1945, retailed by Bailey, Banks & Biddle, Philadelphia, gold, diamonds, and citrines, 3 × 2 in., collection of Elena Alcalay.

have come to light. High-end retailers often forbade manufacturers from using their touchmarks, so as not to compete with their prestige, but occasional examples with these marks slipped through and serve as valuable documents.

In the late 1930s and early 1940s, the use of two-color gold typified Newark jewelry. Krementz produced a stylized modernist bouquet of torchlike pink morganite blossoms, bound with diamonds and rubies (Fig. 196), while Lester & Co. produced similar large-scale modern brooches for retailers like Bailey, Banks & Biddle (Fig. 197). Henry Blank & Co. offered jeweled lapel watches for tailored suits (Fig. 198), and firms such as Allsopp-Steller and Erwin Reu capitalized on the revived popularity of moonstones with new colored gems such as zircons into the late 1940s and early 1950s (Figs. 199, 207).

The clip brooch (or dress clip), paired or single, was perhaps the first truly new form to enter the jewelry world in the twentieth century. Emblematic of the Art Deco period, its great success was due to its versatility. Because it could be worn without piercing holes, the clip brooch could be used anywhere on a garment and on any piece of clothing. Perhaps the most typical Newark clips were the all-gold pairs intended "for daytime and sport wear" (Fig. 200).[159] The two pairs shown here are both variations on the skyscraper or organ-pipe motif that was basic to the "modernistic mode" in the late 1920s.[160] Larter & Sons produced a pair of clips, probably in the late 1930s, that attach to a brooch fitting, thus increasing the wearing options (Fig. 201). Following the traditions established back in the nineteenth century, gem-set platinum clips

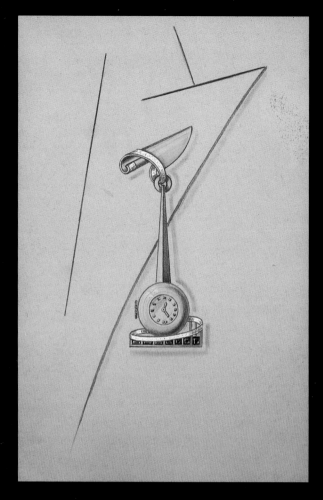

198. Design for a lapel watch, by Henry Blank & Co., 1935–1945, gouache on paper, Henry Blank & Co. papers, New Jersey Historical Society, Newark

200. Two pairs of dress clips in the modern style, 1925–1935. Left to right: by Fritzsche & Co., pink and yellow gold, collection of Nelson Rarities, Portland, Maine; by Harry C. Schick, Inc., yellow gold, 1⅛ × ¾ in., The Newark Museum, Gift of Gary N. Berger and Ulysses Grant Dietz, 1995 (95.58.2)

199. Two spray brooches in the modern style. From top: by Erwin Reu, Inc., 1950–1960, gold, moonstones and rubies, 2½ × 1⅝ in., The Newark Museum, Purchase 1995 Membership Endowment Fund (95.105.5); by Allsopp-Steller, 1940–1950, gold, platinum, moonstones, sapphires, and diamonds, private collection.

202. Dress clip in the Art Deco style, by Krementz & Co., 1925–1930, platinum, yellow gold, sapphires, and diamonds, 1¼ × 1¼ in., The Newark Museum, Purchase 1993 The Millicent Fenwick Fund (93.77)

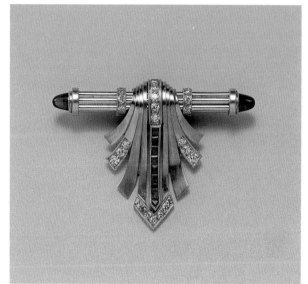

201. Jewelry in the modern style. Counterclockwise from top: necklace convertible into two bracelets, by Larter & Sons, 1940–1950, pink and yellow gold, private collection; pair of ear clips, by Tiffany & Co., 1940–1950, gold, private collection; pair of clips with brooch fitting, by Larter & Sons, 1935–1940, gold, The Newark Museum, Purchase 1994 Stella Goldstein Purchase Fund (94.152)

would have been reserved for evening wear. A rare example from the late 1920s by Krementz & Co. is of platinum, the clasp of yellow gold, set with diamonds and sapphires (Fig. 202). In both its look and its production techniques, it was adapted to suit the Machine Age, and reflects the kind of new jewel-like architectural metalwork that New York's Chrysler building boasted. To cite a trend spotter in 1929: "Dynamic symmetry, the unalloyed delight in the perpendicular line, the ribbed and slotted texture of the modern decorative surface, these are to be carried over from architectural detail and the new furniture into jewelry designing."[161] A more modest pair of Art Deco clips by Krementz demonstrates the use of white gold, carefully faceted to reflect light, to mimic the chic gray finish of platinum that dominated fashionable evening jewelry in the late 1920s (Fig. 203).

203. Pair of dress clips in the Art Deco style, by Krementz & Co., 1925–1930, white gold, diamonds, and sapphires, 1 × ⅜ in., private collection.

204. Three designs for platinum, diamond, and emerald dress clips, ca. 1925–1930, by Henry Blank & Co., gouache on paper, Henry Blank & Co. papers, New Jersey Historical Society, Newark.

205. Design for a dress clip watch, by Henry Blank & Co., 1935–1945, gouache on paper, Henry Blank & Co. papers, New Jersey Historical Society, Newark.

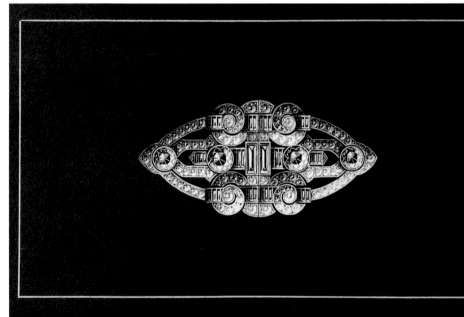

206. Design for a double clip of platinum and diamonds, 1925–1930, by Henry Blank & Co., gouache on paper, Henry Blank & Co. papers, New Jersey Historical Society, Newark.

Although the typical Newark-made clip would have been of the all-gold variety, some firms, notably Henry Blank & Co., would have produced high-end, jewel-encrusted clips in gold and platinum for the most expensive retailers. They also seem to have made pieces designed by New York manufacturers. A trio of Henry Blank designs for single clips in platinum, diamonds, and emeralds (Fig. 204) might have been made to order for a firm like Tiffany & Co. Blank, which specialized in watches, also produced a splendid two-color gold and gem-set clip watch, with a cylinder-faceted topaz or citrine for a crystal (Fig. 205). The grandest surviving design from Henry Blank & Co. is a massive diamond and platinum double clip, probably from the early 1930s (Fig. 206). Set with four large diamonds, this sort of piece would have been unusual for a Newark firm. Given the huge popularity for such grand diamond jewelry among the elite in the early 1930s (for whom the Depression seemed not to exist), it could well have been made to order for a New York firm overwhelmed with commissions, such as Oscar Heyman & Co.

Getting the Goods Out

How did Newark jewelry find its way across the country, into countless little jewelry shops? In the tradition of Isaac Baldwin, who might be considered the first traveling jewelry salesman, Newark's jewelry makers sent out a legion of drummers, poetically known as the "peregrinating Beau Brummels," who created a network of goodwill and salesmanship that put Newark-made jewels into millions of American households.[162] Some manufacturers, such as Kerr, Shanley, Krementz, and Adams, as we have seen, did advertise in consumer magazines like *Vogue*, and Unger Brothers even had a retail shop in its Newark factory.[163] However, most makers depended upon their New York showrooms and their traveling salesmen. The development of the railroad in post-Civil War America made it possible for traveling representatives of jewelry firms to carry their sample cases both to major wholesaling centers, such as Chicago, Pittsburgh, and St. Louis, as well as to smaller cities and even frontier outposts. The jewelry salesmen congregated in hotels that catered to them, and these hotels actively sought salesmen's patronage in trade journals and publications. The Hotel Schenley in Pittsburgh, the Jefferson in St. Louis, the Richelieu in Chicago, and the famed Astor House in New York City—all were homes away from home for the jewelry drummer, who was charged $1 to $5 and up per night.[164] The advent of the automobile made the job even easier, and by the end of World War I, company cars for the salesmen had become an established custom.[165] As early as 1908, it was noted in *The Jewelers' Circular—Weekly* that "Edward E. Allsopp, of Allsopp Bros., Camp and Orchard Sts. [Newark], was touring New York in his automobile, last week."[166]

The Jewelers' Circular (which became a weekly in 1900), ran a column covering the business of the salesmen called "Our Traveling Representatives." A support organization known as The Brotherhood of Traveling Jewelers was founded in 1891 to provide anonymous relief to ill salesmen, and assistance to their families in the event of death. The group proudly claimed that its benefits were intended not just for its members, but for all traveling jewelry men. Among the officers of the Brotherhood, a quasi-secret society limited to one hundred members, were executives from the Newark firms of Kerr, Krementz, Bliss, and Day, Clark.[167] The Commercial Travelers' Club in New York offered a social haven for jewelry drummers, and a special column announced the arrivals of sales representatives in New York each week and listed the hotels at which they were staying.[168] The comings and goings of salesmen around the country were followed in the same column, so that the trade would know who was in what town each week. For example, during the week of February 20, 1895, Day, Clark and Unger Brothers had representatives in Kansas City; Riker Brothers had a salesman in Davenport, Iowa; the Keller and Reddall firms were present in Lancaster, Pennsylvania; and Shafer & Douglas and Glorieux had drummers in Syracuse, New York.[169]

Remarkable among the jewelry manufacturers and their traveling representatives was a sense of fraternity unparalleled in other competitive industries. "Their friendliness towards each other is a unique characteristic of jewelry travelers; whether due to *savoir-vivre* or to companionship for the safety of their respective responsibilities, it is a fact that they incline to gregariousness.

However keen as competitors in business, they seek each other and are more content to travel together than with those of other industries." This sort of fraternal spirit was apparently true at all levels of the industry, from the unions to the board rooms; jewelry bench workers, salesmen, and executives looked out for one another.[170]

The trade journals also helped get Newark goods "out there" by offering extensive resources for retailers of all sizes and in every location in the country. To assist the retailer in attracting customers, special articles were devoted to "scientific principles in advertising." Newly propounded theories about the suggestibility of the human mind were discussed as potential benefits to jewelry dealers.[171] After 1896, *The Jewelers' Circular and Horological Review* encouraged retailers to "know the marks" of the jewelry manufacturers, so that they could special order pieces or lines that customers brought to show them. To this end, the journal offered a special $3 catalogue listing four thousand makers' marks. As one jewelry retailer commented, "Like the cowboy's pistol, 'tis not required every day, but when needed it is wanted quite bad."[172] The weekly also ran a column titled "Storekeeping Department," in which it would offer display and sales tips and also showcase the retail premises of some far-flung jeweler. In 1907, this column highlighted, for example, a jewelry store in Juneau, Alaska.[173] Arnstine Brothers, a Cleveland firm that produced catalogues for retail jewelry stores, ran a continuous series of advertisements in 1909, with photographs promoting their clients' stores in places like Pine Bluff, Arkansas; Portland Oregon; Pocatello, Idaho; Chattanooga, Tennessee; Tipton, Indiana; Corsicana, Texas; and Jackson, Mississippi.[174]

Color printing began to influence retail sales catalogues in the 1890s, allowing jewelry stores to sell goods more effectively without the customer's presence. Such alluring variety, especially when in bright, realistic color, must have fanned the flames of consumer novelty-hunger quite brilliantly. The Blanchard Press in New York produced sixteen pages in color in the 1896 catalogue for J.H. Johnston & Co., a retailer-manufacturer on Union Square in New York City.[175] The Peninsular Engraving Company of Detroit, which advertised in full-color pages, must have produced the catalogue that William

Stolz of Saginaw, Michigan, offered his customers between 1900 and 1910. The Stolz retail catalogue offered twenty-four pages of full-color jewelry, from scarf pins and sapphire crescents to enameled flower pins and gold match safes, from cuff buttons, signet rings, and pocket knives to a whole page of mourning jewelry. The prices ranged from 75¢ for a child's ring to $54 for a man's gold watch.[176]

There is little doubt that most of this jewelry came from Newark shops, having made its way via traveling representatives from the factories on Mulberry Street. The pieces have the "look" of Newark-made jewelry—semiprecious colored stones, skillfully applied enamels in many shades, seed pearls, small diamonds for sparkle—and the names of Larter, Krementz, Alling, Durand, Bippart, Griscom & Osborn, and Hedges all come to mind as one scans the pages. However, the Saginaw matron or bridegroom or widow would not have known where the jewelry was manufactured. Nor would any of them have cared. The ability to choose at leisure, at home, by flipping through pages of bright color, would have been all that mattered. Today it is hard to imagine the impact of such a color catalogue, so accustomed are we to lavish advertising and endless mail-order catalogues. But such catalogues were once a novelty, and the store owner used the advances in transportation, production machinery, printing, advertising, and jewelry design to good effect, offering the American consumer an affordable selection of 14-carat beauty. Epaphras Hinsdale, opening his factory in Newark with six employees in 1801, could never have envisioned the world his little enterprise would lead to.

Epiloque: Survival and Change

The Depression created a wound in Newark's jewelry industry that never healed. However, even during the Roaring Twenties, the beginnings of decline were evident. From a high of 200 jewelry makers, Newark had been reduced to 144 shortly before the stock market crash. The erosion was in part due to the recession of the early 1920s, but no less to the new vogue for costume jewelry. Once worn only by those who couldn't afford anything else, costume jewelry was now being designed and encouraged by such *haute couture* figures as Coco Chanel and

207. Jewelry in the modern style, by Allsopp-Steller, 1940–1950. Clockwise from top: spray brooch, gold and citrines, 3½ × 1½ in., The Newark Museum, Purchase 1994 The Millicent Fenwick Fund (94.19); pair of barettes, gold, private collection; bracelet of dogwood blossoms, retailed by Tiffany & Co., gold and garnets, The Newark Museum, Purchase 1994 Stella Goldstein Purchase Fund (94.150); medallion brooch, gold and zircons, private collection.

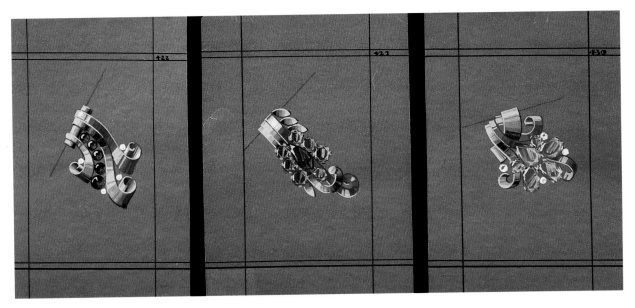

Elsa Schiaparelli. H. Jack Hunkele, writing of his grandfather Achille Bippart's Newark jewelry company, said that "the 1920s were a time when costume jewelry came into vogue, and people were more interested in putting their money into automobiles and other things than expensive jewelry."[177] Even The Newark Museum's 1929 exhibition celebrating the city's fine jewelry industry hinted at this reality. Pointing out that "as a whole, Newark's [jewelry] products are of a superior quality, since no cheap jewelry, for which there is such a fad at present is made here," Julia B. Smith unwittingly exposed the industry's Achilles' heel.[178] Once elite women began to favor imitation jewelry, the dominance of solid-gold jewelry among middle-class consumers was in danger. Moreover, before the crash of 1929, "all classes demanded high-grade merchandise." Bankers, bricklayers, cab drivers, and "every other type of American citizen" had created a demand for solid-gold jewelry that kept Newark's factories busy.[179]

All that ended in October 1929, just seven months after The Newark Museum closed its exhibition. The Depression years continued to erode the industry, with firms either folding or merging with larger, more stable firms, to stay alive.[180] Even those firms that thrived during the 1930s and 1940s faced stiff competition for the first time in their history from costume jewelry producers. Allsopp-Steller, Larter, Sloan, Enos Richardson, and Tiffany & Co. continued to produce stylish solid-gold jewelry that was up to date, wearable, and of the same quality for which Newark had always been renowned (Figs. 207-

209). But these manufacturers were relying on the same nineteenth-century desire for real gold and real gems, and they underestimated the consumer's willingness to accept imitation gold and glass stones. At the middle-class level, jewelry was becoming less intrinsically valued as a sign of wealth and more as a mere accessory to fashion. Even as the middle-class consumer was

209. Non-piercing earrings, by Sloan & Co., ca. 1952, gold, private collection. Designed by Julius Guth in 1950, these spring-mechanism earrings were granted patent number 2,600,251 on September 23, 1952.

turning away from the jewelry made in Newark's factories, the very rich continued to patronize New York jewelry makers. The glamorous end of the jewelry market continued to thrive in Manhattan, as it does to this day.

Krementz & Co. saw the writing on the wall, and as early as the late 1930s began to focus more and more on rolled-gold plate—the very material that William Bagnall sniffed at as "not Newark" in 1882. A promotional booklet published by Krementz for the trade in 1946 gave a brief world history of gold, and then expanded on the firm's production techniques for rolled-gold jewelry, emphasizing phrases such as "correct styling," "more than mere beauty," and "lasting value" (Figs. 210, 211).[181] Krementz also produced a full-color retail catalogue illustrating both its two-color gold overlay and its white-gold overlay jewelry with imitation diamonds in about 1951. But the firm also continued to emphasize its long tradition as a fine jewelry maker.[182] By this carefully crafted sleight of hand, Krementz turned itself from a fine jewelry maker into a costume jewelry maker and thus survived the downward trend. By 1949, the company was famous for such pieces as the two-color gold-wire bangle, which Helga Bendix received as a confirmation gift that year (Fig. 212); they were what the American consumer requested.

In 1954, the annual product of Newark's jewelry factories was worth $50 million.[183] By 1964, the figure had shrunk to $10 million, and it was getting harder and harder to find the skilled workers needed for fine jewelry production.[184] The most recent generation of immigrants, largely German, the last of whom had arrived during the boom of the 1920s, was aging. Some of them had sons to take their places, and occasionally new workers from the German jewelry schools arrived to fill vacancies. But firms were also beginning to look to new communities—Portuguese, Puerto Rican, African-American—for possible apprentices.[185] The old factories in Newark remained virtually unchanged from the nineteenth century—which was not necessarily a disadvantage, for working conditions were still

Krementz styles are created and approved by fashion experts. Located within a dozen miles of the fashion center of New York City, Krementz stylists are in close touch with the newest trends. Because Krementz jewelry will outlast any passing fads, most of the new patterns selected are those chosen by the more conservative style leaders. Fine jewelry like fine music does not change in style too rapidly.

211. A fashion model wearing Krementz rolled-gold jewelry, from Krementz & Co., *The Story of Gold in Modern Jewelry*, 1946, p. 12.

210. Steps in making Krementz jewelry of rolled-gold plate, from Krementz & Co., *The Story of Gold in Modern Jewelry*, 1946, p. 11.

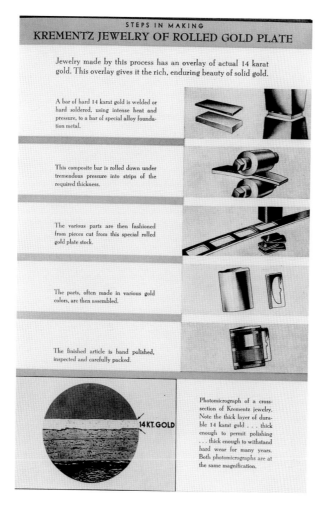

212. Rolled-gold-wire bracelet, by Krementz & Co., 1949, collection of Helga Bendix.

213. Flower brooch of multi-colored gold, by A.J. Hedges & Co., 1890–1900, collection of Doris Weinstein; lifesize pansy brooch, by A.J. Hedges & Co., 1900–1920, gold and enamel, collection of Krementz & Co., Newark.

clean and well-lit. However, by the mid-1960s, jewelry workers no longer enjoyed the highest pay scale in American industry.[186]

A dwindling market, taxation, and a general anti-urban movement gradually forced most of Newark's firms to shut down, sell out, or relocate quietly to other parts of the state. Enos Richardson closed its doors in 1969, after 128 years in Newark. Jabel moved to Irvington, New Jersey, in 1956; Larter & Sons to Laurence Harbor in 1986. Erwin Reu moved to Springfield, New Jersey, in 1966. Henry Blank & Co. had closed by 1986. Tiffany & Co. shut down its large Victorian factory in 1985.

Of all the great Newark jewelry names, Krementz & Co. stands as the oldest and sole standard-bearer today, in its new state-of-the-art factory on McCarter Highway, just a few blocks from the original factory in Newark's old jewelry district. The company's name, visible from the commuter trains that pass through Newark on their way to and from Manhattan each day, is the lone reminder of the former capital of America's fine jewelry industry, the one-time city of gold and precious stones.

NOTES

1 Smith 1929, pp. 4, 5.

2 Bagnall 1882, p. 18.

3 Ibid., pp. 18, 20, for the filling process. The process is also discussed in Fales 1995, p. 154.

4 Smith 1929, p. 4. This is also discussed in "Newark Sparkles Among Cities as Home of Gold and Platinum Jewelry," *Newark Evening News*, January 9, 1917, p. 14.

5 Robert W. Adams, obituary, in *JCW*, vol. 70, June 2, 1915, pp. 59–60. In 1903–1904, Adams, head of Thomas W. Adams & Co. in Newark, was among the first to campaign for a national carat stamping act. The act was finally passed by Congress in 1906; see *JCW*, vol. 52, May 16, 1906, p. 35, and June 20, 1906, p. 43.

6 See the patent notice in *JCHR*, vol. 33, October 7, 1896, p. 16. The best reference for marks is Rainwater 1988.

7 Bagnall 1882, p. 16.

8 Ibid., p. 34.

9 Ibid.

10 Hands Ledger of Alling Brother & Co., 1859–1863, pp. 111, 437, New Jersey Historical Society, Newark, MG435.

11 Ferdinand Herpers, obituary, in *Jewelers' Weekly*, vol. 6, July 26, 1888, p. 39.

12 See Fales 1995, pp. 311, 312.

13 Letter in The Newark Museum archives (52.255).

14 See the notes in a small leather notebook kept by Ferdinand Herpers between December 1863 and May 1864, The Newark Museum archives (52.196).

15 Rainwater 1988, p. 121. Bippart, Griscom & Osborn's patent was advertised in *JCW*, vol. 43, August 28, 1901, p. 14, patent no. 676,640, received June 18, 1901.

16 Herpers ledgers for 1874–1876 and 1877–1881, The Newark Museum archives (52.260, 52.262).

17 Herpers source files, The Newark Museum archives. A suite of jewelry by Mueller of Nome, Alaska, using gold nuggets and fossil ivory, was given to The Newark Museum by the Herpers family.

18 Alling Brother & Co., Day Books, 1865, 1877, New Jersey Historical Society, Newark, MG435.

19 Bagnall 1882, pp. 26, 28.

20 Joseph Krementz, holograph notebook, 1897–1906, p. 99, collection of Krementz & Co. The firms of Balbach and LeLong were the major players in this arena. Edward Balbach, a German immigrant who came to America in 1848, founded his refining plant in Newark in 1850; see Cunningham 1954, p. 59. L. LeLong & Brother also operated a large-scale refining operation, advertising to the national jewelry trade in the late 1880s; see *Alphabets, Monograms, Initials, Crests, Etc.* (New York: E.W. Bullinger, ca. 1887), p. 168.

21 Larter & Sons compared the quality of cast and die-stamped gold for its ring settings in an advertisement in *JCW*, vol. 51, August 23, 1905, p. 15.

22 *Newark Evening News*, January 9, 1917, p. 14, and January 18, 1917, p. 14.

23 Hilary Anderson, "Earning a Living in Eighteenth-Century Boston: Silversmith Zachariah Brigden," M.A. thesis (Winterthur: University of Delaware, 1996).

24 *Godey's Lady's Book*, vol. 47, first semester, 1853, p. 91.

25 *Godey's Lady's Book*, vol. 47, second semester, 1853, p. 94.

26 Cecil B. Hartley, *The Gentlemen's Book of Etiquette and Manual of Politeness* (Boston: DeWolfe, Fiske & Co., 1873), p. 138.

27 Charles Harcourt, *Good Form for Men: A Guide to Conduct and Dress on All Occasions* (Philadelphia: The John C. Winston Co., 1905), p. 42.

28 Alling & Co., cost book, 1886–1887, p. 142, collection of Larter & Sons, Laurence Harbor, New Jersey.

29 J.H. Bentley & Co., cost book, 1885–1891, The Newark Museum (39.445).

30 Cunningham 1954, p. 61; *JCW*, vol. 44, March 5, 1902, p. 19.

31 *JCHR*, vol. 26, June 21, 1893, p. 41.

32 Facsimile of an advertisement for S.F. Myers' line of waist sets, in Rainwater 1988, p. 289.

33 *The Jewelers' Circular-Weekly*, vol. 48, February 3, 1904, p. 64.

34 J.H. Bentley & Co. cost book, 1885–1891, The Newark Museum archives (39.445).

35 Unger Brothers, *Holiday Suggestions 1901–1902*, p. 15.

36 Larter *Gold Book* for 1911; Alling & Co. cost book, ca. 1910, collection of Larter & Sons, Laurence Harbor, New Jersey.

37 Advertisement in *JCHR*, vol. 33, September 16, 1896, p. 7.

38 *JCW*, vol. 40, June 13, 1900, p. 8.

39 *JCW*, vol. 56, February 4, 1903, p. 18.

40 In addition to the Krementz advertisement reproduced in Fig. 18, see also the one in *Vogue*, vol. 47, February 1, 1916, p. 118.

41 *Vogue*, June 1914, p. 38. The actual pieces are marked Pat. Dec. 12, 99.

42 *Vogue*, vol. 47, February 1, 1916, p. 118.

43 *JCW*, vol. 48, February 3, 1904, p. 28.

44 Larter *Gold Book* for 1911, collection of Larter & Sons, Laurence Harbor, New Jersey.

45 The Shanley advertisement appeared in *Vogue*, vol. 56, December 1, 1920, p. 20; the Kerr advertisement in *Vogue*, vol. 48, December 1, 1916, p. 28.

46 Cunningham 1954, p. 60.

47 Alling & Co., cost book, 1886–1887, pp. 113, 118, collection of Larter & Sons, Laurence Harbor, New Jersey.

48 Advertisement for D.F. Briggs Co., *JCW*, vol. 59, November 3, 1909, p. 18; advertisement for S.O. Bigney & Co., *JCW*, vol. 56, February 4, 1903, p. 83.

49 Unger Brothers, *Holiday Suggestions 1901–1902*, pp. 12–15.

50 Larter *Gold Book* for 1925–1926, collection of Larter & Sons, Laurence Harbor, New Jersey.

51 Emily Post, *Etiquette: The Blue Book of Social Usage* (New York: Funk & Wagnalls Company, 1940), p. 730, says categorically: "Nothing is more vulgar than a display of 'ice' on a man's shirt front, or on his fingers." See also Henry Lunettes' advice in 1866, quoted in Jenna Joselit's essay, p. 23.

52 Advertisement for Durand & Co., *JCW*, vol. 51, August 23, 1905, p. 16; Alling & Co. cost book, 1886–1887, collection of Larter & Sons, Laurence Harbor, New Jersey.

53 Larter *Gold Book* for 1925–1926, collection of Larter & Sons, Laurence Harbor, New Jersey.

54 *Jewelry Fashions* 1917, pp. 46, 47.

55 Ibid., pp. 52, 53.

56 *JCHR*, vol. 25, January 25, 1893, p. 34.

57 Post, *Etiquette*, p. 739.

58 Tiffany & Co. archives, Parsippany, New Jersey. Commissions for such jewelry are filed alphabetically, and range from the 1870s to the 1940s. The author has also seen a Mystic Shrine lapel button by Riker Brothers, in the collection of Louis Scholz.

59 Tiffany & Co. archives, Parsippany, New Jersey.

60 *JCW*, vol. 48, February 3, 1901, pp. 22–25.

61 William C. Edge, obituary, 1900, unnamed Newark newspaper, photocopy of clipping in The Newark Museum archives, courtesy of Nancy N. Kattermann.

62 *JCHR*, vol. 33, October 14, 1896, p. 7.

63 *JCW*, vol. 52, February 7, 1906, p. 83.

64 *Vogue*, vol. 30, December 5, 1907, p. 817.

65 *JCW*, vol. 48, February 3, 1904, p. 30. Elsie Bee was probably a pseudonym for someone with the initials L.C.B.

66 *JCW*, vol. 48, February 3, 1904, p. 30.

67 Joseph Krementz, holograph notebook, 1897–1906, pp. 111–119, collection of Krementz & Co.

68 Henry Blank & Co. papers, 1915–1918, New Jersey Historical Society, Newark, MG1273, book #9.

69 *JCW*, vol. 58, February 3, 1909, cover and p. 107.

70 *JCHR*, vol. 23, April 29, 1891, p. 45; vol. 30, February 13, 1895, p. 7.

71 Alling & Co. cost book, ca. 1910, pp. 227–230, collection of Larter & Sons, Laurence Harbor, New Jersey.

72 *Jewelry Fashions* 1917, p. 40.

73 *JCHR*, vol. 32, April 8, 1896, p. 11.

74 *JCW*, vol. 35, December 29, 1897, p. 7.

75 *JCW*, vol. 46, February 25, 1903, p. 12.

76 Hugh Tait et al., *The Art of the Jeweller: A Catalogue of the Hull Grundy Gift to The British Museum* (London: The British Museum, 1984), II, p. 288, fig. 108a.

77 George F. Kunz, *Natal Stones: Birthstones, Sentiments and Superstitions Associated with Precious Gems* (New York: Tiffany & Co., 1909), p. 14.

78 *JCW*, vol. 42, March 20, 1901, p. 7.

79 Pieces by both Carter, Gough and Keller are illustrated in May Langlands, "Styles in Fine Jewelry in 1928," *The Jewelers' Circular*, vol. 98, February 21, 1929, pp. 163, 167.

80 Bishop, quoted in "Better Jewelry More in Demand," *The New York Times*, January 31, 1937, p. 31.

81 *Alphabets, Monograms, Initials, Crests*, pp. 112, 146.

82 Fales 1995, p. 291 n. 111.

83 *JCHR*, vol. 21, January 1891, p. 41.

84 *JCHR*, vol. 33, January 13, 1897, p. 9; vol. 35, December 8, 1897, p. 10.

85 Vivienne Becker, *Art Nouveau Jewelry* (New York: E.P. Dutton & Co., 1985), p. 21.

86 *Vogue*, vol. 38, December 6, 1906, pp. 840–841.

87 Advertisement for Charles L. Trout & Co., New York City, *JCW*, vol. 54, May 1, 1907, p. 32.

88 Alling & Co. cost book, ca. 1910, collection of Larter & Sons, Laurence Harbor, New Jersey.

89 Collection of Louis Scholz.

90 *Jewelry Fashions* 1917, p. 40.

91 Henry Blank & Co. papers, New Jersey Historical Society, Newark, 1987.1, box 7, shelf 20, and drawers 6–18.

92 *JCW*, vol. 42, June 12, 1901, p. 9.

93 The writer has seen an identical band on a Patek Philippe watch case retailed by Tiffany & Co. The mechanism was invented by "a German" who awarded sole rights to its use in the U.S.A. to Whiteside & Blank in 1911. Handwritten notes by Peter Blank, Henry Blank & Co. papers, New Jersey Historical Society, Newark, 1987.1, box 4.

94 The Newark Museum purchased two silver necklaces from Georg Jensen's 57th Street shop in 1929: a choker with moonstones and a lavaliere pendant set with labradorites.

95 The candelabra are in The Newark Museum (85.4).

96 The Newark Museum owns a pair of silver shoe buckles made by Philadelphia silversmith Daniel Dupuy in the eighteenth century (67.152).

97 *JCHR*, vol. 32, February 12, 1896, p. 7.

98 Rainwater 1988, p. 193.

99 *JCW*, vol. 41, September 12, 1900, p. 7.

100 *JCHR*, vol. 32, February 12, 1896, p. 7.

101 Unger Brothers, 1904 catalogue, with 203 pages of photographs, and 23 pages of cut-glass designs, collection of Gladys and Robert Koch. Design 0410 is on p. 164.

102 *JCW*, vol. 41, October 3, 1900, p. 7.

103 *JCW*, vol. 42, June 12, 1901, p. 9.

104 Diane Chalmers Johnson, "Siegfried and the Rhine Maidens, Albert Pinkham Ryder's Response to Richard Wagner's *Gotterdämmerung*," *American Art*, vol. 8, Winter 1994, pp. 23, 27.

105 Unger Brothers, *Holiday Suggestions 1901–1902*, p. 16.

106 *Vogue*, vol. 20, November 6, 1902, p. 609; December 4, 1902, p. 802; *Vogue*, vol. 38, December 6, 1906, p. 841.

107 *JCHR*, vol. 33, December 2, 1896, p. 14.

108 *JCHR*, vol. 32, February 5, 1896, p. 6.

109 *JCHR*, vol. 31, August 14, 1895, p. 8.

110 *JCW*, vol. 40, July 4, 1900, p. 9; vol. 42, March 13, 1901, p. 9.

111 Lillian E. Purdy, "The Trend of Fashion in Jewelry," *JCW*, vol. 58, February 3, 1909, p. 103.

112 *Jewelry Fashions* 1917, p. 42; the cost of platinum is reported in "Newark Sparkles Among Cities as Home of Gold and Platinum Jewelry," *Newark Evening News*, January 9, 1917, p. 14. Gold in the same period sold for $20.59 per ounce.

113 *JCHR*, vol. 31, March 13, 1895, p. 6.

114 *JCHR*, vol. 33, January 6, 1897, p. 7.

115 The writer has seen two of these firsthand, one of which was slated for melting down by the jewelry dealer who owned it.

116 *JCW*, vol. 59, November 3, 1909, p. 44.

117 Rainwater 1988, p. 140.

118 Conversation with Richard Krementz, chairman of Krementz & Co., September 10, 1996.

119 *JCHR*, vol. 31, October 23, 1895, p. 9; vol. 36, February 9, 1898, p. 7.

120 *JCHR*, vol. 31, October 2, 1895, p. 24.

121 *Jewelry Fashions* 1917, pp. 42–43, 50–51. The writer has seen the Carter, Gough examples.

122 *JCHR*, vol. 30, February 6, 1895, p. 7.

123 See Jenna Joselit's essay, p. 27 and n. 71; also *Vogue*, vol. 46, November 15, 1915, p. 101.

124 *JCHR*, vol. 30, February 13, 1895, p. 7.

125 *JCHR*, vol. 32, April 15, 1896, p. 4; also in Unger Brothers 1904 catalogue, item number 9910, "napkin holder."

126 *JCHR*, vol. 30, April 24, 1895, p. 7; vol. 22, February 11, 1891, p. 48; *JCW*, vol. 44, March 26, 1902, p. 26.

127 *JCHR*, vol. 29, November 28, 1894, p. 49.

128 *Vogue*, vol. 30, September 19, 1907, p. 814; December 5, 1907, p. 329.

129 Alling & Co. cost book, 1886–1887, p. 201, collection of Larter & Sons, Laurence Harbor, New Jersey; *Jewelry Fashions* 1917, pp. 34, 35.

130 *JCW*, vol. 59, November 3, 1909, pp. 33, 46.

131 *Jewelry Fashions* 1917, p. 10; *JCW*, vol. 51, August 2, 1905, p. 16.

132 *JCW*, vol. 58, February 3, 1909, p. 55.

133 Maud C. Cooke, *Social Life, or, The Manners and Customs of Polite Society* (Philadelphia: Co-operative Publishing Co., 1896), p. 413.

134 *JCHR*, vol. 35, January 19, 1898, p. 11.

135 *JCHR*, vol. 30, June 5, 1895, p. 8.

136 Cooke, *Social Life*, p. 413; also *JCHR*, vol. 28, February 7, 1894, p. 81.

137 *JCHR*, vol. 30, February 27, 1895, p. 5; April 10, 1895, p. 7.

138 *JCHR*, vol. 29, December 19, 1894, p. 7; vol. 31, September 25, 1895, p. 2.

139 For Lafitte's version, see Tait, *The Art of the Jeweller*, II, pl. 58. Whiteside & Blank's advertisement appeared in *JCW*, vol. 51, August 23, 1905, p. 24. The cost is taken from the Henry Blank & Co. papers, New Jersey Historical Society, Newark, MG1273, book #5, p. 26.

140 *The Jewelers' Review*, vol. 22, September 18, 1893, p. 22.

141 *Modern Design in Jewellery and Fans by the Artist Craftsmen of Paris, London, Vienna, Berlin, Brussels, etc.*, no publishing data given, but a pencil inscription on fly leaf of the Herpers copy reads "M[ar]ch. 8 1909 pd. $1.50."

142 Tait, *The Art of the Jeweller*, I, pp. 148, 149; II, pp. 243, 257, figs. 957, 958, 975–978.

143 Kunz, *Natal Stones*, p. 12.

144 *JCHR*, vol. 25, August 10, 1892, p. 35; *The Jewelers' Review*, vol. 22, October 24, 1893, p. 28.

145 Tait, *The Art of the Jeweller*, I, p. 171; II, pp. 282–284, fig. 107.

146 *Die Perle (The Pearl, La Perle)* (Vienna: Verlag von [Martin] Gerlach und [Charles] Schenk, 1879). The Herpers copy has a color fron-

tispiece dated 1881, and bears a purple ink rubber stamp on the title page indicating that it was published in New York by Charles Schenk.

147 *Christian Science Emblem Jewelry* (Concord, New Hampshire: J.C. Derby Co., ca. 1900), Archives of the Church of Christ, Scientist, Boston, Massachusetts. The Derby firm lists itself as "sole manufacturers," and this design was patented January 9, 1900, but clearly farmed out to Riker Brothers.

148 *JCHR*, vol. 30, February 27, 1895, p. 5; *JCW*, vol. 59, November 3, 1909, p. 33.

149 *JCHR*, vol. 29, October 10, 1894, p. 4.

150 "The amethyst is one of the favored stones of the moment," *JCHR*, vol. 31, October 6, 1897, p. 8.

151 Frederic, a New York jeweler, was advertising his coronation pieces in *Vogue*, vol. 18, October 1, 1901, p. iv; while the crown and heart brooches were reported in *JCHR*, vol. 35, August 25, 1897, p. 8. Heart-shaped amethysts are noted in the same publication, vol. 22, February 4, 1891, p. 57.

152 *JCHR*, vol. 29, October 10, 1894, p. 4.

153 Alling & Co. cost book, ca. 1910, designs 2436, 2437, 2440, collection of Larter & Sons, Laurence Harbor, New Jersey.

154 "Thirteen Charms Against Evil a Fad," *JCW*, vol. 40, March 21, 1900, p. 50.

155 *JCHR*, vol. 28, No. 1, Feb. 7, 1894, p. 81. For French floral brooches of this period, see Tait, *The Art of the Jeweller*, II, pl. 56; I, pp. III, 112.

156 For example, in 1868, *Godey's Lady's Book* published a series of articles entitled "The Language of Flowers," discussing the flowers alphabetically over the course of six different issues.

157 *JCHR*, vol. 25, October 19, 1892, p. 46; vol. 21, November 1890, p. 50.

158 Advertisement for L.A. Wertheimer Co., Importers, 611–621 Broadway, New York City, *Vogue*, July 1902, p. 367.

159 "Milady's Jewels for 1929," *The Jewelers' Circular*, vol. 98, February 21, 1929, p. 135.

160 Ibid., p. 131.

161 Ima Thompson, "Adapting Modern Decorative Themes to Jewelry Designing," *The Jewelers' Circular*, vol. 98, February 21, 1929, p. 102. Illustrated on p. 101 of this same article is a nickel-plated and black glass cocktail table in The Newark Museum's collection (94.41). Designed by Donald Deskey in 1927, it reflects this same machine aesthetic, which was a departure from the lush ornamentalism of earlier modernism.

162 Reese Alberts, "Peregrinating Beau Brummels," *The Jewelers' Circular—Keystone*, June 1969, pp. 24–34.

163 Unger Brothers, *Holiday Suggestions 1901–1902*, p. 2.

164 The Astor House and the Richelieu advertised on full pages with engraved illustrations in *Alphabets, Monograms, Initials, Crests*, pp. 102, 242; the Schenley had a small ad in *JCW*, vol. 51, August 2, 1905, p. 38; and the Jefferson was the site of the jewelry manufacturers' convention in 1907, as reported in *JCW*, vol. 54, June 5, 1907, p. 52.

165 Alberts, "Peregrinating Beau Brummels," pp. 29–30.

166 *JCW*, vol. 57, December 30, 1908, p. 83.

167 "Our Traveling Representatives," *JCHR*, vol. 28, May 23, 1894, p. 30.

168 *JCHR*, vol. 28, July 11, 1894, pp. 24–25; vol. 54, May 22, 1907, p. 72.

169 *JCHR*, vol. 30, February 20, 1895, p. 22.

170 "Fellowship Among Jewelers," *JCW*, vol. 43, August 15, 1901, p. 52.

171 "Retail Jewelers Advertising," *JCW*, vol. 54, May 22, 1907, p. 110.

172 *JCW*, vol. 54, May 1, 1907, p. 94.

173 *JCW*, vol. 54, May 1, 1907, p. 115.

174 *JCW*, vol. 68, May 19, 1909, June 16, 1909, June 23, 1909, June 30, 1909, all on p. 11.

175 J.H. Johnston & Co., New York City, 1896 catalogue, collection of Janet Zapata.

176 William Stolz, Jeweler and Optician, Saginaw, Michigan, ca. 1900–1910 catalogue, collection of Janet Zapata; the Penninsular Engraving Company advertisement appeared in *JCW*, vol. 68, June 23, 1909, p. 20.

177 H. Jack Hunkele, "Achille Bippart, Notes on His Life by One of His Grandsons," unpublished typescript produced for family members, August 30, 1992, n.p., Newark Museum archives.

178 Smith 1929, p. 4.

179 J.B. Bishop, of Bishop & Bishop, quoted in "Better Jewelry More in Demand," *The New York Times*, January 31, 1937, p. 31.

180 Vincent Slavin, "Glittering Trade, Veteran Craftsmen Add Luster to Jewelry Products Made in Newark," *Newark Sunday News*, April 12, 1964, pp. 6–8.

181 Krementz & Co., *The Story of Gold in Modern Jewelry* (Newark: Krementz & Co., 1946), 15 pages.

182 Krementz & Co., *Jewelry: The Perfect Gift for Every Occasion* (Newark: Krementz & Co., ca. 1951). The catalogue gives retail prices.

183 Cunningham 1954, p. 63.

184 Slavin, "Glittering Trade," p. 8.

185 Oral histories from workers at Jabel Inc., Irvington, New Jersey, interviewed and transcribed by Diane Salek, 1995–1996, The Newark Museum archives.

186 Slavin, "Glittering Trade," p. 8.

214. A view of the first Labor Day parade in Union Square, New York City, on September 5, 1882, with Newark jewelry workers in the vanguard. From *Frank Leslie's Illustrated Newspaper*, September 16, 1882, p. 53, detail.

"An intelligent, respectable, well-dressed body of men"

A History of Newark's Jewelry Workers from the Industry's Founding to the Great Depression

Kevin J. Smead

On Tuesday, September 5, 1882, several hundred Newark jewelry workers took the Jersey City ferry across the Hudson River to Manhattan. The trip was to be no ordinary excursion. Invited by New York's Central Labor Union, the men from Newark were set to march in what would later be known as the nation's first Labor Day parade (Fig. 214).

The ferry carrying the Newarkers arrived at Cortlandt Street some twenty minutes late for the 10 am start. Though the organizers had ordered that the parade wait for no one, the Newark men—led by Voss' Military Band of Newark playing a Gilbert and Sullivan tune—were hustled to the front of the procession waiting at City Hall Park.[1] Moving up Broadway and past Washington Square to the reviewing stands at Union Square, the Newarkers and their New York brethren were quite a sight among the marching workers, whose reported numbers ranged from four thousand to twenty thousand. The Newark jewelers, "who presented a very respectable appearance, all wore buttonhole bouquets, and carried canes, which they held as infantry officers carry swords on parade. They marched four abreast" up the avenue, noted the New York *Evening Post*. Even more flattering was the New York *Herald*, which reported that "the Jewellers' Union of Newark came upon the heels of the musicians, and their appearance fully justified their right to the place of honor in the procession. Their name was legion, and for the most part they were young and well dressed, wearing dark clothes, Derby hats and badges on their lapels." The *Newark Daily Journal*, otherwise contemptuous of the banners and general appearance of many of the morning's marchers, commented that the "Newark contingent in the parade made a highly creditable appearance. They were an intelligent, respectable, well-dressed body of men."[2]

The favorable press reaction toward Newark's jewelry workers is perhaps not surprising. By the 1880s, Newark's journeyman jewelers were an elite group among the industrial working class. Well-paid, highly skilled craftsmen in an era of increasing mechanization, they represented an ideal which few other trades were able to attain. Yet even in Newark, the center of the nation's fine gold jewelry industry, all was not as it seemed. For one thing, the marchers did not include children or women, though child labor was common and the employment of women was on the rise in Newark's jewelry shops. For another, the growing size of jewelry firms (with the concomitant decrease in a journeymen's likelihood of successfully becoming his own employer), the advent of steam power, and other forces of the second Industrial Revolution were in the process of depriving the industry of much of its special status. Within two generations, what had once been one of the city's leading industries would fade to a shadow of its former significance, and the esteem in which Newark's journeymen jewelers were held would be considerably diminished.

The history of Newark's jewelry workers and the larger story of this once-leading Newark industry remain largely untold. This essay will explore that history, focusing especially on such questions as: When and why did the manufacture of jewelry begin in Newark? What forces led to its rise and fall? Who were the jewelry workers? What were their lives like? How did the jewelry industry, and these lives, change over the course of a century and a half? And what is the legacy of jewelry workers to the first city of New Jersey? The answers to these questions should provide a window into the lives and work of those employed in Newark's jewelry industry in the nearly two centuries since 1800.

Newark and Manufacturing

Newark in 1800 retained many aspects of its rural, Puritan past. As a regional market town, it was more oriented to its hinterlands than to the larger world. Lacking direct transportation, Newark was isolated from New York, only eight miles distant. As one early historian of the city noted in 1878, "A journey to New York...was attended with greater preparations, and probably more anxiety, than is a trip to St. Louis or the Far West now-a-days."[3] Most people living in the Newark area at the beginning of the nineteenth century were either farmers or craftsmen who made articles in traditional artisanal fashion for home consumption. Shoemaking, an outgrowth of customary home production, introduced as a winter occupation for farmers, grew into the first industry of importance in the area's economy. Gradual improvements in transportation early in the century encouraged Newark's farmers to ship their produce directly to Jersey City for the New York market, and the town's industrial goods also found a broader market, soon becoming the focus of Newark's productive energies. Remarkably, by 1826 over eighty percent of the labor force in Newark was engaged in manufacturing, with thirty-four different crafts being practiced.[4] Newark was poised to become the first large American city whose economy was based principally on industry rather than commerce.

The diversified skill of Newark's artisans encouraged other industries to locate in the city, especially when access to Newark was facilitated by canal and railroad construction in the 1830s. Increasingly, manufacturing shifted from homes and small shops, where apprentices and journeymen worked under the supervision of a master craftsman to produce an entire object, to factory settings where larger numbers of workers, frequently with the aid of specialized machinery, performed specific parts of a manufacturing process. Newark pioneered among American cities in committing itself to factory methods of production, and a municipal ethos in favor of manufacturing developed and was nurtured, particularly under Republican administrations in the latter part of the nineteenth century. Mayor Julius A. Lebkuecher, elected in 1894, was himself a jewelry manufacturer and co-founder of Krementz & Co., with his cousin George Krementz; and Daniel W. Baker, alderman and president of the Common Council in the 1860s, was also a manufacturing jeweler. As manufacturing became more dependent on credit and national markets, Newark was thrust more closely into the orbit of New York City, already the nation's commercial and financial center and the location of twenty-five percent of the nation's jewelry trade. For Newark's jewelry manufacturers, New York's central place in the nation's commerce meant that opening offices in Gotham, as well as establishing wholesale arrangements with New York merchants and jobbers, was essential to survival and growth.[5]

Jewelry-Making in Newark

The history of jewelry manufacture in Newark is usually dated to 1801, when Epaphras (or Ephrais) Hinsdale established the first American factory for the exclusive manufacture of fine jewelry. Located on the east side of Broad Street, north of Lafayette, the firm employed six men and supplied jewelers from Hartford (from whence Hinsdale had removed) to Georgia with brooches, bracelets, earrings, necklaces, and chains. Hinsdale took on John Taylor as a partner; following the founder's death, Taylor joined with Colonel Isaac Baldwin to form the long-lived firm of Taylor & Baldwin.[6] Operating on Franklin Street near Broad, Taylor & Baldwin is credited with being the first jewelry firm in the nation to engage in quantity production, rather than just specialty work and manufacturing for store stock.

The jewelry industry grew relatively slowly in Newark in the early nineteenth century. An 1826 census found just twenty-two jewelry workers; by 1830, there were fifty skilled jewelers employed in the city, and in 1836, the year of Newark's incorporation, four jewelry-making establishments employed a total of one hundred men (out of nearly 5,600 employed in industry in the city) and produced articles worth $225,000.[7] Rapid growth soon followed, and other names to be long remembered in the annals of Newark's jewelry industry—Alling, Carter, Durand—appeared on the scene. By 1845, nine manufacturing firms were in operation in the city, which was gaining a reputation for its fine gold jewelry. (Despite the city's growing reputation for high-quality work, many manufacturers found it necessary to stamp their goods "Paris" or "London" in order to assure their sale in New York—where most of the larger firms kept sales offices—across the country, and around the world.[8]) As the Newark name gained cachet—particularly after Newark's noted Industrial Exhibition of 1872, where jewelry manufacturers like Durand & Co. were acclaimed for

215. Commemorative postcard for the Newark Industrial Exposition of 1912. New Jersey Historical Society, Newark.

their "exquisitely fine jewelry"—such deceit proved less necessary, though it was many years before the practice entirely disappeared.[9]

By 1860, jewelry manufacture was the fourth largest industry (in terms of the value of its product) in the nation's seventh largest manufacturing city. Over eight hundred workers—most of them native-born Americans—were employed in some twenty-seven establishments. The number

of heads of households who listed their occupation as "jeweler" in the federal Census had tripled since the decade of the 1850s.[10] The figures above are somewhat deceiving, however. Jewelry workers made up only 3.7 percent of the manufacturing population of Newark, consistent with the industrial diversification of a city where it could be said that "almost every thing is made in Newark that is made by man." The percentage of jewelry workers peaked in 1880 at 7.2 percent. Journeyman jewelers were, nonetheless, an elite class among Newark workers, earning over fifty percent more than the average Newark industrial employee in 1860.[11]

By 1890, jewelry employed the second greatest number of workers (nearly two thousand) in Newark (behind leather), with an annual product valued at over $4.6 million, ranking third in the city—a position the jewelry industry would maintain until after World War I.[12] Into the early twentieth century, jewelry—along with leather, brewing, hat- and clothes-making, and (increasingly) foundry and machine-shop products—ranked among the city's leading products.[13] But the diversification of the city's manufacturing—leather, still the top product in 1900, amounted to only eight percent of the city's total production—meant that no one industry dominated in Newark. The nearly 2,500 establishments in the city produced over two hundred distinct classes of manufactures at the turn of the century, reported the *Newark Evening News*.[14] As late as 1945, one chronicler could remark on the city's "bewildering variety of small, medium, and large-sized concerns producing almost every sort of article."[15]

At the time of Newark's second great Industrial Exhibition, in 1912, the city's reputation as a center of fine gold jewelry manufacturing had been entrenched—along with that of New York City—for decades (Fig. 215). While Gotham led in precious-stone work, seven-eighths of the "solid" (10- to 14-carat) gold items produced in the nation were made in Newark, as was half of the highest quality (18- to 24-carat) merchandise; a majority of platinum goods was produced along the Passaic as well.[16] In the mid-1920s, an article on the city's jewelry industry could reasonably refer to Newark as "the city of gold and platinum and precious stones."[17] However, the growing popularity of cheaper costume jewelry, produced principally in the New England towns of Providence and the Attleboros, was at that moment relegating Newark to a declining share of the nation's total jewelry production.[18] Whereas between 1850 and 1923, Newark had never produced less than about an eighth of the nation's jewelry (measured in product value), peaking in 1880 at eighteen percent, the mid-1920s saw a swift fall-off. In 1927, the city manufactured less than half the product of only four years earlier; its 6.5 percent share of the nation's jewelry production that year fell to five percent a decade later.[19]

Jewelry was among many Newark industries in decline—including leather, hat-making, corset-making, fertilizer, and brewing (due to Prohibition)—in the years following World War I.[20] The decline in jewelry production, however, actually antedated the war; in 1929, the *Journal of Industry and Finance* dated the problem back to 1913—though in 1925 Newark's 144 jewelry manufacturing establishments (the most of any single industry in the city) still employed 2,430 people, second among Newark industries.[21] By 1933, in the depth of the Great Depression, only fifty-nine jewelry factories with 1,200 employees were operating in all of New Jersey; wages paid dropped to $1 million, from $6 million four years before.[22] It was a slump from which Newark's jewelry industry never really recovered.

Jewelry Workers: Origins and Evolutions

The original proprietors of Newark's jewelry shops were nearly all American Protestants of British origin, themselves trained in the jeweler's art. As late as the 1860s it could be stated that

most of the employers are natives of New Jersey, and reside here, although attending to the business of their firms in New York, where the bulk of the articles manufactured is disposed of. With few exceptions, too, they are all practical workmen, and at some time in their lives were employed as apprentices and journeymen by the older establishments.[23]

However, it was not long before significant numbers of immigrants and their children became not just employees in the jewelry factories, but manufacturing jewelers in their own right. Over time, well-known names of shop owners like Hinsdale, Taylor, Baldwin, Carter, and Alling were joined by those of Krementz, Herpers, Champenois, Schuetz, and Unger.

Most of those who augmented the group of "native" American jewelry makers in Newark were immigrants, particularly from Germany. Though Germans made up less than two percent of Newark's 1835 population of 18,201, they soon became a major force in the jewelry industry, and in the city generally. The great influx began when many left the Old World following the failed revolutions of 1848. Lager beer brewing was not the only industry in which the German presence was felt; in the Censuses of 1850 and 1860, Germans already constituted a quarter of the city's jewelry workers, and continued to increase their share over time. A glance at the Alling Brother's Hands Ledger in the early 1860s turns up, among the otherwise largely Anglo-American names, those of journeymen jewelers such as Charles Schuetz, Gottfried Woolf, George Rudolf, John Buhler, E. Ladenburger, G. Kraemer, Frederick Froelich, Christian Wedekind, and Rudolph Stecher; a good number of other continental names—Champenois, Boteaux, and Rabineau—could be found as well. Indeed, this should not be surprising since jewelry firms specifically recruited European craftsmen, particularly from Germany and France.[24] A smattering of other nationalities, from British to Scandinavian to Eastern, Central, and Southern European, also worked at the bench in Newark throughout the nineteenth and twentieth centuries.

The 1890 Census found that two-thirds of Newarkers were foreign-born or had parents who were immigrants. By 1902, it could be reported that in New Jersey "fully one-half of the number employed in the [jewelry] business are foreigners, Germans being the most numerous."[25] On the eve of World War I, German-Americans and German immigrants, still the dominant ethnic group in the city, were also among the most active jewelry workers in the labor movement. In 1907, the international officers of the International Jewelry Workers Union of America (IJWUA) included second vice president H.A. Schoellhamer and treasurer Herman Grote, both of Newark. IJWUA Local 2's officers that year included Frederick J. Engel, George Bessinger, Julius F. Jack, Harry Taylor, R. Schueler, H. Greve, William Reinhart, F. Marshovitz, Frederick Mess, and Schoellhamer and Grote.[26] The IJWUA's successor, the International Jewelry

Workers Union (IJWU), also had a strong German presence in Newark. Among its officers and delegates in the late 1910s were men like Charles Schwartz, Thomas Wier, Edward Kiepe, William Seeger, Herbert Holzhauer, and Theophilus Stauber.[27]

The first decade and a half of the twentieth century saw a heavy influx into Newark (as in other American cities) of Southern and Eastern Europeans. Many of these newcomers were Italians or Russian and Polish Jews, some of whom

216. Signature page of Herman Grote's IJWUA dues book, 1906-1907. The Newark Museum, Gift of the Estate of Gertrude L. Grote, 1987, in memory of Herman E. Grote (87.62c)

were skilled jewelry workers whose talents (and traditions of labor activism) enlivened the trade (Fig. 216). Conspicuously absent from Newark's jewelry shops were African-Americans. When asked about blacks in the industry, one officer of the IJWUA reported in 1903 that he had "never heard of a Negro being employed as a mechanic in any branch of the jewelry business, [though there was] nothing in the law of the union to prevent his becoming a member or working at the business if properly qualified."[28] In an industry where the craft was often passed down from father to son, little was ever done to overcome the industry's lily-white traditions.

The Geography of Newark Jewelry

Where in Newark was the jewelry industry located? And where did Newarkers who made jewelry live? As noted by one early twentieth-century historian of Newark industry, the city's early tradition of industrial home work led to the development of workshops and factories near the homes of ambitious industrialists.[29] While this led to the dispersal of some of the city's industries, in the jewelry industry a long-lasting pattern of geographic concentration resulted. Initially, this concentration meant that both factories and workers' residences were in close proximity to one another. In the late 1830s, some forty-two percent of jewelry workers were living in the Ninth Ward, just south of downtown. By the Civil War, this area was clearly the jewelry manufacturing section of the city. However, residential concentration was not as persistent. Over time, workers increasingly chose to live elsewhere; only thirty percent of jewelry workers lived in the district in 1860.[30] Neighborhoods clustered by wealth (and by ethnicity), rather than occupation alone, increasingly became the norm in the industrial era in Newark as in most American cities.

Newark's Germans, for example, tended to live in the Sixth Ward. The Teutonic presence in the city was notable enough for *Harper's New Monthly Magazine* to exclaim in 1876 that "a wondrous tide of Germans has flooded Newark, dropping into all the vacant lots about the factories, and spreading itself over the flats to the east and the hills to the southwest, until it numbers about one-third of the voting population." The German quarter in the Hill district was described as "a section of nearly two miles square; . . . a snug, compact, well-paved city within a city, giving evidence of neither poverty nor riches. The Germans who dwell [t]here are chiefly employed in the factories, and nearly all own their houses (Figs. 217, 218)."[31]

Following the early lead of firms such as Taylor & Baldwin, Newark's jewelry manufactories, with a few notable exceptions, were centered in the blocks stretching south along Mulberry Street, in the area bordered by Market, Broad, and Chestnut Streets, and New Jersey Railroad Avenue (now McCarter Highway). Even the IJWU chose as its headquarters an office in this

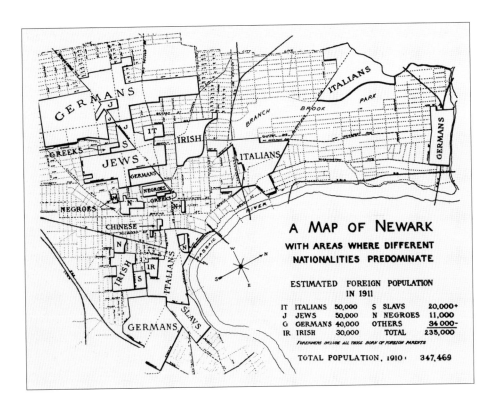

217. Map of Newark, 1911, showing neighborhoods divided by ethnicity. Newark Public Library.

218. A view of the German neighborhood in Newark, 1876. In *Harper's New Monthly Magazine*, vol. 53, October 1876, p. 671.

area, at 277 Mulberry Street. As noted below, the proximity of shops to one another facilitated the interchange of ideas and of workers, and often led to situations where smaller firms (or even individuals) would lease space in competitors' factories.

The Work Process

Descriptions of the jewelry-making process in Newark in the nineteenth century are remarkably few. Some, such as William Bagnall's illustrated description of the manufacturing process in 1882 at Enos Richardson & Co., are tantalizingly brief.[32] For the most part, information on the work life of these craftsmen must be teased from scattered papers, newspaper accounts, and official documents. While various articles of jewelry boasted their own special techniques for manufacture, a general idea of the industry's production methods can be drawn from the historical record.

Initially, the production of a piece of jewelry in Newark was in the hands of an individual craftsman, working at his bench, virtually from start to finish. "Originally," noted *The Newarker* magazine, "a jewelry factory was composed of a melting furnace, a few upright drills, some polishing wheels, and a long line of benches for the workers, who made practically all of each article by hand with file, saw, and blowpipe [used in sol-

dering]."[33] Over time, skills became more differentiated. Specializations such as chain- and watch case-making, stone cutting and mounting, ring-making, polishing, engraving, and enameling developed. Some employers early on turned to "team work," which involved "a number of men and boys, generally two men to each boy working under a foreman[;] in this way each individual workman [was] allotted some part of each job to do." With the introduction of steam power and tool and die work, even greater specialization developed and piecework became more prevalent.[34] Some firms even began to specialize in only parts of the jewelry-making process; for example, in 1865 Ferdinand Herpers began a successful business of manufacturing jewelers' findings (settings) in quantity.

Still, changes in the actual process of making fine gold jewelry in Newark tended to be gradual. The first in a remarkable series of articles in 1869 on the Newark jewelry industry by the *Newark Daily Journal* described the manufacturing process at that time as follows:

Before the [Civil] war all the jewelers manufactured from gold coins, but now they make their purchases of gold from the Assay Office in New York.... As soon as the gold bars reach the manufacturers they are alloyed to whatever carat may be required for the work at hand, then are put though rolls and fashioned into the several shapes and sizes desired. Thence the gold goes into the makers' hands; they work it up according to the designs given them, and prepare it for the polishers, who in turn send it to the engravers. From this point it goes back again to the makers ... to have the final touches given and last ornaments put on. At this point ends the labor of the manufacturer, and when next seen, the articles are in the velvet lined cases of the wholesale and retail jewelers.[35]

Limited specialization was apparent in the physical arrangement of Newark's jewelry factories by the time of the Civil War. The Carter, Howkins & Dodd factory at Park and Mulberry Streets in 1869 had four floors for its more than three hundred workers, two consigned to "general jewelry" making, another to chain-making, and the fourth split between the two; separate areas were also set aside for polishers and engravers (see Fig. 6). Enos Richardson & Co., at the corner of Columbia and Green Streets, had a quite similar layout in its four-hundred employee factory in 1882 (Figs. 38a, 219). Also in 1869, the three-and-a-half story Durand & Co. building on Franklin Street, near Broad, had its basement "used for enameling, refining, and smelting; the first floor for getting out stock, and tool-making; the second floor for manufacturing jewelry and watch cases, and the third floor for making, engraving, polishing, and lapidary work."[36] The Alling Brother & Co. factory, a brick structure three stories tall at 13 Orchard Street, had on its first floor the offices and the engine room, "where the polishing and steaming for enamel-

ing is nearly all done. On the second floor manufacturing, melting, rolling and press work, and on the third floor enameling, turning and engraving."[37]

Most jewelry shops had even more limited specialization. While large factories may have served as industry leaders, the fact remains that well into the twentieth century, some ninety percent of Newark's jewelry factories had fifty or fewer workers—and most had under twenty. In 1909, the typical Newark shop had 18.4 workers,

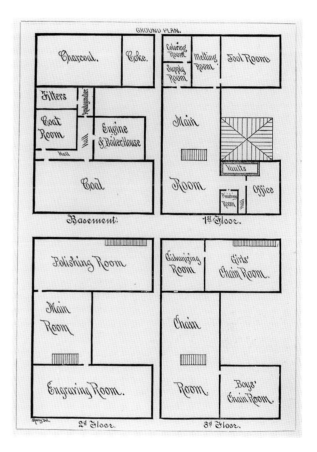

219. Floor plans of the Enos Richardson & Co. factory, Newark, woodcut from Bagnall 1882.

who produced a bit under $50,000 worth of jewelry during the year. Indeed, as the industry succumbed to increasing fragmentation and competition, the percentage of the industry's workers employed in the largest factories actually declined.[38]

Changes in the work process were noted with considerable anxiety by jewelry workers in the latter part of the nineteenth century. When asked in 1879 by the New Jersey Bureau of Statistics of Labor and Industry if labor-saving machinery had been introduced into his trade, one jewelry worker replied that "ten years ago we made everything by hand, now much [is made] by steam," with a related ten percent reduction in the work force.[39] Still, the handicraft nature of jewelry production in Newark lingered. Describing the Enos Richardson factory in the early 1880s, an observer noted that "a visitor of the establishment, acquainted with the conduct of mechanical industries in general, readily notes the fact that in it machinery supersedes hand

220. Boys making gold chains in the Enos Richardson & Co. factory, Newark, woodcut from Bagnall 1882.

labor to a less extent than in most other industries. Used wherever desirable, it is rather to facilitate and supplement than to take the place of the manual dexterity and skill of operatives. Automatic machinery—so effective, and so marvelous in many industries—is not used."[40]

A reporter for the *Newark Sunday News* visited the factory of Krementz & Co. in 1901 to observe the manufacture of "gold novelties," and his account is notable for its descriptions of a mixture of newer and more traditional methods. Both were evident as the reporter followed a popular design from its original conception in the art department, to its modeling in wax, to the creation of a die for its production. The different parts of the object would be stamped from the appropriate dies and then given to a worker for assembly.

Some twenty-five years ago a workman would be furnished with a bar of gold and be expected to work up the design himself, but machinery is now used for a large portion of this work.... The artisans all sit on low wooden benches, in a well-lighted room. With the design in front of them, and their tools ready at hand, they rapidly join each piece, wiring it in place with a very fine wire. When the design is completed, it is placed on a small asbestos tray and taken to a metal oven.... The workman places a minute particle of solder, composed of an alloy of gold, silver, and copper, at each joint where the parts have previously been wired. Then, by the aid of a small metal blow pipe, held between the teeth, he blows the flame directly on the joints, thereby melting the solder. When cool the wire is removed, and the piece of jewelry is ready for the finishing touches.[41]

These finishing touches could include a chemical bath and boiling, polishing by machine, washing, electroplating (if the object was to be colored), and packing. Some pieces would also have stones set in them, done by men who "in this capacity become extremely expert, and are usually the largest wage-earners in the factory." Other work was enameled; this was "done entirely by girls and closely resembled china painting." As had been the practice for generations, the Krementz factory closed twice a year, generally in January and July, to clean the building and recover particles of precious metal lost in the manufacturing process. At the Krementz factory, watch chains were also made, with much of the work being done by hand (Fig. 220).

Owing to the extreme delicacy of a great deal of [the chain-making work] large numbers of girls are employed. One of the chief requisites for this branch of the jewelry business is good eyesight. The work is extremely trying on the optic nerve.... It is a most interesting sight to see them at their wooden benches, rapidly assembling these minute circles of gold under the guidance of the naked eye (Figs. 221, 222).[42]

An interesting picture of a Newark jewelry factory over time—and of some of the changes occurring in the jewelry industry at large in the late nineteenth century—is given in the report issued by the state's Bureau of Statistics of Labor and Industry in 1898. The 1886 and 1896 figures for a single, moderate-sized (twenty-eight workers in 1886, thirty-four in 1896) jewelry factory were presented, and they illustrate several trends. The most significant increase in employment was among apprentices—especially those under eighteen—and among women, who were employed exclusively as polishers (and who saw their average wage decline over the decade). Certain skilled work was eliminated, as the four enamelers and engravers who had been paid by

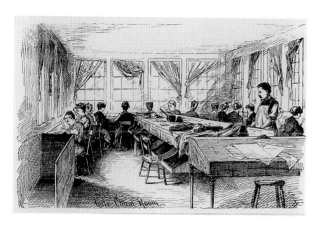

221. Girls making gold chains in the Enos Richardson & Co. factory, Newark, woodcut from Bagnall 1882.

222. Workmen in 1953 at a long bench in an unnamed Newark jewelry factory. From John T. Cunningham, "Global Jeweler," *Newark Sunday News Magazine*, December 6, 1953, p. 22.

four-story loft buildings in a one-mile radius at the south end of Mulberry Street near McCarter Highway"[45]—offered the visitor a glimpse back to an earlier era of craftsmanship. In 1953, the *Newark Sunday News Magazine* commented that "many of Newark's jewelry makers are small plants with only a few employees working in a second or third story loft. This . . . was how Durand and Carter and Krementz and nearly all others began."[46] The article was illustrated with pictures of jewelers (many of them silver-haired) working at the bench, another setting a stone, an owner sketching a ring design, and other workers otherwise engaged in processes such as melting, rolling, stamping, and fashioning jewelry (Fig. 223).

As had been true for more than a century, the city's precious-metal workmen continued (and continue) to produce high-quality gold jewelry, most designed in-house and struck from dies rather than cast. Jewelers still remained "prone to stick together and it is not unusual to find more than one firm located in the same building."[47] A 1964 feature on the industry in the *Sunday News*

the piece were reduced to a single engraver, paid a (lower) hourly wage. A new skilled position, machinist, was added to the payroll, perhaps in the place of the others. An area where skilled work did climb—perhaps because of changing fashions—was stone setting, where the number of such craftsmen increased from one to four, at a piece rate that continued to net $30 per week on average. And while the number of "jewelers" employed remained constant at seven, their average wage declined from over $20 per week to less than $17.[43] Increasing female and youthful (if not child) labor, wage pressures on the average jeweler, and the elimination of certain skilled work through the use of advanced machinery—such were the trends in the jewelry shops at the end of the nineteenth century, and they continued into the twentieth.

By the 1920s, deskilling in the jewelry-making process was well in evidence. One observer found that "modern methods have changed the entire routine, and today the delicate machinery and dies do most of the preliminary work, so that the workers have merely to assemble the various pieces together."[44] Still, as late as the mid-twentieth century, a visit to one of Newark's jewelry factories— "in drab-looking three or

223. A workman rolling gold into workable sheets in the Krementz & Co. factory, ca. 1953. Krementz & Co. archives, Newark.

Magazine noted that "one problem facing the industry is development of new craftsmen," as an aging work force (averaging twenty-five to thirty years with their firms) was being replaced neither by sons, who now were interested in college degrees, nor by immigration, as had been true until the 1920s (Fig. 224).[48] Manufacturers

224. Workers from Whiteside & Blank on a company outing, 1904, Henry Blank & Co. papers, New Jersey Historical Society, Newark. Henry Blank is in a vest and cap in the middle row, with his two sons seated at his right.

continued to mechanize processes wherever possible. "As in most craft industries," stated Krementz & Co. president Robert Krementz darkly in 1971, "people today would just as soon drive a truck at $5 an hour as learn a skill. So we've got to engineer operations around the workers."[49] Also seemingly unchanged was the seasonality of the business and its vulnerability to economic downturns. Philip Blank, retired president of Henry Blank & Co., sounded little different from his nineteenth-century precursors when he complained that sixty to seventy percent of his business was handled in the last four months of the year, and that his luxury goods were "the first to feel the slackening of the economy."[50]

One respect in which jewelry-making compared favorably to other metalworking occupations was in the relative absence of gross threats to workers' lives and health in the years prior to occupational safety legislation. This is not to say that there were no occupational hazards. Certainly the sedentary nature of the work, with jewelers bent over their benches, could lead to health problems. The eyesight of many workers deteriorated. "The jeweler's work, in all its branches, is particularly trying to the eyes, and it not infrequently happens that defective sight compels men to abandon the trade, who are in every other respect capable and competent to follow it for years to come," reported the state Bureau of Statistics of Labor and Industry around the turn of the twentieth century.[51] Respiratory disorders were also common—common enough to be a leading cause of death among jewelers. Though large factories tended to be well ventilated, the impetus was as much to catch and trap particles of precious metal as to protect workers' health. Small shops, as the federal Public Health Service reported in 1917,

[were] often . . . overcrowded, and poorly ventilated; the air in them impregnated with the precious dust gathered in the process of hammering, cutting, and polishing, and polluted with products of respiration, animal effluvia, and smoke. The windows [were] opened very seldom, as that would interfere with the use of the mouth blow-pipe, and also on account of the ignorance of the employees themselves, who [were] prejudiced against open windows.[52]

One firm located on the Passaic River blamed "the polluted condition of that stream and the stench which is a natural result of its foulness, as the principal ill health producing factor having any relation to its business or surroundings."[53]

Acid poisoning, from powerful chemicals used in processes such as coloring, gilding, and refining, was a threat to workers who came into contact with such substances and their fumes, especially in improperly ventilated areas.[54] The increasing mechanization of the industry created its own dangers. Small shops in buildings not originally intended to serve as factories were said to be more dangerous than those in larger, more modern structures. Accidents were said to be greatest in the machine shop and the press room, and "careless" workers were usually blamed for their own injuries, frequently to their hands.[55] For example, in 1905 Charles Limbacker, who worked at the Unger Brothers jewelry factory, suffered a compound fracture of the right arm when the limb was caught in a stamping machine.[56] Such accidents as these were generally not life-threatening; a 1902 survey of the industry in Newark found not a single fatal accident in the previous year.[57]

Jewelry Workers: Description and Perception

Newark's jewelry workers were part of an elite among the city's industrial working class, and they carried themselves as such. A journalist shortly after the Civil War noted that

the journeymen jewelers of Newark, as a class, are very respectable men socially and otherwise. A considerable percentage of them we find to be real estate owners, and in tolerably comfortable circumstances. They dress with more taste than other mechanics, and although employed ten hours out of the twenty-four, manage to keep as well informed on the topics of the day as those of other trades.[58]

The city's journeymen jewelers took obvious pride in the objects they produced. They advertised to the world who they were and how they made a living by displaying on their person the work of their own hands. In 1869, a contemporary noted that they "adorn themselves with curiously fashioned ornaments in gold and silver, and may be generally recognized from this peculiarity, while daily walking through the public streets."[59] These manifestations of pride in craft also indicated that jewelry workers had the wherewithal to purchase the luxury goods they produced.

The character of Newark's journeymen jewelers frequently received favorable comment. Employers found the jewelers a fairly sober lot, and others celebrated a litany of virtues—including the fact that they were seldom to be seen in court on charges of stealing the valuable goods with which they worked every day. The journalist who described the respectability of jewelers in 1869 also noted:

The working jewelers, also, are for the most part natives of this State, and are as fine a body of men as can be found. Their wages average $25 per week,...a large portion of which is expended in this city. Some, to be sure, goes to the savings banks, and of this thriftiness we have every reason to feel proud, because it shows a character of temperance and economy combined, and it would be well if the same could be said about the workmen in every other branch of trade.[60]

Most jewelry workers were thus able to afford more than the mere necessities of life; some even vacationed away from home, a practice virtually unheard-of among working people of the day. In 1869, the *Daily Journal* described the return of the jewelers after the annual July factory closing: "the men, nearly all, g[a]ve evidence of having bathed [swam] a good deal and exposed themselves to the scorching rays of the sun at quiet rural retreats. They are jollier, happier, and more inclined to work, and wait for another 'resting spell' about New Year."[61]

As early as the 1840s, jewelry workers began, in a limited way, to share a common social life outside the factory walls, from factory-sponsored baseball teams to fraternal organizations to the German Turnverein. However, there is little evidence that leisure hours were enjoyed in the company of those of different ethnic heritages. The labor movement, which in other industries helped to break down ethnic insularity among workers, for many years made few inroads in the jewelry industry. Leisure itself was at a premium for workers who averaged nearly sixty hours of work per week in the nineteenth century. And as "labor aristocrats," many workers subscribed to the reigning Victorian middle-class domestic ideals and spent a good deal of leisure time within the bosom of their family.

An 1880 study by New Jersey's Bureau of Statistics of Labor and Industry compared the living expenses of a group of the state's jewelry workers with those of individuals in other industries. The picture painted by this predominantly German sample indicates that jewelry workers earned more, and lived better, than most of their contemporaries. Like the machinists and other elite trades, they spent well above average on clothing, food, "sundries," and rent or board, and were even able to set aside a sizable portion of their wages in savings—despite on average losing a month or more each year to enforced idleness due to shop closings. And jewelry workers tended to be the sole support of their family. Only one quarter of the married men had children or spouses who brought in significant additional income.[62] In 1888, the Bureau profiled a single, and apparently typical, Newark jewelry worker. Born in New Jersey, married with six children—three of whom were under twelve years of age—this journeyman was the sole support of his family. Working ten hours a day, six days a week, he earned a daily wage of $3. Though he lost twenty-one days during the year, six to "slackness of the trade" and fifteen to illness, his semimonthly pay nonetheless added up to $720 for the year, about average for a skilled male jewelry worker at that time. Perhaps because of his large family, he was unable to save any money during the year, and in fact ran a deficit for 1888. Though he belonged to no building and loan or beneficial association, nor to any labor organization, he did carry a $1,000 life insurance policy to protect his family in case of his untimely demise.[63] Such was the life of a journeyman jeweler at the peak of the trade's influence and esteem in the city of Newark.

Jewelry Work, Jewelry Workers

The Industrial Revolution of the nineteenth century affected Newark's jewelry industry more subtly than it did other industries, especially those where the production of staple items for national markets demanded increasing mechanization and specialization. Jewelry-making in Newark clung to its artisanal class heritage, both in ideology and in practice, long after other crafts found themselves stratified by growing class divisions in the nineteenth century. The artisan, or "mechanic," class of pre-industrial Newark was the bulwark of local society through the 1820s. Boys usually were indentured as apprentices (often living with their masters), became journeymen, and aspired to be masters with their own shops, which frequently were located in or near their own homes. "Independence and skill were the artisan's chief virtues, and these were possessed by all mechanics," writes a historian

of early Newark industry.[64] These independent artisans mixed intense labor with leisure, setting their own pace (which not infrequently meant breaks for liquid refreshment from the local tavern) and enjoying time off during dull periods in the trade.

As production began to move out of the household or small shop and into the factory, the nature of the work experience for Newark's jewelry workers slowly began to change. More haltingly than in easily mechanized industries, such as leather, Newark's jewelry workers gradually shifted in status from a pre-industrial "mechanic" class to wage workers, for whom the potential for economic independence grew less likely over time. As the average size of firms became larger, and as showrooms shifted from Newark to New York, it became clear to many of Newark's jewelry workers that the move from craftsman to successful manufacturing jeweler was one that fewer would be able to make. Increasingly, "a journeyman had only a gambler's chance to succeed as an entrepreneur." While 42.3 percent of jewelry workers were self-employed in 1840, the figure fell to 22.2 percent in 1850, and 14.3 percent—one in seven—in 1860; the decline accelerated in later years.[65]

Nevertheless, the classic artisanal structure of master, journeymen, and apprentices retained some of its currency in Newark's jewelry industry, even after the inroads of industrialization had begun to redefine those roles—and to include women in the work process as well. Well into the twentieth century, most Newark jewelry manufacturing concerns were organized as partnerships. Frequently, one of the partners—himself usually a master craftsman—supervised the factory operations, while one or more attended to sales in offices in Newark and New York. For example, in the late 1860s, the factory owned by Charles L. Nesler and Thomas H. Redway, at 14 Oliver Street, had two dozen year-round employees (manufacturing breast pins, solid and filled rings, studs, sleeve buttons, and earrings), whom Nesler superintended at the factory while Redway handled business and sales in New York; William Howkins played the same role in the large firm of Carter, Howkins, & Dodd.[66] Nor was it unheard-of for talented workmen to rise within a firm from the bench to an ownership position. Ferdinand Meerbot, employed since mid-century by Aaron Carter, was by the early 1890s not only superintendent of the Carter, Sloan & Co. factory, but he also received a portion of the firm's profits (Fig. 225).[67] Jewelry workers seemed to expect the owner-supervisor to be a "practical workman" as well as a capitalist. One jewelry worker complained in 1902 that he "noticed that the treatment of men grew worse the less the manufacturer himself knew of the technical side of the business, and with the evolution of the old-fashioned shop into the modern

225. Ferdinand Meerbot, foreman of the Carter, Sloan & Co. factory, 1895. Howe Family papers, New Jersey Historical Society, Newark, MG427, scrapbook folder 2.

factory, or mercantile establishment, the number of such places is growing rapidly. They leave the running of their shop to a superintendent or foreman, who receives a very good salary and who in turn has to grind it out of the men again."[68]

Working-class consciousness, evident among many journeymen in Newark industries by the mid-1830s, was slower to appear among jewelry makers. While shoemakers, hatters, silver platers, construction tradesmen, and others organized and confederated, jewelry workers remained aloof from such collective action. Historian Susan Hirsch has noted the peripatetic life of many journeymen craftsmen in Newark in the antebellum era, finding a rootlessness which may have inhibited their development of class consciousness.[69] Many journeymen spent only a few years in Newark, traveling at times to New

York or New England in search of employment and the chance to learn new skills. Several other factors help to explain jewelry workers' quiescence. First, jewelry-making retained through much of the nineteenth century many elements of its traditional "craft" status, despite innovations in manufacturing and shop organization. Jewelry-making required skills that could be obtained only through years of experience. Hence, true apprenticeship was practiced long after "apprentices" had become simply exploited, inexpensive labor in other industries, and even after mechanization had begun in jewelry-making. (By the 1880s, however, one journeyman jewelry worker could complain bitterly, when asked if his shop had a system for training apprentices, "to get all the work possible out of the apprentices, so that the journeymen will lose all the time possible, is the only method in my shop."[70])

The second factor that inhibited the growth of a working-class consciousness among journeyman jewelers was the size of the shops. Although after the 1840s some shops grew to large size—a hundred or more workers—most remained much smaller, headed by an owner who was not merely an investor but a true master of the craft. "As late as 1845," declared the *Newark Daily Advertiser* in 1858, "the shop which employed 15 or 20 hands was considered a large concern; and the establishment of Messrs. Taylor & Baldwin, the oldest jewelry manufacturing house in the country, with perhaps 50, was at that time viewed as a monster manufactory."[71] The free-labor ideal of economic independence did not yet seem too remote a possibility for Newark's mechanic jewelers, who with a little capital could open their own shop in this relatively unmechanized industry. Finally, as the producers of luxury goods for which the cost of skilled labor—itself only a minor part of the cost of the finished product—could more easily be passed on to the consumer, jewelry workers (at least males) were relatively well paid, with men earning significantly above the average for Essex County manufacturing workers in 1860.[72] The combination of high wages and the jewelry industry's vulnerability to economic fluctuations and changing fashion made Newark's labor aristocrats generally reluctant to organize for better wages, hours, or working conditions.

Following the Civil War, Newark's jewelry industry expanded tremendously. Manufacturing establishments increased in number and size, steam machinery grew more prevalent, and markets grew more extensive. Steam—used for stamping, grinding, rolling, and polishing metal—though available earlier, was not in widespread use before the 1860s. Manufacturer Aaron Carter is usually credited with being the first jewelry maker in the city to use steam power (though others credit Palmer, Richardson & Co. in 1849 with the distinction); Carter even acquired for his factory the steam engine built by famed Newark inventor Seth Boyden for the 1853 Crystal Palace Exposition in New York.[73] As the jewelry industry grew larger, it spurred the development of related industries. Fine silver, watches and watch cases, optical goods, jeweler's tools, settings, and the refining of precious metal—including the valuable sweepings of Newark's jewelry shops—all developed as significant elements of the Newark economy.

What did not change was the high level of skill required of Newark jewelry workers in order to meet the constantly changing demands of a product subject to the whims of fashion. "Jewelry manufacturing in the 1860s," says business historian Philip Scranton, "was a craftsman's domain." Increasingly, however, beginning in the Civil War era— "the real starting point of industrial growth under the stimulus of labor-saving machinery"—jewelry-making took on the character of what Scranton has termed "batch" production.[74] Unlike mass and bulk production, which dominated in industries (such as steel plate or shoemaking) that could benefit from the efficiencies available in large-scale, routinized production, batch production characterized industries (such as jewelry) where demand was narrow and seasonal, and labor processes were not infinitely divisible.

Facing the fickle demands of fashions, batch producers such as jewelry manufacturers made many different products, finding it too risky to focus on any one product or to subdivide tasks. They located in proximity to one another to benefit from networks that provided "economies of agglomeration." And they set prices—derived from prior experience—designed to cover costs and profits, rather than make and stock staples and let the market set prices for them.[75]

As was typical of batch producers of consumer goods, jewelry manufacturers seasonally circulated samples (through their own sales force or via jobbers and wholesalers) among middlemen, shop owners, and department store buyers. Orders received determined production schedules and labor needs; seldom were items produced for inventory. A successful jewelry manufacturer was one whose workmen designed items that could snatch a segment of market demand and produced those items in a timely fashion and in whatever quantity was required.[76] Central to batch methods of production were versatile, skilled workers who could make product diversity a reality, individuals "on whose judgment and experience rested firm capacities for quality and timely production."[77] The concentration of fine gold jewelry firms in Newark led to the development of a corps of highly skilled craftsmen, many trained as apprentices in Newark shops; in addition, the steady immigration of workers who had learned the craft in Europe broadened the pool of available skills.

Factories with space for several manufacturing jewelers, such as the one built by veteran craftsman John R. Pierson (Goldsmiths Hall on Maple Place, off Green Street) facilitated both entry into the industry by ambitious journeymen or immigrants who had earned a stake and the expansion of existing firms.[78] With large manufacturers generally willing to buy the product of smaller firms for sale through their own distribution networks, setting off on one's own was feasible, though seldom a sure road to success. For example, in 1869 three-year-old Krementz & Co., later known worldwide for its one-piece collar buttons, rented space on the second floor of the building owned by the manufacturing jewelers Nesler & Redway, at 14 Oliver Street.[79] Firms like Nesler & Redway "routinely built beyond their needs, leasing the extra space.... The practice was further refined by tenants who sublet 'bench space' to tiny, often one-person, firms that focused on sample-making, designing, or custom work."[80]

As noted above, the realities of uncertain demand in the jewelry trade meant that long periods of unemployment were not uncommon. Seldom were the traditional factory closings of two weeks each year (after Christmas and in July) the only times Newark's jewelry factories shut down. Personal relationships between the most highly skilled workers and their supervisors (frequently an owner) helped firms retain their best workers in slack times. This was especially true of the larger firms, which were more able to ride out slow seasons. Not coincidentally, such personalism also served to mitigate labor organizing. The proximity of other jewelry firms in Newark also allowed laid-off workers to seek employment nearby, and gave journeymen the chance to learn new skills in a different setting.

By the last decade of the nineteenth century, Newark's jewelry-making shops were affected by changes in the market for and marketing of jewelry. Inexpensive jewelry, produced largely in Providence and the Attleboros with less-skilled (and often female) labor, had begun to be fashionable before the Civil War and eventually undercut Newark's production of fine gold jewelry. "By vastly cheapening the article, without any apparent loss of beauty or value," noted the *Daily Advertiser* around mid-century, "the farmer's daughter and the kitchen maid may now vie in splendor of ornament with the belles of the Fifth Avenue."[81] The manufacture of costume jewelry was also more adapted to mass-production techniques than the fine jewelry industry, which continued to require a high level of skill. Yet it was precisely the need for this skill that somewhat mitigated the effects of competition from the costume jewelry industry. Newark's skilled jewelry workers did not suffer from technological and economic change as much as their less-skilled New England counterparts.

But suffer they did. During economic downturns (such as the lengthy depression and gold drain of the 1890s), fine jewelry faced greater decreases in demand than did cheaper varieties.[82] Jewelry workers who were ambitious or desperate "repeatedly tried to outflank the trade's notorious seasonality by opening their own shops," placing buyers in an advantageous position and flooding markets with cut-price duplicates of popular styles. Through the first three decades of the twentieth century, "the trade became progressively more demoralized and chaotic, even as the number of manufacturing firms escalated." The industry became divided into "up-market craftsmanship" (Newark and New York) and "low-market sweatshop" (New England) segments.[83] To

counter calls for higher wages or shorter hours, Newark employers tried to show their workers how much better off they were than their New England counterparts. Industry leaders cited the exploited condition of workers in New England, where unions had less impact, the growth of industrial home work, and the increasingly feminized and deskilled work force—fifty percent of New England jewelry workers in 1920 were female (virtually all unskilled), forty-seven percent were unskilled males, and only three percent were skilled males. "The objection frequently raised by New York and Newark employers," declared the *Jewelry Workers Monthly Bulletin* in January 1919, "consists in pointing out to inhuman labor conditions prevailing in Providence, R.I., and in the Attleboros, Mass."[84] The New England formula of "cheap silver, new techniques and styles, lowered wages for factory hands, outwork labor, and wider demand for inexpensive jewelry" was not one that fine-gold oriented Newark was willing to follow.[85]

Skilled metalworkers, attracted by the steadier employment in other industries, began to leave jewelry manufacturing. Though *The Jewelry Worker* declared in June 1910 that "the number of mechanics leaving the workshops in the past month to become retail jewelers is an encouraging sign of the times and speaks for the interest they take in their vocation," the meaning of such departures was actually more ominous.[86] One jewelry worker and labor activist described the conditions in Newark in the years between 1903 and 1916 as follows:

We who loved our trade shed bitter tears as we saw it, driven by unjust competition, from pillar to post, commercialized as no trade ever was before, machines and tool work introduced in every branch, child labor and female help put in every corner of the shop. Wages reduced to almost half, short time all the year around and piece work and sweat shop conditions wherever you went. Thus did we jewelry workers of Newark suffer the agony of Hell as we tried to make ourselves understand the why and wherefor [*sic*] of such conditions.[87]

During World War I, "skilled workers deserted their benches in droves, returning, if at all, only after the 1920-21 depression to start new firms that further intensified competition.... Jewelry employment had always been erratic, but after 1914 those workers who could were moving out entirely."[88] Manufacturers were more than ever at the mercy of unfaithful jobbers or hard-driving department store buyers. "By 1910 more than a thousand firms were trying to reach millions of customers through a thousand wholesalers courting over ten thousand retailers," notes Philip Scranton. With "a market power shift toward distributors," who capitalized on the extreme seasonality of the industry, the decade of the 1920s was for jewelry manufacturers characterized by a "profitless prosperity."[89] When the Great Depression struck, the industry collapsed.

Wages and Hours

While wage and hour statistics for Newark's jewelry industry were not gathered systematically until the twentieth century, the evidence available demonstrates a clear pattern. Jewelry workers tended to be well paid, earning twenty percent or more above the average for New Jersey industrial workers. Women, a growing minority of jewelry workers, earned considerably lower wages than their male counterparts—often half or less, even for comparable work. High wage rates were balanced by the heavily seasonal nature of the work, often compressed into the months from September through December (this seasonality was characteristic of many consumer goods industries of the period). In 1881, one jewelry worker complained to a state investigator that "working overtime is a great injury to our trade. The bosses have a custom of withholding work as long as possible, and then crowd it into a few months, when we are compelled to work late. This necessarily results in idleness during the remaining time, of which advantage is taken by reducing wages." The worker argued that an eight-hour-a-day law would greatly benefit jewelry workers (Fig. 226).[90] Long hours—generally ten hours per day, plus nine on Saturday—were the norm. As late as 1909, more than four out of five jewelry workers put in between fifty-four and sixty hours per week. Not until the labor activism spurred by World War I reinvigorated Newark's jewelry union did the eight-hour day (plus four on Saturday) become common.[91]

Employers tended to favor the highest skilled workers in hiring and wage practices. Such workers were usually the last let go in bad times and the first to be rehired. For example, in 1859 the Alling firm agreed to pay German-born

226. A view of the first Labor Day parade in Union Square, New York City, on September 5, 1882, with Newark jewelry workers in the vanguard. From *Frank Leslie's Illustrated Newspaper*, September 16, 1882, p. 53, detail.

Charles Schuetz and Isaac Champenois, both of whom later became successful manufacturing jewelers, weekly wages equivalent to $1,100 and $1,000 per year, respectively—a considerable sum in an era when highly paid machinists averaged $500 annually, and the average Essex County industrial worker earned $281. Alling Brother's arrangement with these key employees continued until the factory failed to reopen after the 1860 Christmas season, due to the economic dislocations associated with the impending Civil War. When production resumed in September 1861, Champenois returned, only this time at piecework rates. Even so, he earned $694.28 in 1862 and was soon returned to a weekly wage. Schuetz fared equally well, returning as a machine operator and earning $1,053.08 in the same year. Less favored employees were engaged even less regularly, and at lower wages.

The Alling shop's female employees tended to work more consistently and to have less turnover than most of the men. Whether because of their skill or, equally likely, the low piecework rates they were paid, women like Matilda Passmore, Charlotte Krauss, Sarah Taylor, Anna Price Butler, and Susan Davenport were kept working as much as possible, earning on average a bit over $250 per year each in 1860 and 1862.[92] Though in 1860 such women made up just under ten percent of Newark's jewelry workers, by the end of the century this figure would nearly triple. Generally, women were relegated to tasks like polishing, chain-making, and production work, all of which required extremely fine hand-eye coordination—tasks deemed appropriate to the female sex and which paid considerably less than the jobs assigned to men. However, the number of women employed in Newark never matched that of New England, where women comprised about half the total employees in Rhode Island plants in 1922.[93] As with the growing feminization of the work force, piecework would also become a much more common—and contested—phenomenon for all workers.

As noted earlier, wage rates for men in the jewelry industry continued to be high following the Civil War. The pay scale in 1869 reportedly ranged from $15 per week up to $100 per week, with pieceworkers able to earn up to $40-$50 per week, and engravers, precious-stone setters, and designers earning the most. On average, journeymen's wages were said to be $25 per week. However, the 1870 Census showed Essex County jewelry workers earning on average over $650 per year, or just over $13 per week for fifty weeks, which would indicate that workers were employed not much more than half the year. Still, the wages were well above the Newark average, and were "remunerative enough to prevent those strikes and combinations from which other branches of business so frequently suffer," according to the *Daily Journal*.[94] "While at exceptionally busy times the men were worked overtime and as many new men as possible were engaged," noted one critic of the labor system employed in the shops, "as soon as the season was over the new men were dismissed or, in fact, some of the old ones in their stead and the rest very often put on short time until another rush came; and the employees who had to go were left to shift for themselves or go and underbid someone else."[95]

New Jersey's Bureau of Statistics of Labor and Industry reported in 1882 that jewelry workers' yearly wages ranged from $1,150 to $2,200 for foremen, $1,200 for colorers, $850 to $900 for toolmakers, $900 for melters, while other mechanics averaged $650 to $800—all considerable sums for working people in that era. (The cost of living in 1880 was approximately one tenth of what it would be a century later.[96]) Women's wages, as was typical in the nineteenth century, continued to lag well behind those of men. For example, in 1888 female chain makers were reported to average $7 per week and males $12; female polishers $8.70 and males $14.74; and female enamelers' helpers $7.50 and their male counterparts $16.50. That same year, while seven-eighths of men earned $15 or more per week, seventy percent of women earned under $8 per week or less.[97]

While the wages paid (male) jewelry workers were recognized as being well above those of most Newark industries, the constant struggle between owners and workers over wages—and, increasingly, over piecework rates—grew as the industry became more competitive throughout the nineteenth and into the twentieth century. Even in 1869, it was reported that in Newark's largest jewelry factory (Carter, Howkins, & Dodd, with 312 workers) "half the employees are paid by the week, and the other half by the piece."[98] Though piecework did not necessarily mean that wages earned would be lower (in fact, in 1890 pieceworkers reportedly earned more than those being paid an hourly wage), the increasing division of labor that it often entailed was seen as an infringement on the craftsman's independence, and the potential for squeezing workers to produce more at lower rates became a reality in the hypercompetitive decades around the turn of the century.[99] Jewelry workers recognized that their product was less sensitive to labor costs than other industrial goods, and argued that this justified higher wages. "As far as the public is concerned," declared one worker and labor activist, "they would not be able to detect the difference if the price of labor were doubled, as that is the smallest item in the manufacture of jewelry."[100] While this statement was somewhat exaggerated, one early twentieth-century estimate put wage costs at slightly over one-fifth of total expenses in the New Jersey jewelry industry—much lower than in other industries, and consistent with past figures in the jewelry industry.[101]

Apprentices and Children

Formal apprenticeship remained important in the jewelry industry and lingered into the twentieth century, though in its later years the apprentice

227. Staff of the Carter, Sloan & Co. factory, including young boys, ca. 1880. Howe Family papers, New Jersey Historical Society, Newark, MG1362.

system often shaded into mere child labor. Around the time of the Civil War, Alling Brother & Co. maintained the traditional five-year apprenticeship in its shop, beginning when a boy was sixteen. At that age, he received $33 per year, plus board and washing; each year until he was twenty-one his wages increased $5 annually. Unlike the early days of the industry, boys boarded away from their masters, no longer receiving the benefit of his "moral guidance." While at times such apprenticeships appeared to be much like those of the pre-industrial past— the 50¢ deductions from the pay of Henry Crique and Charles Keller in 1859 for the "Library Association" recall the era of Benjamin Franklin—apprentices were just as much subject to dismissal during economic downturns as were journeymen.[102] Moreover, an institution like the library served a social control function for apprentices, as it was "the only place young workers could go at night that was free of liquor, gambling, or prostitutes."[103]

On the whole, children never formed a large portion of Newark's jewelry workers; those under seventeen constituted nine percent of the work force in 1870 (Fig. 227)—higher than average in Newark, but they were much more likely to be serving genuine apprenticeships leading to well-paying skilled work than were, say, the twenty-one percent of the state's glassware workers or the nearly one-third of silk workers who were children.[104] Still, in 1883, one underemployed Newark jewelry worker complained that "the cause of this idleness is due, to a great extent, to the system of boys' labor, the competition of which is so great that, when business is dull, the journeymen are given only such work as the boys cannot do.... The introduction of machinery has also displaced a great amount of skilled labor of late years." His recommendation—like that of another jewelry worker cited above—was the enactment of an eight-hour law.[105] Another jewelry worker complained in 1881 that "child labor is a great evil in our trade."[106] Nevertheless, the percentage of children in the shops diminished over time, particularly after the 1880s, indicative of the declining significance of traditional apprenticeship (and of the success of factory legislation enacted in that decade).

True apprenticeship remained more important in jewelry-making, however, than in more easily deskilled crafts. Numerous were the Newark jewelry manufacturers who prided themselves on their rise from a "boy" in someone's shop, to the rank of journeyman, and ultimately to the status of master craftsman with his own shop. One manufacturer nostalgically recollected that "fully 80% of our manufacturers left the bench and the forge to start [a] business with limited capital," though the number who successfully rose from apprentice to manufacturing jeweler was undoubtedly small, and grew smaller over time.[107]

A classic example of a Horatio Alger-type success story was that of David Dodd. In later life a noted industrialist, the fifteen-year-old Dodd was apprenticed to Aaron Carter in 1853, agreeing in his indenture that in return for learning the trade of jeweler, plus $20 per year (to increase by $5 each year until he reached twenty-one) and $2 per week (later $2.25) board, he would

his Master faithfully serve, his secrets keep, and his lawful commands obey; he shall do no damage to his Master, nor suffer it to be done without letting or giving notice to his Master; he shall not embezzle nor waste his Master's goods, nor lend them without consent; he shall not play at cards, dice, or any unlawful game; he shall not frequent taverns, tippling houses, commit fornication, nor contract matrimony; he shall not absent himself from his Master's service without his said Master's consent; but in all things behave himself as a good and faithful Apprentice, during the said term.

Dodd rose through the ranks and eventually became a partner of Carter, and moved on to operate several successful manufacturing businesses. When Carter, Sloan & Co. celebrated its golden anniversary in 1891, Dodd's indenture was deemed enough of a curiosity that it was reproduced in the firm's program for its gala celebration at Delmonico's (Fig. 228).[108]

Left unstated in Dodd's indenture was the delicate matter of who would supervise the "morals" clauses of the contract while the teenager boarded separately from his master's home. The problem of the control of apprentices was an ongoing one. As late as 1883, the proprietors of the firm of Carter, Sloan & Howe offered, in traditional paternal fashion, a series of "frequent evening meetings, at which music, recitations and addresses were had" during the

winter months "for the purpose of affording proper amusement and instruction to their large number of apprentices."[109] Other firms, especially those considerably smaller than the mammoth Carter firm (in the 1870s it was considered the largest jewelry factory in the world), lowered their costs through the increased use of younger workers without providing such amenities.

With the eventual demise of genuine apprenticeship by the early twentieth century, manufacturers, once reluctant to encourage the

228. Facsimile of David Dodd's indenture to Aaron Carter in 1853, printed for the semi-centennial banquet of Carter, Sloan & Co. in 1891. New Jersey Historical Society, Newark, pamphlet file, N671 C246.

teaching of jewelry designing in technical schools, found themselves encouraging such courses. The Newark Technical School, for example, began a three-year, four-evening-per-week program for factory artisans (with no restriction on age) in 1902. The program, which charged $20 for the first year and $30 each for the second and third years, was instigated by George R. Howe, the senior partner of Carter, Howe & Co. and a trustee of the school—and this despite maintaining in his own shop what he called "a genuine apprenticeship system." In a 1905 interview, the school's chief instructor and director, Prof. Charles A. Colton, commented indirectly on the program's limited success (and on the unstable nature of the Newark jewelry trade) when he noted that few students completed the entire course because, in order to support their families, many were forced to find employment in locations outside Newark. That year the program had only seventeen students.[110]

Howe also pushed for more technical education in public schools, where a course in the design of silver jewelry was instituted in 1907. He believed that the public schools placed "too much stress on preparation for college and on bookish education, slighting the development of industrially intelligent men and women," and he "looked forward to the day when a boy of 12 to 14 [could] enter a school in Newark and graduate later a skilled, alert, enterprising, ambitious jeweler."[111] Jewelry workers were less enthusiastic, however, viewing school-based programs as a way of "producing cheap labor in our trade at the expense of the government."[112] But given Newark's ongoing municipal efforts to encourage manufacturing interests, from industrial exhibitions to tax policy to infrastructural development, the involvement of the schools—particularly at the height of the "industrial education" movement—is not surprising.[113]

Collective Organization

Though manufacturer George R. Howe wistfully remembered in 1911 that in 1860 "a strong bond of sympathy [existed between] employers and men," a growing gulf in fact developed between workers and their employers over the course of the nineteenth century.[114] Despite their significant place in the local economy, Newark's jewelry workers were notably unsuccessful in organizing for higher wages and shorter hours. "The industry we represent," claimed one union official in the 1920s, in a statement as true then in seeking to explain jewelry workers' organizational difficulties as it had been three-score years earlier, "is the first to be hit by panics and last to be affected by tides of prosperity."[115]

The first recorded effort of Newark jewelry workers to organize collectively did not come until the eve of the Civil War (and in the shadow of the Panic of 1857, which had by early 1858 reduced the number of jewelry workers employed in Newark from over 1,000 to fewer

than 100). It was in 1859 that journeymen jewelers first sought—unsuccessfully—to organize for higher wages.[116] A mutual benefit association, the Jewelers' Assurance Company, was organized in lieu of a union; "warmly approved of by the stable men," it collected a benefit of $1 from each member, to be paid to the survivors of a deceased member.[117]

In the 1880s, with the rise of the Knights of Labor—the nation's first mass organization of the working class—Newark jewelry workers again organized. The Knights, who espoused moral and political education and promoted cooperative enterprise, served as a vehicle for trade union action in Newark and across the nation. Little is known about the Newark men who marched in the 1882 Labor Day parade, or of the delegates who presented the credentials of a "Jewellers' Union" to the Knights-affiliated Newark Trades Assembly in May 1886, at the peak of the Knights' influence.[118] Nor do we know much about the 250 members of the United Jewelers' Association and the Silver Platers' Union who were among the 20,000 who marched in the September 1886 Labor Day parade in Newark.[119] In 1887, the state Bureau of Statistics of Labor and Industry reported the existence of a single Newark Knights jewelry workers local (which had been established that same year), with 500 members—ninety percent of whom were currently employed—paying annual dues of three dollars. The members reportedly included 200 Germans, 100 English, 75 Americans, and 25 each of Irish, Scots, Swiss, French, and Italians. Reportedly, there were a further 1,500 unorganized workmen in the vicinity, 1,000 of whom were unemployed.[120] Following the Knights' 1887 collapse, nothing further was heard from these organizations; the Essex Trades Council, the successor to the Trades Assembly and a coordinating body for Newark-area trade union activity, had nothing to say about jewelers when it published its history in 1899.[121]

In 1899, a short-lived craft union of jewelry workers organized some 870 members in order to combat piecework, an effort in which they had some success, and to reduce the standard fifty-nine-hour week; this latter effort failed. It was not until the American Federation of Labor (AFL) chartered the International Jewelry Workers

229. The double acorn logo of the International Jewelry Workers' Union of America. From the IJWUA Constitution, printed in English and in German, 1903, private collection.

Union of America (IJWUA) in September 1900, and recognized its "double acorn" union label, that a jewelry workers union existed more than fleetingly (Fig. 229). The union's constitution declared that "the objects of this Union, for which it is organized and which are ever to be kept in view, are the welfare of the individual members, sought to be attained by a reduction in the number of hours of their labor, discouraging and if possible finally abolishing piece work and generally whatever tends to improve the condition of labor and to increase wages."[122] From the remnant of the 1899 group, Local 2 was organized in Newark, growing quickly in visibility. It took part in two large Newark labor parades held in 1901.[123] Local 2 soon did more than march; the following year, the members agitated for a nine-hour day (with ten hours pay) and even sponsored a Labor Day excursion that year for 750 members, family, and friends to Chimney Rock Glens in the mountains.[124] Still in 1902, leveraging their power in the busy pre-Christmas manufacturing season, the growing union demanded a fifty-four-hour week and an increase in piecework rates. By October, the union claimed 1,400 of the city's 1,559 journeymen jewelers.

The first strike called by Newark's jewelry workers began on October 3, 1902, at the Mulberry Street factory of Larter, Elcox & Co., when twenty-four men walked out. Krementz & Co. was also struck on October 7. Though few of the large firms were willing to accede to the union's demands, a number of smaller shops capitulated. It was not until after Christmas—and

hence, after the seasonal rush of business—that a "verbal understanding" was reached with the manufacturers, who refused to formally submit the agreement to the IJWUA.[125] According to a state report, the nine-hour movement largely had achieved its goal of reducing hours without reducing wages, while increasing employment in the jewelry industry.[126]

With the fifty-four-hour week in place, two thousand Newarkers joined the IJWUA by late summer 1903. However, when employers launched a nationwide open-shop offensive in 1904, the union was among many which were unable to withstand the onslaught; previous gains were rapidly lost. Though they continued to meet every second and fourth Tuesday at Aurora Hall, on William Street, and even put on an annual social dance there, the officers of Local 2 had little success in expanding the IJWUA's membership, especially after the Panic of 1907 and with a growing immigrant population in the shops. By 1913, the IJWUA had surrendered its AFL charter and disbanded, leaving a few locals (including Newark's) independently federated with the AFL. Three years later, as war in Europe tightened labor markets, union veterans organized the International Jewelry Workers Union (IJWU), which was again chartered by the AFL as an industrial union, this time identifying itself with an encircled diamond as its union label (Fig. 230).[127]

Local 2—chartered on February 22, 1916— again grew to be a force on the local labor scene. With labor markets tight, Newark workers successfully negotiated a forty-eight-hour week (with time-and-a-half for overtime) from their employers, without reduction in pay. Content with their gains, they declined to take part in a (failed) general strike begun in February by New York jewelry workers to gain a forty-four-hour week. The largest labor local in the State of New Jersey, Local 2 counted 1,832 members in good standing (312 of whom were females or apprentices) by the end of 1916. Men paid dues of 65¢ per month, and women and apprentices 40¢ per month; the initiation fee, which was at first was only $1, rose to $10 (later $25) for men and $2.50 for women and apprentices. This both served as inducement for apprentices to join the union early and subsequently to control entry into the craft.[128] By the time America entered World War I, wages had risen to 50¢ per hour, and Local 2 discussed establishing technical classes and a scientific trade library at its offices on Court Street.[129] By mid-1917, 111 of the 116 shops in Newark were said to be organized.[130] A strike against Carter, Gough & Co., one of the "Big Six" manufacturers which sought to maintain an open shop, was begun in September 1917; the strike led to a lockout of union members by a number of other jewelry firms. Though Carter, Gough declared that "it is undoubtedly a fact that our union workmen are controlled by a few radicals," the relatively conservative local was able to organize eighty percent of the firm's skilled mechanics (and ninety-five percent of those in the city).[131] The strike and lockout ended inconclusively, though they led to much rancor among the rank-and-file and even suggestions of infiltration of the union's executive board by employer interests.[132]

The wartime shortage of materials (including restrictions by the federal government on the use of precious metals) slowed the trade and led to periodic unemployment, but also spurred a number of successful job actions aimed at keeping wages apace with wartime inflation. Many members took work outside the jewelry trade, whether for lack of jewelry jobs or because of the higher wages being paid elsewhere. Newark's jewelry workers were also hurt because wartime calls to "Hooverize," or eschew luxuries, cut demand for fine gold jewelry.[133] Perhaps the high point in the history of the IJWU in Newark came in July 1918, when the city hosted the third annual convention of the IJWU, whose meetings were held in the Council Chambers at City Hall. The three-day session opened with an address by Mayor Charles P. Gillen and other local officials.[134] Among other things, the meetings served to display union strength to Newark's manufacturing jewelers and demonstrated the high degree of respect in which public officials held the jewelry workers and their union.

Immediately following the armistice, the number of jobs in the jewelry industry increased as precious metals again became available for

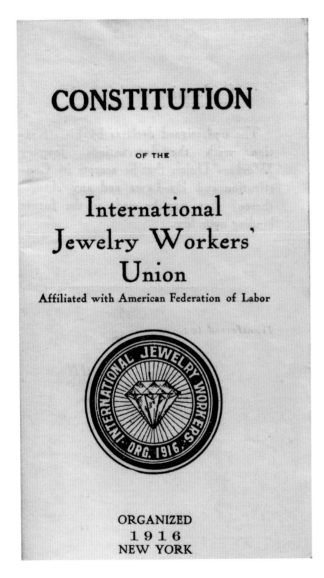

CONSTITUTION

OF THE

International Jewelry Workers' Union

Affiliated with American Federation of Labor

ORGANIZED
1916
NEW YORK

230. Title page of the International Jewelry Workers Union Constitution, for 1916-1917. The Newark Museum, Gift of the Estate of Gertrude L. Grote, 1987, in memory of Herman E. Grote (87.62a)

civilian uses. The work week in Newark and elsewhere was cut to forty-four hours, and further wage increases agreed to; double pay for overtime and the abolition of piecework also topped the agenda of Newark unionists after the war.[135] But such gains were not to last. The influence of the Newark union waned in the early 1920s, partly due to poor leadership and partly to the inroads made by the powerful and aggressive New York Local 1, no less than to a downturn in the economy, jurisdictional disputes with other unions, and the force of a coordinated employer anti-union offensive. By May 1922, when membership had dropped to under two hundred, Local 2 could only report that "business is quiet, the local is alive, and...we hope to accomplish something in the line of reorganizing this city."[136]

The union lay dormant for much of the 1920s, when the "campaign for the open shop launched by the National Association of Manufacturers was felt heavily in the Jewelry Industry."[137] Collective action picked up again during the Great Depression. A four-month strike by seven hundred Local 2 members in 1933-1934 largely failed, but did lead to an agreement under the authority of the National Recovery Administration. The IJWU and Local 2 in particular remained weak, however, and could not prevent the blacklisting of some one hundred union activists, a sore spot until well after World War II. By 1947, Local 2 was moribund and the city was largely unorganized, facing a "tougher bunch of manufacturers in the City of Newark" than even in aggressively anti-union, low-wage Providence.[138] By the 1950s, the IJWU itself

existed for the most part only in New York City, where the taint of criminality and charges of selling out low-paid members surrounded the union's leadership, which was reportedly connected to organized crime.

Conclusion

From humble beginnings, the jewelry industry in Newark grew to be one of the city's major employers until the time of the Great Depression. The "glitter" associated with this product attached itself as well to the men and women of Newark who fashioned the fine gold goods which would adorn so many across the nation and around the world. Possessing skills which afforded them a higher standard of living than most Newark craftsmen, jewelry workers—a fairly conservative group—lived relatively well and received the esteem of Newarkers both above and below them on the social scale.

Though they struggled mightily to maintain the world as they knew it, the nature of the industry and the impact of larger social and economic forces inexorably transformed the lives of jewelry workers, particularly beginning in the late nineteenth century. Squeezed by more aggressive marketing practices, driven from pillar to post by relentless competition and pressures to deskill the manufacturing process, Newark's jewelry industry declined. However, it has never quite disappeared; the few hundred workers who remain today are the heirs of a long, proud tradition—the sons and daughters of those Newarkers who marched in that first Labor Day parade.[139]

NOTES

1 Richard P. Hunt, "The First Labor Day," *American Heritage*, vol. 33, August–September 1982, p. 109.

2 New York *Evening Post*, September 5, 1882, p. 1; New York *Herald*, September 6, 1882, p. 4; *Newark Daily Journal*, September 6, 1882, p. 2.

3 Joseph Atkinson, *The History of Newark, New Jersey* (Newark: William B. Guild, 1878), p. 154.

4 Susan E. Hirsch, *Roots of the American Working Class: The Industrialization of Crafts in Newark, 1800–1860* (Philadelphia: University of Pennsylvania Press, 1978), p. 4.

5 Samuel H. Popper, "Newark, N.J., 1870–1910: Chapters in the Evolution of an American Metropolis," Ph.D. diss. (New York: New York University, 1952), p. 30.

6 Fales 1995, pp. 153–154; "Newark: The City of Gold and Platinum and Precious Stones," *The Keystone*, vol. 52, May 1925, p. 163. Taylor & Baldwin was dissolved in November 1868; it was succeeded by Thomas G. Brown & Sons; see *Newark Daily Journal*, July 3, 1869, p. 3.

7 James M. Reilly, "Rise and Growth of Manufactures," in *A History of the City of Newark* (New York: Lewis Historical Publishing Co., 1913), II, pp. 896–897.

8 Atkinson, *The History of Newark*, p. 230; William F. Ford, *Industrial Interests of Newark, N.J.* (New York: Van Arsdale & Company, 1874), p. 148; *Newark Evening News*, March 10, 1900, p. 11.

9 See the later reprint, *Report and Catalogue of the First Exhibition of Newark Industries* (Newark: Holbrook's Steam Printery, 1882), p. 37.

10 Raymond M. Ralph, "From Village to Industrial City: The Urbanization of Newark, New Jersey, 1830–1860," Ph.D. diss. (New York: New York University, 1978), p. 105. The increase was from 1.6 percent to 5 percent.

11 Reilly, "Rise and Growth of Manufactures," pp. 902, 910–911; U.S. Census Office, *Census of Manufactures*, 1860, 1890. The quoted passage is from Martha J. Lamb, "Newark," *Harper's New Monthly Magazine*, vol. 53, October 1876, p. 673.

12 Reilly, "Rise and Growth of Manufactures," pp. 914–915.

13 Popper, "Newark, N.J., 1870–1910," pp. 22–23.

14 *Newark Evening News*, March 5, 1900, p. 2.

15 Robert G. Albion, "Modern Industry," in William S. Myers, ed., *The Story of New Jersey* (New York: Lewis Historical Publishing Company, 1945), III, p. 34.

16 Newark Board of Trade, *Newark: The City of Industry* (Newark: Newark Board of Trade, 1912), p. 109.

17 See note 6 above.

18 Albion, "Modern Industry," p. 23.

19 U.S. Census Office, *Census of Manufactures*, 1850–1937.

20 Paul A. Stellhorn, "Depression and Decline: Newark, New Jersey: 1929–1941," Ph.D. diss. (New Brunswick, New Jersey: Rutgers University, 1982), p. 12.

21 "Jewelry a Traditional Newark Industry," *Journal of Industry and Finance*, vol. 3, April 1929, p. 58.

22 "Are Diamonds Safer than Paper Money?," *Journal of Industry and Finance*, vol. 9, April 1935, p. 9.

23 *Newark Daily Journal*, July 15, 1869, p. 2.

24 Hands Ledger of Alling Brother & Co., 1859–1863, New Jersey Historical Society, Newark, MG435; Hirsch, *Roots of the American Working Class*, p. 48.

25 "Annual Report," *NJBSLI*, vol. 25, 1902, p. 369.

26 *The Jewelry Worker*, vol. 1, August 1907, p. 4; vol. 1, November 1907, p. 4.

27 *JWMB*, passim, 1917–1919.

28 *NJBSLI*, vol. 26, 1903, p. 201.

29 Reilly, "Rise and Growth of Manufactures," p. 892.

30 Hirsch, *Roots of the American Working Class*, pp. 96, 99.

31 Lamb, "Newark," p. 675.

32 Bagnall 1882.

33 "Simple Facts in Jewelry Manufacture," *The Newarker*, vol. 1, December 1923, p. 7.

34 *JWMB*, vol. 1, January 1917, p. 6.

35 *Newark Daily Journal*, July 2, 1869, p. 3; see also Ford, *Industrial Interests of Newark*, p. 151.

36 *Newark Daily Journal*, July 2, 1869, p. 3.

37 *Newark Daily Journal*, July 8, 1869, p. 3.

38 U.S. Census Office, *Census of Manufactures*, 1909–1919.

39 *NJBSLI*, vol. 2, 1879, pp. 63, 64.

40 Bagnall 1882, p. 34.

41 *Newark Sunday News*, October 6, 1901, p. 4.

42 Ibid.

43 *NJBSLI* vol. 21, 1898, p. 181.

44 "Simple Facts in Jewelry Manufacture," *The Newarker*, vol. 1, December 1923, p. 7.

45 *Newark Sunday News Magazine*, April 12, 1964, p. 7.

46 *Newark Sunday News Magazine*, December 6, 1953, p. 26.

47 *Newark Sunday News Magazine*, April 12, 1964, p. 8.

48 Ibid.

49 "Newark's 24-Karat Business," *Newark!*, vol. 16, July–August 1971, p. 30.

50 Ibid., p. 46.

51 *NJBSLI*, vol. 25, 1902, p. 369.

52 International Jewelry Workers Union, *Almanac* (New York: IJWU, 1923), p. 126.

53 *NJBSLI*, vol. 25, 1902, p. 366.

54 International Jewelry Workers Union, *Almanac*, p. 127.

55 *NJBSLI*, vol. 25, 1902, pp. 367–368.

56 *NJBSLI*, vol. 28, 1905, p. 257.

57 *NJBSLI*, vol. 25, 1902, p. 365.

58 *Newark Daily Journal*, July 12, 1869, p. 2.

59 Ibid.

60 *Newark Daily Journal*, July 15, 1869, p. 2.

61 *Newark Daily Journal*, July 13, 1869, p. 2.

62 "Annual Report," *NJBSLI*, vol. 3, 1880, pp. 31, 62.

63 "Annual Report," *NJBSLI*, vol. 11, 1888, pp. 362–363, 394–395.

64 Hirsch, *Roots of the American Working Class*, p. 7.

65 Ibid., pp. 92, 79.

66 *Newark Daily Journal*, July 8, 1869, p. 3; July 2, 1869, p. 3 (Howkins); George R. Howe, notes for Board of Trade speech, February 28, 1911, Howe Family papers, New Jersey Historical Society, Newark, MG427, scrapbook folder 2; *Newark Daily Journal*, July 3, 1869, p. 3 (Leonard P. Brown's role as a partner in Enos Richardson & Co.).

67 *Jewelers' Weekly*, vol. 13, January 27, 1892, p. 12.

68 International Jewelry Workers Union of America, *Official Jewelry Workers' Annual* (New York: IJWUA Local No. 1, 1902), p. 9.

69 Hirsch, *Roots of the American Working Class*, pp. 92–93.

70 Ibid., p 74; "Annual Report," *NJBSLI*, vol. 4, 1881, p. 105.

71 *Newark Daily Advertiser*, January 27, 1858, p. 2.

72 Hirsch, *Roots of the American Working Class*, pp. 26, 67; *Newark Daily Journal*, July 3, 1869, p. 3.

73 *Newark Daily Journal*, July 3, 1869, p. 3, for Palmer, Richardson & Co.

74 "Annual Report," *NJBSLI*, vol. 30, 1907, p. 184; Philip Scranton, "Diversity in Diversity: Flexible Production and American Industrialization, 1880–1930," *Business History Review*, vol. 65, Spring 1991, p. 79, for the quoted passages, and passim.

75 Scranton, "Diversity in Diversity," pp. 34–38, 74.

76 Philip Scranton, "Manufacturing Diversity: Production Systems, Markets, and an American Consumer Society, 1870–1930," *Technology and Culture*, vol. 35, July 1994, pp. 486–487.

77 Ibid., p. 491.

78 *Newark Daily Journal*, July 7, 1869, p. 2; July 9, 1869, p. 3.

79 *Newark Daily Journal*, July 8, 1869, p. 3.

80 Scranton, "Diversity in Diversity," p. 79.

81 *Newark Daily Advertiser*, January 27, 1858, p. 2.

82 *Newark Evening News*, March 10, 1900, p. 11.

83 Scranton, "Diversity in Diversity," pp. 61, 77.

84 *JWMB*, vol. 3, January 1919, p. 1.

85 Scranton, "Diversity in Diversity," p. 75.

86 *The Jewelry Worker*, vol. 4, June 1910, p. 4.

87 *JWMB*, vol. 1, January 1917, p. 7.

88 Scranton, "Diversity in Diversity," pp. 80–81.

89 Ibid., pp. 83, 84.

90 *NJBSLI*, vol. 4, 1881, p. 89.

91 U.S. Census Office, *Census of Manufactures*, 1909–1919.

92 U.S. Census Office, *Census of Manufactures*, 1860; Hands Ledger of Alling Brother & Co., 1859–1863, New Jersey Historical Society, Newark, MG435.

93 *JWMB*, vol. 6, July 1922, p. 1.

94 *Newark Daily Journal*, July 2, 1869, p. 3; U.S. Census Office, *Census of Manufactures*, 1870, vol. III, table IX, p. 694.

95 International Jewelry Workers Union of America, *Official Jewelery Workers' Annual*, p. 9.

96 *NJBSLI*, vol. 5, 1882, p. 12.

97 *NJBSLI*, vol. 11, 1888, pp. 285, 300.

98 *Newark Daily Journal*, July 2, 1869, p. 3.

99 U.S. Census Office, *Census of Manufactures*, 1890.

100 International Jewelry Workers Union of America, *Official Jewelery Workers' Annual*, p. 11.

101 U.S. Census Office, *Census of Manufactures*, 1909; *NJBSLI*, vol. 11, 1888, p. 313.

102 Hands Ledger of Alling Brother & Co., 1859–1863, New Jersey Historical Society, Newark, MG435.

103 Hirsch, *Roots of the American Working Class*, p. 75.

104 U.S. Census Office, *Census of Manufacturers*, 1870.

105 *NJBSLI*, vol. 6, 1883, p. 122.

106 *NJBSLI*, vol. 4, 1881, p. 99.

107 George R. Howe, notes for Board of Trade speech, February 28, 1911, Howe Family papers, New Jersey Historical Society, Newark, MG427, scrapbook folder 2.

108 Carter, Sloan, & Co., "Souvenir of the Semi-Centennial Banquet," January 23, 1892.

109 *Newark Daily Journal*, November 12, 1883, p.3.

110 "Jewelry Department in the Newark Technical School," *JCW*, vol. 50, February 1, 1905, p. 41; *Manufacturing Jeweler* (1902), p. 382 (from Howe Family papers, New Jersey Historical Society, Newark, MG427, scrapbook folder 2).

111 *Newark Evening News*, September 28, 1907, p. 10; "President of Newark Manufacturing Jewelers' Association Expresses His Views on the Apprenticeship Question," *JCW*, vol. 97, 1908 (page proof of this article, in Howe Family papers, New Jersey Historical Society, Newark, MG427, scrapbook folder 2).

112 International Jewelry Workers' Union, *Almanac*, p. 89.

113 Popper, "Newark, N.J.," pp. 75–76.

114 Howe, notes for Board of Trade speech.

115 *JWMB*, vol. 6, September 1922, p. 1.

116 *Newark Daily Advertiser*, January 27, 1858, p. 2; March 26, 29, 1859, p. 2; *Newark Daily Journal*, July 3, 1869, p. 3.

117 *Newark Daily Journal*, July 7, 1869, p. 2.

118 *Newark Daily Advertiser*, May 27, 1886, p. 2.

119 *Newark Daily Advertiser*, September 6, 1886, p. 2.

120 *NJBSLI*, vol. 10, 1887, pp. 28, 43, 54; Charles Minard, "History of the Newark Local," *JWMB*, vol. 1, January 1917, p. 6, offers a contrasting set of figures.

121 Essex Trades Council, *Illustrated History of the Essex Trades Council* (Newark: Essex Trades Council, 1899).

122 International Jewelry Workers Union of America, "Constitution Governing Local Unions," article II, 1903.

123 *Newark Evening News*, May 30, 1901, p. 7; *Newark Daily Advertiser*, September 2, 1901, p. 2; *JWMB* vol. 1, January 1917, p. 6.

124 *Newark Evening News*, April 14, 1902, p. 10; August 29, 1902, p. 7; September 1, 1902, p. 2.

125 *Newark Evening News*, October 3, 1902, p. 10; October 5, 1902, p. 7; October 7, 1902, p. 1; December 27, 1902, p. 3.

126 *NJBSLI*, vol. 28, 1905, pp. 231–232.

127 Gary M. Fink, ed., *Labor Unions* (Westport, Connecticut: Greenwood Press, 1977), p. 164.

128 *JWMB*, vol. 1, March 1917, pp. 11–12.

129 *JWMB*, vol. 1, May 1917, pp. 12–13. The offices were later moved to Mulberry Street.

130 *JWMB*, vol. 1, November–December 1917, p. 50.

131 *JWMB*, vol. 1, September–October 1917, pp. 3–5.

132 *JWMB*, vol. 2, August 1918, pp. 41–42.

133 *JWMB*, vol. 2, February 1918, p. 11; March 1918, p. 9; August 1918, p. 2; September 1918, pp. 11–12; September 1918, p. 9.

134 *JWMB*, vol. 2, August 1918, passim.

135 *JWMB*, vol. 3, September 1919, p. 22.

136 *JWMB*, vol. 6, March 1922, pp. 7, 12.

137 *JWMB*, vol. 8, June 1924, p. 4.

138 International Jewelry Workers Union, *Proceedings*, vol. 9, 1942; vol. 11, 1947.

139 In 1992, New Jersey had some 1,200 production workers in the precious metal jewelry industry; U.S. Department of Commerce, Bureau of the Census, "1992 Census of Manufactures: Industry Series-Jewelry, Silverware, and Plated Ware," Table 2, May 1995.

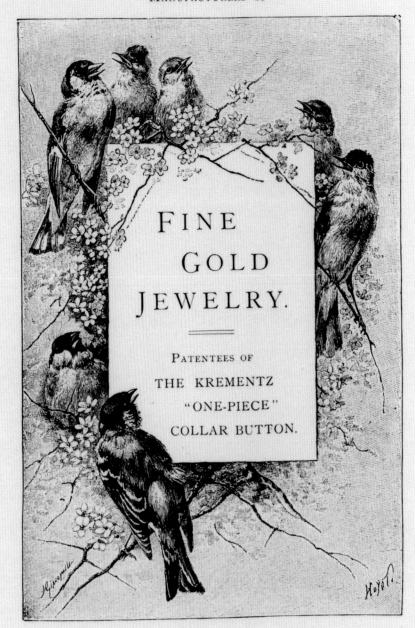

231. Advertisement for Krementz & Co., ca. 1887, in *Alphabets, Monograms, Initials, Crests, Etc.* (New York: E.W. Bullinger, ca. 1887).

The Names Behind the Jewelry

Summary Biographies of Newark Jewelry Makers

JANET ZAPATA

ABELSON & BRAUN

In 1920, Julius Braun was recorded in the Newark Directory as a steel engraver at 296 Chadwick Street. He was not listed again until 1935, when he became president of Abelson & Braun, a ring manufacturer, in partnership with Louis Abelson, who was secretary-treasurer. Their factory was located at 449 Washington Street. Abelson & Braun specialized in bridal jewelry. When the business was purchased by Krementz & Co. in 1940, this expertise was absorbed within the parent company.

232. Julius Braun at his bench, 1920–1930, collection of Buddy Braun.

THOMAS W. ADAMS & CO.

Thomas Weir Adams was born on August 12, 1822. He entered the jewelry trade as a young man, serving an apprenticeship with Stephen Alling, whose brothers founded Alling & Co. After learning the trade, in 1844 he went into partnership with R.A. Harriott. Known as Harriott & Adams, the firm's shop was located at 35 Walnut Street. In 1854, the firm merged with John C. Jennings, a manufacturing jeweler since 1844, to form Jennings, Harriott & Adams. The factory was located at 83 Union Street and a New York City office was at 182 Broadway. Upon Harriott's death in 1855, Adams and Jennings continued under

the name of Jennings & Adams. Between this date and 1861, there were several partnership changes and, in 1861, with the addition of William Greathead, the name became T.W. Adams & Co.; other partners included Henry James and H.C. Ostrander. Although the company continued to maintain the factory at the Union Street address throughout its history, the New York office moved several times, first to 15 John Street, then to 22 John Street, 14 John Street, 11 John Street and, finally, to 15 Maiden Lane.

Robert W. Adams was born on August 24, 1851. He joined his father's firm in 1876, learning all phases of the jewelry business before serving as a traveling salesman for the company. Upon Greathead's and Ostrander's retirement in 1878 and 1879, respectively, Robert became a partner, as did his brother, J. Woodhull Adams, in 1880. From this date until the death of Thomas Adams on January 9, 1901, the business was run by the father and his two sons.

Robert Adams was a leader in the jewelry industry, encouraging improvements in all areas of the business. When, in 1903–1904, a movement was started for a national stamping law, he gave his unqualified support and was one of the first Newark manufacturing jewelers to join the committee. He continued to support this act until the National Stamping Law was passed in 1906. He managed the firm until his death on May 26, 1915. By this time, his brother, J. Woodhull, had retired from active participation in the business. The firm closed its doors in 1915.

ALLING & CO.

Alling & Co. was founded in 1843 when two brothers, Isaac A. and Joseph C. Alling went into partnership, establishing Isaac A. & J.C. Alling for the manufacture of jewelry at 347 Broad Street. The firm moved, in 1846, to 6 Orchard Street. A younger brother, Horace, who was born in Newark on September 24, 1822, entered into an apprenticeship with the company and, in 1850, was admitted into partnership, assuming the responsibilities of salesman. At this time, the name of the company became Alling Brothers. In 1858, Joseph left the firm to open his own business. About this time, Isaac L. Blauvelt joined the company, remaining for only a few years.

In 1859, another brother, William R., born June 16, 1831, became a partner and the name became Alling Brother & Co. The factory had relocated to 11 Walnut Street; by 1864, it had moved to 13 Orchard Street, where it remained throughout the life of the company. In 1881, when Isaac Alling retired to form another company, Horace and William Alling and William B. Kerr, who held a small interest in the company, entered into partnership and the firm's name became Alling & Co. Kerr withdrew in January

ALLING & CO.,

170 BROADWAY,

Factory at Newark, N.J.   NEW YORK.

Manufacturing Jewelers

A COMPLETE LINE OF EVERY STYLE OF

14 KT. JEWELRY

Specialties,

LOCK BANGLES AND SCARF PINS,

PLATINUM AND GOLD BUTTONS.

233. Advertisement for Alling & Co., ca. 1887, in *Alphabets, Monograms, Initials, Crests, Etc.* (New York: E.W. Bullinger, ca. 1887).

1884. In February 1886, when Horace Alling retired, the firm was restructured with William R. Alling and his son, John D., and Frank M. Welch of Brooklyn, becoming junior partners. The firm maintained an office at 170 Broadway in New York City. Horace Alling died on July 7, 1902.

John Alling was born on September 16, 1860. He started in the jewelry trade as an office clerk with Aiken, Lambert & Co. before joining Alling & Co. as a salesman. Beginning in June 1883, he made annual trips to London and Paris, where he purchased colored drawings, designs, and models of artistic jewelry suitable for die-stamping in the manufacture of jewelry. In March 1905, Alling & Co. announced its dissolution and reorganization as a stock company under the same name. William Alling was the president and Frank Welch was secretary and treasurer. John Alling was also on the board of directors.

Matthias Stratton, who joined the company in January 1898, had been with J.E. Caldwell & Co. in Philadelphia. When the company reorganized again a year later, he became the president and manager, succeeding Frank M. Welch, who resigned from the business. John D. Alling was vice president and F.H. Buhler, who had been with the company for five years, became secretary and treasurer. Mrs. Emma Downing Alling and W.A Seidler, the designer and foreman of the factory, were elected to the board of directors.

On September 14, 1915, Alling & Co. declared bankruptcy and was placed in the hands of a receiver. All debts were paid

in full, with monies remaining to pay stockholders. It must have been at this time or shortly thereafter that Larter & Sons purchased the drawings, dies, and goodwill of the company. The following year John Alling died (February 22, 1916).

Alling & Co. were manufacturers of fine gold jewelry, offering a range of selections, from tubular bracelets, ear drops, pendants, cuff buttons and cufflinks to small novelties such as knives and matchboxes. Alling made jewelry for such firms as Starr & Marcus; J.E. Caldwell & Co.; M.W. Galt Bros.; Bigelow & Kennard; Wood & Son; Aiken, Lambert & Co.; Mermod & Jaccard & Co.; C.D. Peacock; Theodore B. Starr; Samuel Kirk & Son; Bailey, Banks & Biddle; Clark & Biddle; and Tiffany & Co.

ALLING, CLEVELAND & CO.

In 1843, Joseph Alling entered into a partnership with his brother, Isaac A., to establish Isaac A. & J.C. Alling for the manufacture of jewelry at 347 Broad Street. Another brother, Horace, joined this company in 1850, when it was known as Alling Brother & Co. and had relocated to 6 Orchard Street. Joseph remained with the company for several years before embarking on his own business in 1858 at 202 Mulberry Street. In 1860, he formed a partnership with Thomas B. Cleveland under the name of Alling, Cleveland & Co., with a factory located at 73 Columbia Street and another at 212 Broadway in New York City. In 1868, Cleveland was listed in the Newark Directories as a jeweler at 85 Columbia Street. From 1888 to 1892, his occupation was still given as jeweler, but with no business address, suggesting that he worked in this capacity for another firm.

ALLING, HALL & DODD

Stephen B. Alling was the grandson of Isaac Alling, who had been a member of Wheeler's Grenadiers (organized on April 17, 1776), and had, along with other members of the Alling family, fought in the Revolutionary War. Stephen Alling's family originally lived in New Haven, where another descendant, Roger Alling, was the treasurer of the Connecticut Colonies.

Stephen Alling first began making jewelry in 1836 at 31 Walnut Street. In 1838, his brother, Isaac A., joined him, remaining until 1843, when he left to form a partnership with another brother, Joseph, in a concern known as Isaac A. & J.C. Alling. By this time, Stephen Alling had moved his shop to 35 Walnut Street. In 1846, he took in a partner, Edward A. Crane, and the name was changed to Alling & Crane. In 1850, John Hall joined the company and the name became Alling & Hall. The following year David C. Dodd, Jr., was admitted as a partner and the firm became known as Alling, Hall & Dodd. A year after Stephen Alling died in 1860, the name became Hall, Dodd & Co., with John and David Hall, David Dodd, and Daniel W. Baker as principals. This partnership lasted until 1867, when Dodd left to go into business with A.J. Hedges, and the Hall brothers formed John Hall & Co., a business located at 54–56 Hamilton Street.

In 1869, the company's name became J. Hall & Co. In 1871, Hall went into partnership with William D. Maxwell and the name was changed to Hall, Maxwell & Co. By 1874, the principals in the company were David A. and R. Finley Hall and William Maxwell; their factory was located at 359 Mulberry Street. The last listing for this company appears in the 1875 Newark Directory, with David Hall and William Maxwell in charge of the business.

Isaac A. Alling & Co./A. Alling Reeves/ Reeves & Browne

Isaac A. Alling was born in Newark on February 17, 1814. After learning the trade of silverplating, he entered the jewelry business, working for his brother, Stephen, at 35 Walnut Street. He remained for five years; in 1843, he went into partnership with another brother, Joseph C., to establish Isaac A. & J.C. Alling for the manufacture of jewelry at 347 Broad Street. In 1850, another brother, Horace, was admitted into the firm, which had relocated to 6 Orchard Street. With the addition of another brother, the company was renamed Alling Brother & Co. In 1858, Joseph left to open his own business. Another brother, William R. Alling, entered the business in 1859. In July 1881, when Isaac Alling retired, the firm's name became Alling & Co.

On August 15, 1881, Isaac Alling, along with James A. Holmes and Thomas B. Cleveland, organized a new company, known as Isaac A. Alling & Co., with a factory at 50 Walnut Street. The firm maintained a New York office in the Bryant Building at Nassau and Liberty Streets. Isaac A. Alling & Co. manufactured fine gold jewelry, specializing in wire bracelets, bangles, and American Lever Sleeve Buttons. In the early 1890s, the company made a variety of bracelets, including padlock, knife-edged, chain, diamond, link, flower, adjustable wire, and children's bracelets.

Upon the retirement of James Holmes and Thomas Cleveland from the firm, Alling's nephew, A. Alling Reeves, was taken in as a partner. He assumed control of the business when Isaac Alling retired in 1889, two years before his death on April 10, 1890. By 1890, the name had been changed to A. Alling Reeves, with an office at 21 Maiden Lane in New York City.

In 1892, Reeves entered into a partnership with W.S. Sillcocks under the name Reeves & Sillcocks at the 35 Walnut Street address, keeping the New York office at 21 Maiden Lane. By 1897, Sillcocks had left the firm, and the following year Reeves went into partnership with James A. Browne under the name Reeves & Browne. They remained in business until 1913.

In 1902, a member of the firm, Louis D. Frenot, patented an ornamental leonine head for brooches and other articles. Reeves & Browne advertised a complete array of this "oddity" in 14-carat gold brooches, buttons, scarf pins, lockets, charms, bracelets, hatpins, fobs, pin sets, and boa clasps.

Allsopp & Allsopp

The firm Allsopp & Allsopp was founded in 1901 by two brothers, Thomas and Edmund F., with a factory at 50 Columbia Street, which, four years later, relocated to 18–20 Columbia Street. By 1905, two other brothers, Albert and Frank, had joined the firm. Both Edmund and Frank had been stone setters before joining this business.

In 1906, Thomas patented an adjustable collar holder to be used to support collars of lace, velvet, or other soft material. At the 1916 Newark Industrial Exposition, the firm contributed a display of platinum and gold jewelry, along with its "Original" flexible bracelet. Among the articles on exhibition were platinum lavalieres set with diamonds, pearls, and other colored gemstones; gold and platinum link bracelets set with diamonds and other gemstones; specially designed brooches with intricate workmanship; bar pins of green gold; pendants; scarf pins; neck chains; knives; and baby pins. One brooch was made up of pearls forming a cluster of grapes; another a fruit basket; and a third, a flower basket.

In 1926, Thomas Allsopp was listed as president of the company with Edmund F. as secretary and treasurer. Allsopp & Allsopp went out of business in 1933.

Allsopp Bros.

Henry Allsopp was first listed in the Newark Directories as a jeweler in 1885. In 1889, he became associated with Schlosstein & Co. and, the following year, went into partnership with Frederick A. Schlosstein and Andrew O. Keifer, at 93–95 Green Street, for the manufacture of jewelry. Two years later, Allsopp left that firm, forming a partnership with his brother, George A., under the name of H. Allsopp & Co. at 60 McWhorter Street. In 1894, the name was changed to Allsopp Bros. In 1904, the firm erected a new building at 26 Camp Street which was specially equipped to manufacture jewelry.

By 1922, George Allsopp was president of Allsopp Bros. That year, he took over management of Allsopp-Bliss and, in 1929, moved the manufacturing operations of that company to the Camp Street facility. In 1937, the two firms merged, with Edward E. Allsopp, president; Arthur Steller, vice president and treasurer; and Clifford Allsopp, secretary. The following year, the name was changed to Allsopp-Steller and the factory moved to 81 Warren Street. The firm was acquired by Krementz & Co. in 1956.

Allsopp Bros. manufactured 10- and 14-carat gold and platinum rings.

Arch Crown Manufacturing Co.

The Arch Crown Manufacturing Co. succeeded Schrader-Wittstein, a Chicago-based company founded in 1904 by Alfred H. and Charles T. Wittstein and Edward Schrader of Chicago. Their first factory was located at 26 Camp Street, specializing in diamond mountings. Patented on November 3, 1903 and first introduced on January 1, 1906, the firm's arch crown mounting has prongs shaped like arches with a concave tip to secure the stone, thus allowing more light to the stone. Arch Crown proudly advertised that this was the first mounting ever offered in a fully completed state, ready for setting a stone in only five minutes.

In 1920, the company built a plant at 81 Warren Street, but maintained offices at 31 North State Street in Chicago and at 209 Post Street in San Francisco. Arch Crown went out of business between 1932 and 1934.

Baker & Co.

Daniel W. Baker was born in Derian, Georgia, in 1828, moving as a youth to Newark, where he worked as an apprentice in the jewelry trade. After successfully mastering all phases of the industry, in 1875 he established Baker & Co. with his son, Cyrus O., to manufacture gold jewelry. Within a few years, a refining department was added to the business which quickly became the mainstay of the firm. On August 3, 1891, Daniel Baker died, and the business continued under the management of his son. Within a short period of time, another son, Charles W., entered the company, located at that time at 408 Railroad Avenue.

The 1890s witnessed the rise in use of platinum, and Baker & Co. was the first firm in America to process this ore, imported from the Russian Ural Mountains. For many years, the company remained the only one involved in refining platinum commercially. Other departments were established to produce jeweler's settings, findings, ring blanks, as well as a variety of products outside the jewelry industry. By 1925, the firm was also known as the Baker Platinum Works, with a factory at 121 Liberty Street in Newark, and offices at 30 Church Street in New York City and 5 S. Wabash Avenue in Chicago. In 1928, the firm participated in an exhibition of platinum, held at The Newark Museum. By 1934, Baker & Co. was located at 54 Austin Street and, in 1942, at 113 Astor Street. In the Newark Directory for 1957, Charles W. Engelhard is listed as chairman of the board and Gordon V. Richdale as president.

BATTIN & CO.

In 1894, George and John Battin established Battin & Co. at 106 Ogden Street, specializing in gold and silver novelties. Battin also maintained an office in New York City at 3 Maiden Lane. In 1901, John Battin was listed in the Newark Directory as the sole proprietor. Battin & Co. remained at the Ogden Street address until the firm went out of business between 1928 and 1931.

Battin & Co. manufactured novelty items such as belts, calendars, razor strops, emery bags, key rings, comb cases, whisk brooms, thermometer cases, cigar cases, lorgnettes, cigar cutters, nail file cases, jeweled matchboxes, knives, silk winders and, at Easter time, a selection of Lenten goods. In 1896, it patented a matchbox and miniature case in which one side opened to reveal the miniature.

BIPPART, GRISCOM & OSBORN

Achille Bippart was born on December 21, 1857 in Eisenach, Germany. At the age of fourteen, he emigrated to Providence, Rhode Island, where he learned the jeweler's trade. In 1880, he moved to Newark to join his father. By 1882 he was listed in the directories as a jeweler at 41 Lillie Street. In 1885, he graduated from New Jersey College of Business and, that same year, established Bippart & Co. with Andreas Kienle at 34 Crawford Street. Two years later, Theophil Roos, who had also emigrated from Germany, joined the company and the business moved to 481 Washington Street. In 1890, Bippart & Co. relocated to the corner of Marshall and Halsey Streets; by 1891, the firm had eighty employees working in the factory. Bippart & Co. maintained an office at 19 Maiden Lane but, on May 1, 1894, this facility was closed and all business was conducted from the Newark factory.

Bippart & Co. offered creatively designed jewelry with excellent worksmanship. As early as 1891, it was advertising jewelry in 14-carat gold with enamel work as its specialty. The company sold gold jewelry, with or without diamonds, in such articles as brooches, lace pins, scarf pins, earrings, bracelets, chatelaines, hatpins, link buttons, cuff pins, necklaces, rings, mounted tortoiseshell combs, and belt buckles in gold and sterling silver. Several members of the firm applied for patents for new devices or techniques. In 1890, Andreas Kienle invented a mechanism to hide the catch on bangle bracelets. Achille Bippart patented many devices for collar buttons and link buttons and, in 1901, invented a process for recessed enamel work. In 1893, he and a fellow worker, John H. Theberath, patented a pearl fastener for retaining the whole pearl without clamps. In 1901, Theberath and Charles L. Uhry invented an automatic safety catch for pins and brooches that the firm illustrated in much of its advertising at the turn of the century.

After the death of Andreas Kienle on July 11, 1897, at the age of thirty-seven, Bippart took in another partner, Bennet Osborn, Jr. In 1901, Benjamin F. Griscom from Philadelphia, who had joined the company in 1893, became

a partner and the name was changed to Bippart, Griscom & Osborn. Griscom and Osborn represented the company as salesmen. In 1903, Alfred P. Hinton became associated with the company and, in 1909, was admitted as a partner, the same year that the firm moved to 6 Garden Street. In 1912, the firm employed 125 workers and its jewelry was sold throughout the country and in several Canadian cities as well as exported to many European cities.

In 1913, Lawrence H. Smith became a partner, but it is not known in what capacity he served. In 1917, the officers were listed as Achille Bippart, president; Benjamin Griscom, vice president; and Bennet Osborn, secretary and treasurer. By this time, the company had relocated to 2–4 Garden Street. In 1918, the factory employed seventy-five

234. Advertisement for Bippart, Griscom & Osborn in *Jewelry Fashions* 1917, p. 35.

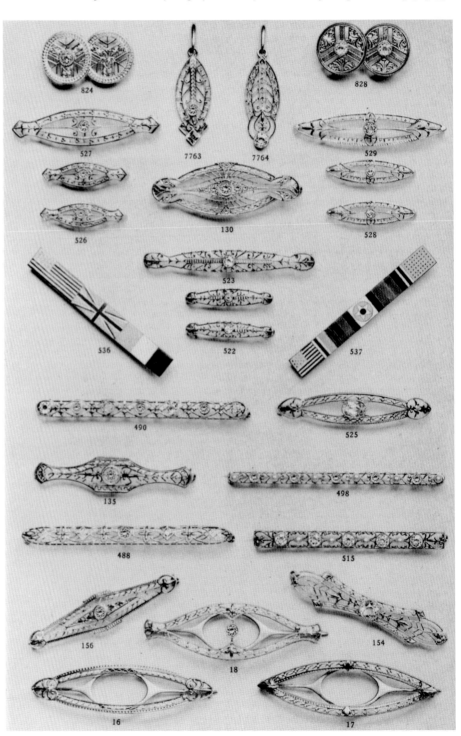

235. Advertisement for Block & Bergfels, ca. 1887, in *Alphabets, Monograms, Initials, Crests, Etc.* (New York: E.W. Bullinger, ca. 1887).

workers. In 1927, the firm's name became Bippart, Bennett & Co., and by the early 1930s, it went out of business. Krementz & Co. purchased the company's tools and dies.

BISHOP & BISHOP
John J. Bishop was first mentioned in the Newark Directories as a jeweler in 1890. In 1906, he and his brother, Henry W., worked for the manufacturing jewelers, Bergfels & Co., located at 336 Mulberry Street (this firm's name had been Block & Bergfels in the late 1890s). By 1910, Bishop & Bishop was listed in Newark Directories at the Mulberry Street address. The firm operated as a small jewelry manufacturing business, with only six employees in 1918. Bishop & Bishop produced fine gold and platinum jewelry and remained in business until at least 1965.

HENRY BLANK & CO./WHITESIDE & BLANK
Newton E. Whiteside worked for A.J. Hedges & Co. as a salesman for over twenty years. In February 1890, he formed a partnership with John W. Fahr (who had been previously employed with Riker & Sons and Carter, Sloan & Co.), under the name N.E. Whiteside & Co. at 54 Columbia Street. In 1895, this partnership was dissolved, with Whiteside continuing the business. By 1895, he had relocated to 93–95 Green Street and, in 1900, he moved to 17 Liberty Street while maintaining an office at 14–16 John Street. For the first fifteen years of business, the firm manufactured 14-carat gold brooches, scarf pins, sleeve buttons, studs, and bracelets, accented with enamel. In 1895, Whiteside also advertised silver goods, guaranteed 937-1000 fine.

In 1899, Henry M. Blank entered the business as a junior partner and the name was changed to Whiteside & Blank. Blank had not worked in the jewelry trade; before his association with Whiteside, he had been a district supervisor for the Prudential Insurance Co. in Newark. In February 1903, the firm incorporated with Newton E. and Elizabeth Whiteside and Henry and Phoebe Blank as shareholders. The firm quickly expanded, producing high quality

jewelry in platinum, as well as continuing to offer its gold line. Whiteside & Blank was one of the few firms that made jewelry with *plique à jour* enameling.

In 1911, the company was awarded the exclusive license to sell the expansion watch bracelet that had been invented in Germany. This venture became immediately successful and Whiteside & Blank devoted more and more of its operation to the watch business, becoming the first in the United States to make wrist watches for ladies, diamond watches, sautoir watches, ring watches, watches with diamond crystals, and watches with colored gemstones. The firm produced its own line of jewelry, which was sold to retailers throughout the country, while also making jewelry on special order for such retailers as Grant A. Peacock, Neiman Marcus, and Tiffany & Co. In the 1916 Newark Industrial Exposition, Whiteside & Blank contributed a display of diamond lavalieres, platinum bar pins set with diamonds and other gemstones, and wrist watches with either platinum or ribbon bands.

In 1917, Whiteside left the business and the name became Henry Blank & Co. By the following year, the officers were Henry Blank, president; D.B. Pickering, vice president; Edwin McElvery, secretary and treasurer. Throughout the 1920s and 1930s, Henry Blank was listed in the Newark Directories as an officer of Davis & Lowe. In 1938, Blank became president of the Cresarrow Watch Co. The Cresarrow movement fit into small ladies' watches that were adjusted to three positions. The movement also sold under the C.H. Meylan and International Watch Co. names.

By 1947, Henry Blank's son, Philip E., had joined the business and was listed as the treasurer on the board of directors, with Henry Blank continuing as president, Bert Lowe, vice president, and Andrew C. Becker, secretary. In 1965, Philip Blank was president, with Ralph E. Blank as vice president. The last Blank to run the business was Peter, who remained with the company until it closed its doors in 1986, continuing to occupy the factory at 17 Liberty Street

until the end. The firm's archives, including drawings, employee and business records, castings, molds and dies, were given to the New Jersey Historical Society, Newark.

THE BRASSLER CO.
Hans Brassler was born in Germany. He studied jewelry designing in Paris "under the greatest masters of the time and, for his original and artistic work, received a gold medal from the Paris Exposition," according to a 1905 article in *The Jewelers' Circular—Weekly*. When he first arrived in this country, he entered into a partnership with A. Heineke and C. Appeldorn in the firm of Heineke & Co. at 48 West 22nd Street in New York City, specializing in platinum mountings and fine gold jewelry. By 1909, he had left this company and established his own shop in Newark at 6 Garden Street under the name The Brassler Co. From 1910 through 1914, he was listed as vice president of this firm. In 1916, Brassler left the company and William H. Jones, Theodore M. Woodland, and Louis Jackes continued to run the business. On October 9, 1933, Jones & Woodland purchased the assets and liabilities of The Brassler Co.

Hans Brassler made highly original designs that were often portrayed in *The Jewelers' Circular—Weekly*. His drawing of a woman, wearing imaginative diamond-set jewelry,

was featured on the cover of that magazine's thirty-sixth anniversary issue on February 1, 1905.

THOMAS G. BROWN & SONS
Thomas G. Brown was born in New York in 1813. He began his career working with a gold and silver refiner on Maiden Lane in New York City. When he was in his twenties, he became a salesman for Platt & Brothers, journeying to the south and west before railroads were available, often traveling on steamboats and stagecoaches to sparsely settled areas. After learning the various aspects of jewelry manufactory, he and James A. Dwight, another employee of Platt & Brothers, opened a factory to manufacture jewelry and silverware at 10 Cortlandt Street in New York, operating under the name Brown & Dwight. Five years later, Stephen H. Palmer joined the firm and the name was changed to Brown, Palmer & Dwight. At this time, the premises were moved to the corner of Broadway and Maiden Lane.

In 1860, Thomas Brown withdrew from the firm and became a member of Baldwin & Co., successors to Taylor & Baldwin in Newark. At this time, Wickliffe Baldwin was in charge of the company. In 1865, due to ill health, Baldwin withdrew from the business, selling his interest to Brown. The factory was located at the corner of Halsey and Marshall

Streets. Brown operated the business by himself until 1878, when his two sons, Thomas B. and William A., were admitted as partners and the name became Thomas G. Brown & Sons, with a New York office first at 5 Bond Street and then at 860 Broadway.

Thomas G. Brown & Sons manufactured "ring" jewelry, including necklaces, lockets, bracelets and sleeve buttons. In 1877, the firm advertised itself as the sole manufacturer of a souvenir from Rome, the "Campanello Margherita" bell, made in brooches, shawl pins, veil pins, earrings, and charms. Brown & Sons made silverware and some sterling silver articles for the Gorham Manufacturing Co. When Brown retired in 1892, his sons continued to run the business. In 1896, William left the company to form a partnership with Frederick T. Ward to manufacture sterling silver novelty items at 127 West 32nd Street in New York City. Thomas Brown died on December 2, 1903.

M.B. BRYANT & CO.

In 1859, John H. Bentley and Monroe B. Bryant, who had worked with the E. Ira Richards & Co., formed a partnership, with a factory at 170 Broadway in Newark. When Bentley left the company in 1886, James A. Smith and Bryant's son, William Allen, joined the firm, and the name become M.B. Bryant & Co. The following year, the firm moved to New York City, first to 10 then, in 1900, to 7 Maiden Lane. The company incorporated in 1922. By 1932 the officers were Floyd R. Smith, president; John A. Potter, vice president; John H. McKinnery, second vice president; and Ralph Goble, secretary. Sometime after 1932, M.B. Bryant was acquired by Church & Co.

M.B. Bryant & Co. specialized in rings. In 1903, it advertised a selection of "fine struck Tiffany mountings" based on the prong setting.

CARRINGTON & CO.

In 1891, Alfred P. Mayhew and Charles L. Carrington formed a partnership to establish Mayhew & Carrington at 19 Green Street. They set up an office at 1 Maiden Lane in New York City. In February 1900, articles of incorporation for Carrington & Co. were filed with the county clerk of Essex County to acquire the business of Mayhew & Carrington. The incorporators were Charles L. Carrington, president, F.M. Eppley, vice president, and E. Torrey Carrington, secretary and treasurer. In 1901, when the firm's factory location was torn down to make room for the new City Hall, the premises were moved to 42 Walnut Street. Carrington & Co. continued to operate an office at 1 Maiden Lane in New York and specialized in sleeve buttons, cufflinks, dress sets, lockets, cigarette cases, matchboxes and vanity cases.

In 1926, E. Torrey Carrington was president of Carrington & Co. and another relative, Charles B. Carrington, who was listed as a jeweler in the city directory in 1901, was treasurer. Fleetwood Lanneau (also spelled Lannau), who had been listed in the directories as a jeweler, joined the company sometime during the 1930s. By 1937, he became president of the company, Charles B. Carrington having retired and moved to Tucson, Arizona. In 1941, Lanneau was still president, Harry A. Freeman, secretary, and Waring C. Carrington, treasurer. Six years later, only Waring is noted as a principal in the firm, which remained at the same location through 1950.

CARTER, GOUGH & CO.

The firm of Carter, Gough & Co. was one of the oldest manufacturing jewelers in Newark. One of the founders, Aaron Carter, was born in Newark on January 17, 1817. On March 6, 1832, at the age of fifteen, he entered into an apprenticeship with Taylor & Baldwin, remaining for seven years, during which time he mastered all phases of the jewelry trade. In 1839, he joined D. Colton, Jr., and after two years, on November 1, 1841, went into business with two other past workmen of Taylor & Baldwin, A. Pennington and Michael Doremus, under the name of Pennington, Carter & Doremus with a shop located at 369 Broad Street. Carter served as salesman for the firm, traveling to New York, Boston, and Philadelphia.

Two years later, Pennington left and Carter and Doremus continued to run the business together for another year; in 1844, Doremus left. After a brief period of seeking employment elsewhere, Carter decided to continue the business under his own name, Aaron Carter, Jr., until 1845 when he was joined by Anthony C. Beam. In 1847, the name was changed to Carter, Beam & Pierson.

By 1843, Carter had opened a manufacturing facility at 1 Green Street, remaining at this address until 1853, when he relocated to 2 Park Street and, in 1856, to the corner of Mulberry and Park. Other partnership and name changes include the following: 1848, Carter & Pierson; 1853, Carter, Pierson & Hale; 1856, Carter, Hale & Co.; 1867, Carter, Howkins & Dodd; 1875, Carter, Howkins & Sloan; 1881, Carter, Sloan & Co.; 1896, Carter, Hastings & Howe; 1902, Carter, Howe & Co.; on January 1, 1915, the name was finally changed to Carter, Gough & Co.

In the 1850s, the Carter firm was the first jewelry manufacturer to use a steam engine. Aaron Carter reputedly purchased an engine that Seth Boyden had made for the 1853 New York Crystal Palace Exposition. By 1878, a reviewer noted that Carter's firm was among the largest factories in the world, producing $2 million worth of jewelry annually.

Aaron Carter was involved in various aspects of the jewelry trade, serving as president or board member of many organizations devoted to the advancement of the jewelry trade. He remained an active member of the firm until his death on January 31, 1902; his obituary lauded him as an "honored member" of the manufacturing jewelry trade of the United States.

One of the principal partners of the company, Augustus K. Sloan, was born in Cleveland, Ohio, in 1838. His family moved to Syracuse, New York. At the age of sixteen, Sloan relocated to New York City, where he found employment as a salesman with Carter, Pierson & Hale, entering the business on July 25, 1854. He was admitted into partnership in 1867, remaining with the company until 1895. George R. Howe entered the business on March 4, 1866, while C.E. Hastings, who had worked for the jeweler George A. Mudge in Boston, followed him in February 1867. The son of the founder, William Tuttle Carter, joined the business after his graduation from Princeton.

Howe, Hastings, and the younger Carter were admitted into partnership on January 1, 1876. Four years later to the day, William Carter left the business, entering into partnership with Henry Henze as Henze & Carter, this partnership lasting until 1885, when he was readmitted to his father's company. He served the company as a traveling salesman. Howe, who also had been a traveling salesman for the firm, assumed the role of plant manager of the Newark factory on January 1, 1880.

William T. Gough was born in England on January 25, 1854, emigrating to this country at the age of seventeen. The following year, he began his career in the jewelry industry and, in 1872, launched his long association with Carter, Howkins & Dodd as a bookkeeper. In January 1880, he assumed the role of saleman as a successor to George R. Howe and, a year later, took over Hastings' western territory. On January 1, 1885, he took an interest in the company, eventually becoming a partner in 1892. In 1902, he took over as active head of the business.

Other employees who were given an interest in the company in 1892 included F.R. Horton, who represented the house in the western territory; F.S. Wood, whose responsibilities included Philadelphia and Boston; James S. Franklin, the New York City representative; and Ferdinand Meerbot, who had worked in the factory for twenty-five years. It was recorded that Edward A. Thiery was a designer for the company.

Carter, Gough & Co. promoted itself as a manufacturer of gold jewelry, offering a "comprehensive, complete and varied assortment of articles"; in 1902, the firm took a double-page spread in *The Jewelers' Circular—Weekly,* advertising all the products it sold, mostly in 14-carat gold, with a few selections in 10-carat gold, silver, and platinum. At the 1916 Newark Industrial Exposition, the firm displayed a range of white and green 14-carat gold and platinum jewelry set with diamonds and gemstones as well as lorgnettes, jeweled vanity cases and mesh bags, gold cigar cutters and knives, and gold watch chains.

Business locations included an office at 11 Maiden Lane in New York City in 1852 which, by 1854, had relocated to 2 Maiden Lane; in the 1870s at 9 Bond Street; in 1879, at the corner of Broadway and 4th Street; by 1883, to 15 Maiden Lane; and by 1900, to 9–11–13 Maiden Lane, remaining at this location until August 1, 1925, when the New York salesroom was closed and the operation moved to the Newark factory. In 1915, the factory was located at 46 Mulberry Street.

After the death of William T. Carter on February 6, 1923, Carter, Gough & Co. was run by William T. Gough, until his death on January 25, 1925. Other members included J. Nelson Carter, Herbert T. Farrow, and R.F. Gough. By 1930, only Carter and Farrow were listed in the directories as principals in the company. Their last listing appeared in the 1932 Newark Directory. Shortly afterwards, Carter, Gough & Co. closed its doors and the tools, dies, and goodwill of the company were purchased by Krementz & Co.

CHAMPENOIS & CO.
On April 23, 1844 at the age of seventeen, Isaac Champenois became an apprentice to Isaac Alling of the firm of Isaac A. and J.C. Alling. After finishing his apprenticeship, he continued to work for Alling, rising to the position of foreman. In 1865, he entered into partnership with Charles McIntire, formerly with Dodd & Hedges, the firm named McIntire & Champenois. The following year, Horace Bedell became affiliated with the firm and the name was changed to McIntire, Champenois & Bedell, located at 40 Mechanic Street. That same year, Champenois' son entered the business as an office boy. In 1876, Champenois left this company, forming a new concern with his son, Charles, under the name of Champenois & Co., with a factory on Court Street and an office in New York City, first at 11 Maiden Lane, and in 1877 at 1½ Maiden Lane, and 1884, at 5 Maiden Lane. Champenois & Co. advertised a full line of gold jewelry, including engraved and enameled goods, imi-

tation diamond and pearl jewelry, sleeve and collar buttons, ear knobs, jet cluster and onyx goods, and the "Best Lever" sleeve buttons. In 1889, the manufacturing facility was moved to 50 Walnut Street.

In 1894, Charles Champenois patented several mechanisms for cuff buttons or studs; in 1898, he patented the "Best Lever Collar Button," in which the post and back were made in one piece while the head turned in two directions. In 1899, Isaac Champenois retired from the business; after his death on April 22, 1902, the company continued under the direction of Charles, who was joined by his two sons, Harry W. and Charles Edgar. Sometime around 1940, the name was changed to C.E. Champenois. The last listing found was 1950.

CHURCH & CO., INC.
Charles H. Church and Otto Goetzke worked for M.B. Bryant & Co., a ring manufacturer in New York City; Church as a traveling salesman and Goetzke as the factory superintendent. In 1922, they formed a partnership, establishing Church & Co. on the second floor of the building at 336 Mulberry Street. At this location, they maintained two desks and bench space for six jewelers and were permitted access to the landlord's machinery when it was not in use. The company grew, eventually occupying the entire building. By 1950, Church & Co. had moved to 2 Garden Street and, in 1967, relocated to 400 Kennedy Drive North in Bloomfield, New Jersey. Sometime after 1935, the firm purchased the assets and goodwill of M.B. Bryant & Co.

In 1963, both Goetzke and Church died and Stanley Church, son of one of the founders, who had started working for the company in 1927, took over ownership of the firm. His nephew, John R. Hopkinson, began his tenure with the company in 1966, eventually acquiring the business in 1982. Today, his son, David, runs Church & Co. which, in 1992, relocated to 2121 Whitesville Road in Toms River, New Jersey. The officers of the company are David and Douglas Hopkinson, president and vice president, respectively.

Church & Co. specializes in signet rings, but also produces other rings, pendants, bracelets, brooches, and earrings in 14- and 18-carat gold.

W.F. CORY & BROTHER
William F. Cory and Alva W. Osmun founded Cory & Osmun in 1889, with a factory at 27 Marshall Street. In 1898, Cory's brother, John C., entered the business and the name became W.F. Cory & Brother. By 1909, William was no longer listed as a partner; John was president and treasurer of the company. In 1910, Cory entered into partnership with Louis F. Clark and Walter S. Noon, the name of the firm changing to Cory, Clark & Noon and, by 1915, to Clark & Noon. In 1918, the company employed eleven workers. By the 1930s, the premises had been relocated to 50 Walnut Street. In 1936, the firm was out of business.

William F. Cory manufactured fine gold jewelry, set with colored gemstones.

CRANE & THEURER
David N. Crane and E.F.C. Theurer worked with A.J. Valentine in the firm of A.J. Valentine & Co. On May 1, 1895, this association was dissolved, with Crane and Theurer assuming the liabilities of the firm and continuing to manufacture jewelry under the name of Crane & Theurer, located at 13–15 Franklin Street and, by 1915, at the corner of Orchard and Scott Streets. On February 14,

1910, the partners, along with Louise E. Theurer, filed a certificate of incorporation in the office of the Secretary of State to produce jewelry, canes, umbrellas and novelties. By 1918, the firm had relocated to 68 Orchard Street, employing fifteen workers. Crane & Theurer went out of business between 1939 and 1942.

DAY, CLARK & CO.

John Crane Day was born in 1843 in New Providence, New Jersey. As a young man, he worked for Thomas Davis, who maintained a dry goods store in Newark, eventually becoming a partner in his firm. In 1874, he left the dry goods business and established Obrig, Day & Co., with John Obrig, Winton C. Garrison, and James Cox, to manufacture

237. Advertisement for Day, Clark & Co. in *Jewelry Fashions* 1917, p. 41.

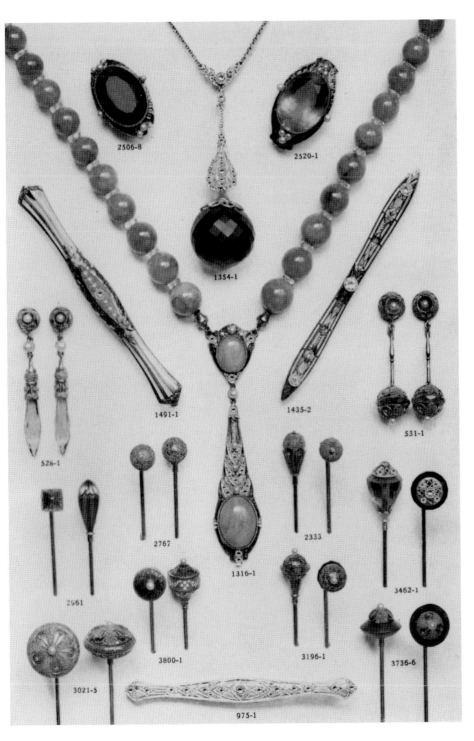

jewelry. When this company was dissolved, John Obrig entered the firm of A.J. Hedges & Co.

Samuel Clark was born in Summit, New Jersey, in 1846. Two years later, the family moved to Newark. As a young man, he served an apprenticeship in the jewelry industry, after which he entered the employ of Alling Brother & Co., remaining there until 1876. In 1877, when he entered into a partnership with John Day at Obrig, Day & Co., the name was changed to Day & Clark. The factory was located on Marshall Street, and offices were also maintained in New York City, first at 10 Maiden Lane and then at 23 Maiden Lane. As early as 1890, the firm had a San Francisco office at 116–120 Sutter Street. On February 1, 1895, Day's brother, Franklin, Wallace S. Campbell, Walter R. Shute, and William A. Cobb were admitted as partners and the name became Day, Clark & Co. Upon the death of John Day on October 31, 1900, additional partners in the company included his son, Irving C. Day, and Addison Rauband. In 1913, Day, Clark moved its factory to 449 Washington Street. The firm closed its doors in 1941.

Day, Clark & Co. specialized in 14-carat gold jewelry novelties, including sleeve links, ear studs, waist pins, sash brooches, curb and link bracelets, bead necklaces, hairpins, and back and side combs. In 1890, the firm advertised a line of bead necklaces in either plain or Roman gold finish or with a vermiculated finish. In 1914, Day, Clark advertised its Juliet Gift Set, which included a boxed set of two hatpins and two veil (hair) pins. In 1915, the company was making rondelle jewelry with amethyst, crystal, or topaz rondelles (faceted beads).

DAVID C. DODD CO.

David C. Dodd, Jr., was born in Bloomfield, New Jersey, on November 7, 1825. In 1841, at the age of sixteen, he began an apprenticeship with Stephen and Isaac Alling at 35 Walnut Street. In 1843, Isaac left this concern to form a business with another brother, Joseph. Stephen continued with the original business and, in 1846, formed a partnership with Edward A. Crane under the name Alling & Crane. In 1850, John Hall joined the company and the name was changed to Alling & Hall. The following year, David Dodd was admitted into partnership and the name became Alling, Hall & Dodd. In 1860, Stephen B. Alling died and David and John Hall, David Dodd, and Daniel W. Baker established Hall, Dodd & Co. By 1865, Baker had left the company. The business lasted until 1867, when Dodd went into business with Andrew J. Hedges under the name Dodd & Hedges at 58 Mechanic Street. In 1877, the partners separated, with Hedges forming his own company and Dodd continuing the business under his own name, David C. Dodd Co. The factory was located on Marshall Street.

In 1888, Dodd's son, Parker, entered the business, rising to assume control of the firm until his untimely death at the age of thirty-six on August 5, 1903. After Dodd's death on December 29, 1906, the business continued to manufacture jewelry. In 1947, W. Irving Royce was recorded as president and treasurer and Mrs. Emmie Royce, secretary. By this date, the factory was located at 51 Lawrence Street. The company went out of business in the early 1950s. David C. Dodd Co. produced a variety of diamond and gem-set brooches and bar pins.

E.A. DREHER & SON

As early as 1885, Ernest A. Dreher was listed in the Newark Directory as a diamond setter. On February 15, 1895, he went into partnership with Joseph R. King, of the firm of King & Co., under the name of King & Dreher, with a factory located at 355 Mulberry Street; by 1905, the firm had moved to 42 Walnut Street. In 1907, Dreher's son, Ernest, Jr., entered the company as a salesman. In 1911, King left the firm and, the following year, the name was changed to E.A. Dreher & Son. It was a small company that employed ten workers in 1918 and went out of business in 1932.

E.A. Dreher & Son produced fine gold jewelry, set with precious and colored gemstones. Among its pieces were festoon necklaces, set with colored gemstones and pearls; strung bead necklaces in coral, garnets, and amethysts with pearls or crystals; and brooches and pendants with colored stones, accented with diamonds. The firm made moonstone cameos and platinum bar pins, set with diamonds. In 1920, Dreher was making jewelry for Gorham, including link buttons, diamond brooches, and gold cigarette cases, set with sapphires and diamonds.

DURAND & CO.

The Durand family of jewelers dates its origins in the industry to 1756, when Samuel Durand was working as a watchmaker and jeweler in Jefferson Village, now Maplewood, New Jersey. After his death in 1787, he was succeeded by his son, John, a soldier in the Revolutionary War, who had moved the shop to 9 Washington Street in Newark and, subsequently, by his grandson, Henry, who added the manufacture of silverware to the business.

James Madison Durand, son of Henry Durand, was born in 1814. He learned his trade with Taylor & Baldwin before opening a shop in 1838, under his own name, for the manufacture of jewelry. Two years later, he joined with Isaac Baldwin, his former employer, to establish Baldwin & Durand, a company which lasted until 1850. A few years later, Major James Carter entered into partnership with James Durand and the name of the company became Durand, Carter & Co.; this arrangement lasted until 1869, when Durand took sole control of the business under the name Durand & Co.

James Durand was one of a small group of gifted artisans who laid the foundation for Newark's jewelry industry. He is known for his innovative approach to jewelry design, preferring to offer only "the exceptional in jewelry." He frequently traveled to Europe to buy diamonds and to study the current jewelry fashions. In 1868, he was the first to introduce strung pearl necklaces to this country. His uncle, Asher B. Durand, was the celebrated American artist and one of the founders of the Hudson River School.

James Durand's son, Wickliffe Baldwin Durand, entered the business at a young age, eventually assuming the position of salesman. He was said to have been the first man in the jewelry industry to personally visit his customers. In 1880, he assumed the direction of the company, two years before his father retired. Another son, Wallace, entered the company in 1869 and, upon the firm's incorporation in 1892, assumed control of the business. A third son, Henry, joined the firm in 1882, taking over the financial end of the business. His son, Henry, Jr., entered the corporation in 1916 as a salesman. The company was located at that time at 49–51 Franklin Street.

Joseph G. Ward worked for Durand & Co. for fifty years, beginning at the age of fourteen as an apprentice and eventually rising to a partnership position. He introduced many machines for the manufacture of jewelry and, in 1897, patented a process for stamping signet rings from gold using hydraulic pressure. He remained with the company until his death in 1902.

Sometime in the late 1870s or early 1880s, Charles L. Tiffany, of Tiffany & Co., entered into a partnership with Durand & Co., an arrangement that lasted until 1886, when Tiffany withdrew from the partnership.

Durand & Co. participated in the Newark Industrial Exhibition of 1872, contributing a display of fine, mounted and unmounted diamonds and other jewelry, valued at $120,000. Not only was the company a manufacturing jeweler, but it also imported precious gemstones. Durand, like many other

238. Advertisement for Durand & Co. in *Jewelry Fashions* 1917, p. 43.

239. Business card of W.C.
Edge, ca. 1886, collection
of Nancy N. Kattermann.

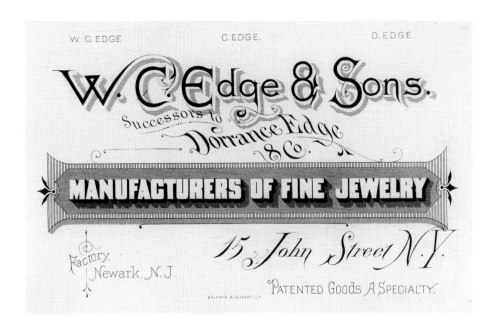

W. C. EDGE   C. EDGE.   D. EDGE.

W. C. Edge & Sons.

Successors to Dorrance Edge & Co.

MANUFACTURERS OF FINE JEWELRY

Factory, Newark, N.J.   15 John Street N.Y.

PATENTED GOODS A SPECIALTY.

Newark firms, made jewelry for other concerns, often one-of-a-kind items. One example is a gold peacock brooch with Cyprian glass fragments, sapphires, and peridots, made for the designer F. Walter Lawrence, which was exhibited in the 1904 Louisiana Purchase Exposition in St. Louis. In 1916, Durand & Co. was one of only nine jewelers who contributed a display at the Newark Industrial Exposition. The display included gold brooches set with large Australian black opals; mesh bags of gold or a combination of gold and platinum, mounted with diamonds and other gemstones; and platinum lorgnettes with diamonds and other gemstones.

Durand & Co. relocated to 72–74 East Kinney Street in 1932, remaining in business until 1936.

ECKFELDT & ACKLEY

Edward H. Eckfeldt was born in Philadelphia on August 5, 1859. On October 1, 1882, at the age of twenty-two, he entered the employ of Carrow, Bishop & Co. as its western representative. Upon the closing of this business in 1885, he went to work in the same capacity for Unger Bros. and then for Kerr & Battin.

In 1896, Eckfeldt opened a business with E.H. Ackley under the name Eckfeldt & Ackley at 49 Chestnut Street. In 1898, another partner, E.H. Rhodes, was taken into the firm, remaining with them for only three years. In 1903, the factory was moved to 51 Lawrence Street. By 1909, it had moved to 102 Murray Street and, by 1934, to 47 Chestnut Street. The firm remained open until 1937, when its assets were acquired by Krementz & Co.

W.C. EDGE JEWELRY MANUFACTURING CO.

William C. Edge was born in England in 1828. His father was a jeweler and it was from him that he learned the fundamentals of the trade before working for several London concerns. While employed with these jewelers, Edge began a career as an inventor, patenting such inventions as the method of using the pedal for propulsion of a bicycle as well as a technique for making foxtail (woven wire) chains by machinery, reducing the cost from $1 per foot to 40¢ per foot. In 1889, he patented another process that lowered the cost to 2¢ per foot.

In 1865, Edge emigrated to the United States and he began working for Chatellier & Spence in Boston, where he perfected a satin finish for gold. Shortly afterwards, he moved to Newark and entered the house of Durand & Co., remaining for several years before opening his own business. This endeavor soon failed, due to a partner's misappropriation of funds, forcing Edge to return to employment with Miller Bros., a manufacturer of buttons. While there, he invented a method for turning the edge of rings, pins, etc., a technique that became quickly accepted in the industry.

A few months later, Edge joined Smillie, Dorrance & Co., located on Maple Street. In 1871, he became a partner in the firm and the name became Smillie, Dorrance & Edge. In 1878, the firm was known as Dorrance, Edge & Co., with a factory at 46 Green Street and an office at 9 John Street in New York City. In the 1884, the name was changed to William C. Edge & Sons and, by 1886, the office had moved to 15 John Street.

In September 1889, the company incorporated as William C. Edge Co., with Edge's son, Charles, president; another son, Frank, vice president; and William C. Edge, secretary and treasurer. The firm specialized in products invented by the founder, including the Edge excelsior reinholder, the aluminum horseshoe and, in jewelry, the scarf ring. William Edge is credited with patenting between forty and fifty inventions, among them techniques and machines for weaving metal fabrics.

Upon Edge's death on October 6, 1900, his sons, Charles and William C., Jr., continued the business. When Charles, who had entered the firm in 1877, died on January 2, 1902, the company continued under his brother and the other stockholders. In 1910, the name was changed to the W.C. Edge Jewelry Co. and moved to 480 Washington Street, remaining there through 1965. The company then moved its business to 918 North 20th Avenue, Hollywood, Florida.

In 1912, another company, the Edge Chain Co., was listed in the Newark Directory at 93 Lafayette Street. In 1913, it had moved to 393 Mulberry Street. The last listing found for this company appeared in the 1920 Newark Directory.

F. & F. FELGER, INC.

After serving a six-year apprenticeship with Krementz & Co., Frederick F. Felger, with $200 borrowed from his father, Frederick D., opened the manufacturing firm of F. & F. Felger on January 15, 1880. The son handled the operational side of the business while his father served as the office manager and bookkeeper. Frederick H. Felger, grandson of the founder, joined the company in 1900. He served as a traveling salesman for the firm, journeying throughout the Midwest. He was assisted by Fred C.D. Bonner, who joined the company in 1905, eventually rising to become vice president. Felger became president and managed the firm until his death in 1958, when it was taken over by his son-in-law, Martin Stone, who had entered the company in 1936. By 1980, Stone's son-in-law, Brad Garman, assumed the title of vice president, serving as manager of production and design.

The firm maintained a factory at 42 Marshall Street, relocating by 1943 to 480 Washington Street, and in the 1960s to 193 Mountain Avenue in Springfield. In the spring of 1986, Jabel Ring purchased the assets of F. & F. Felger, which today constitutes Jabel's Jacor Products Group.

F. & F. Felger made earrings, rings, necklaces and bracelets with the following gemstones: star sapphires, rubies, cat's eye, emeralds, white and black opals, aquamarines, peridots, precious topaz, antique cameos, cultured pearls, amethyst, garnet and topaz quartz. At the outset, the firm made bracelets, pendants, and birthstone rings. Ladies rose-cut diamond cluster rings with ruby doublet centers were soon added to the line, selling to the trade for $5 to $7.50. By 1910, this line had changed to mountings and mounted diamond rings and, within a few years, colored stones were featured in Felger's jewelry. By 1929, this line represented a good percentage of the firm's business. Due to the restrictions of gold and platinum during World War II, mountings became smaller, forcing the firm to reconsider its stock and change to a colored stone jewelry house.

F. & F. Felger won two jewelry awards: a first prize in the Diamonds International Competition for a diamond brooch, and an award in the Diamonds Today Competition for an unusual men's ring using baguette diamonds and ebony. Felger also made an amethyst and diamond ring for the American Gem Society American Gemstones Jewelry Collection that was designed by Aldo Cipullo.

ROBERT S. FISHER & CO., INC.
In 1908, Joseph G. Fisher became a partner with William H. Ziething and Charles G. Klein in Ziething & Co., the factory initially located at 85 Columbia Street and moving to 68 Orchard Street in 1910. In 1914, Fisher left this concern, establishing his own business at 14 Oliver Street under the name Fisher & Co. In 1942, the firm moved to 19 Liberty Street and remain there today.

In 1945, Walter Edmondson started working for the company as a jeweler. When the brother of the founder, Albert Fisher, left the firm, he assumed the job of foreman of the factory, eventually becoming a vice president. A year after Edmondson entered the company, Fisher's son, Robert S., began his long tenure. He took control of the business after his father retired. Sometime after 1965, the name was changed to Robert S. Fisher. In 1977, the company was sold to American Gemsmith and Jaffe & Co. of New York, with Donald Roth joining the firm. He and his son, David Roth, continue to manage the business as president and vice president, respectively. They have always employed a small staff, fifteen in 1918 and nineteen in 1996.

Robert S. Fisher & Co. makes fine quality jewelry in 14- and 18-carat gold, set with precious gemstones and cultured pearls. The firm has been producing beautifully crafted jewelry since the Art Nouveau period. In the 1940s and 1950s, Fisher made jewelry in the then current floral style, featuring fine wire work. The firm produces all types of jewelry with the exception of rings.

L. FRITZSCHE & CO.
L. Fritzsche & Co. was founded in 1905 by Lebrecht Fritzsche and Fred, Frank, and Richard Thaler. At the outset, the firm specialized in engraving but, in 1909, turned to jewelry manufacturing. Fritzsche's first location was at 73 Hamilton Street; in April 1910, the firm moved to the fourth floor of the Herpers building at 480 Washington Street. In 1918, Fritzsche & Co. employed twenty-four workers.

By 1920, Richard Thaler was president; Fred Thaler, vice president; Frank Thaler, secretary; and Lebrecht Fritzsche, treasurer. In 1957, Frank Thaler was president. The company continued to operate from the Washington Street address, remaining open until at least 1964.

L. Fritzsche & Co. manufactured 10- and 14-carat gold and platinum jewelry, specializing in flexible bracelets.

J.A. & S.W. GRANBERY
The firm of J.A. & S.W. Granbery was founded in 1895 as Cutler & Granbery, in Attleboro, Massachusetts. In 1900, John. A. Granbery and his brother, S.W., bought out the Cutler interest, continuing the operation of the house on Jay Street until April of that year, when they moved the entire plant and business to 26 Beecher Street in Newark. In February 1902, the brothers formed a limited partnership. Five years later, in 1907, the factory relocated to 31–33 East Kinney Street. The firm maintained offices at 13 Maiden Lane in New York City and at 342 South Broadway in Los Angeles, remaining in business until 1931.

Granbery specialized in 10-carat gold jewelry, including brooches, scarf pins, bracelets, hatpins, fobs, bib pins, belt pins, veil pins, tie clasps, pendants, neck chains, bead necklaces, and lockets.

A.J. HEDGES & CO.
Andrew J. Hedges, born on July 1, 1828 in Florham Park, New Jersey, learned the jewelry trade with Aaron Carter. Subsequently, he worked with Field & Keep, becoming a partner in this company in 1859, the name changing to Field & Co. In 1867, he left this firm to join David C. Dodd in a new company under the name Dodd & Hedges, at 58 Mechanic Street. In 1877, the partners formed separate companies, with Hedges establishing A.J. Hedges & Co. Working with him were his brother, Wallace M., and John Obrig, a designer and inventor of jewelry manufacturing techniques who joined the company in 1881.

Obrig was a member of the firm until his death in 1900, two years before Andrew Hedges died on November 10, 1902. The business was carried on by Hedges' son, Andrew Jr., along with William M. Kaas, an employee of the company. By 1916, Kaas had left the company and Christina, mother of Andrew, Jr., became a partner. This arrangement remained unchanged until 1926, when Philip H. and Robert C. Hedges were listed as partners. By 1951, the company had moved to 2 Garden Street, with Philip and Andrew Hedges, Jr., as officers. In 1965, only Philip was recorded as an officer.

In 1877, Hedges' manufacturing plant moved to 90 Mechanic Street and, by 1912, had relocated to 178–182 Emmet Street. By 1916, the firm was listed at 72–74 East Kinney Street and, by 1950, at 2 Garden Street. Hedges maintained an office in New York City, initially located at 6 Maiden Lane and, in 1900, at 14 John Street.

A.J. Hedges & Co. offered a line of 14-carat gold jewelry, advertising such novelties as fancy enameled jewelry set with diamonds, pearls, and other stones; "odd jewelry" featuring insects, lizards, butterflies, and turtles; black and white enameled goods; and mourning jewelry.

HERPERS BROTHERS

Ferdinand Joseph Herpers was born in Linz, Austria, on February 21, 1819. At the age of fourteen, he began a four-year apprenticeship with a jeweler in Bonn, after which he entered the Prussian army, serving for three years. At the end of his tour of duty, he returned to the jewelry trade in Bonn, then Cologne, before taking a position as a jeweler in Pforzheim, where he remained for four years. While working there, he learned the art of die-sinking. In 1845, he emigrated to New York, working for a year as a die-sinker for George Downing. The following year, he moved to Newark and joined Baldwin & Co. Ten years later, he entered into a brief partnership with a gentleman by the name of Cavalin before opening his own shop. This move proved unsuccessful, so he returned to the bench, working for Durand, Carter & Co.

In 1857, Herpers patented a scale for detecting counterfeit silver and gold coins, an invention which was soon outdated when, during the Civil War, coins were replaced with paper money. In August 1865, he entered into his own business for the manufacture of machine-made jewelry set-

tings, the first of its kind in the nation. Prior to this, settings were either imported from France or handmade in local shops. Herpers' first shop was located to the rear of his home at 476 Washington Street. After purchasing an adjoining property in 1867, he erected a small brick building. On January 1, 1869, Herpers' thirteen-year-old son, Henry, joined his father; another son, Ferdinand Jr., entered the business in June of that same year. By 1871, Herpers had purchased additional land to expand his factory to 18 Crawford Street.

On September 3, 1872, Ferdinand Herpers patented an improved diamond setting, forecasting the type of mounting which would eventually be called the "Tiffany setting." Up until that time, diamonds had been mounted into collet or bezel settings. The new pronged setting elevated the stone away from the mounting, allowing light to penetrate, thus accentuating the brilliance of the stone. Another important invention, the safety catch, was patented by a member of the firm, August Knaus, on December 3, 1901.

In 1877, Ferdinand Herpers retired from business; he was succeeded by his two sons, who operated the company under the name of Herpers Brothers. They maintained an office in New York City at 41–43 Maiden Lane. In 1917, Henry died and the business was run by Ferdinand Jr.'s sons, Ferdinand and Henry. By the 1920s, many jewelers were making their own settings; in 1936, with business slow, the firm ceased production.

Herpers Brothers produced findings for such jewelry firms as George O. Street & Son, J.E. Caldwell, Jacques & Marcus, Kirk & Sons, and Tiffany & Co. and contributed a display of jewelry mountings and other findings at the 1901 Pan American Exposition in Buffalo.

E. Hinsdale & Co.

Epaphras Hinsdale was born in 1769 in Hartford, Connecticut, and it is believed that he opened his first shop in that city sometime between 1790 and 1795. A few years later, he and five other goldsmiths moved to Newark, where in 1801 he reportedly established the first factory for the exclusive manufacture of jewelry. He specialized in rings, watch charms, seals, and brooches and, according to Martha Gandy Fales in *Jewelry in America*, supplied jewelers "...not only in Newark, but in Norwich and Hartford, Connecticut; New York City and state; Philadelphia; Alexandria, Virginia; and Augusta, Georgia." He expanded his stock to include bracelets, necklaces, chains, and earrings. By the time of his death in 1810, Fales explains, "the company's assets in gold and tools were worth over $6,000, there were accounts due of almost $16,000. Among his customers were Marquand & Harriman and J. & A. Simmons of New York; Chaudron & Co. and John J. Parry in Philadelphia; and Charles A. Burnet in Alexandria." In 1804, John Taylor, Jr., a journeyman who worked for Hinsdale, became a partner, the firm known as E. Hinsdale & Co., with a New York office under the name of Taylor & Hinsdale. In 1810, Hinsale died and the company was continued under the direction of his son, Horace, and Taylor. In 1818, Horace retired from the business and went to New York, where he opened a retail establishment. The business continued to be run by Taylor, who took Isaac Baldwin as a partner and the name became Taylor & Baldwin.

Jabel Inc.

Jack J. Abelson worked as a stone setter with Jones & Woodland before opening his own business in 1916, known as Jabel Ring Manufacturing Co., at 23 Marshall Street. He developed a technique for setting stones, called the "illusion" setting, which appeared to magnify the size of the stone as well as its brilliance. In April 1923, the factory relocated to 401–07 Mulberry Street. Jabel maintained a West Coast branch at 133 Geary Street in San Francisco.

Jack Abelson remained as president of the company until his death on December 26, 1976. His daughter, June Herman, worked for Jabel for many years before assuming a full time position in 1965 as the advertising director. Today, she is vice president of the company and her two sons, Alan H., Jr., and Daniel D., are president and secretary-treasurer, respectively. In the spring of 1986, Jabel purchased the assets of F. & F. Felger, Inc., to form its Jacor Products Group, specializing in colored gemstone jewelry.

Jabel Inc. maintains a full jewelry shop in its factory, where all phases of production are carried out, from rolling the gold, to die-stamping, stone setting, polishing, and finishing. In 1954, the firm moved to 365 Coit Street in Irvington, New Jersey. Jabel produced a full line of jewelry, including rings, bracelets, necklaces, and brooches.

Jones & Woodland

On January 1, 1895, William H. Jones and Theodore M. Woodland founded Jones & Woodland, with an office and factory at 49 Chestnut Street, located in the Krementz building. Both partners had originally worked for Larter, Elcox & Co. Their first advertisement in *The Jewelers' Circular and Horological Review,* on January 2, 1895, listed their line as "children's, ladies' and gentlemen's plain and fancy rings. A large assortment of improved spring back studs in new designs: link buttons, stone seals, etc." By 1904, the

company had relocated to 365 Market Street and, by 1915, to 2 Garden Street.

On January 9, 1906, Jones & Woodland incorporated, with Jones, Woodland, Louis A. Jackes, and E. Cooper Stone as members of the board of directors. Sometime after 1904, the firm decided to specialize solely in the manufacture of rings. At the 1916 Newark Industrial Exposition, the firm contributed a display of rings for men and women in 14- and 18-carat gold and platinum, set with precious and colored gemstones. By this date, the company was well-established and, according to *The Industrial Directory of New Jersey*, its staff numbered 110 workers.

On October 9, 1933, Jones & Woodland purchased the assets and liabilities of Tierney & Co., Weigle & Rose Co., and The Brassler Co. In 1938, the firm was acquired by Kre-

241. Advertisement for Jones & Woodland in *Jewelry Fashions* 1917, p. 47.

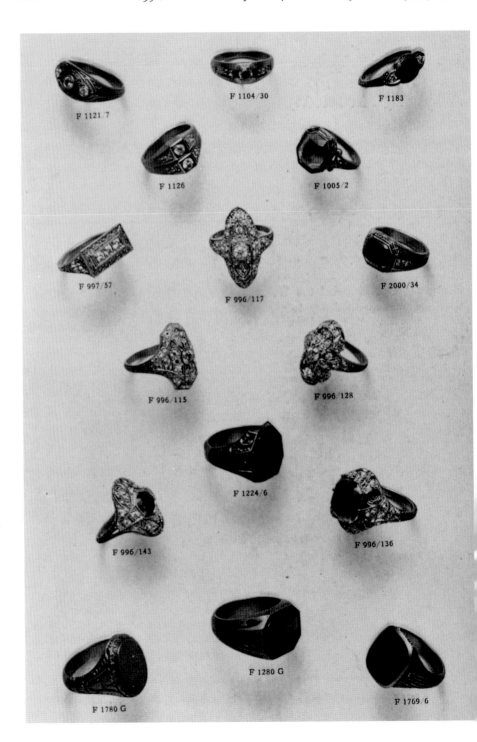

mentz & Co., providing the parent company with a line of precious stone rings and other jewelry. By this date, Jones & Woodland had relocated, back to the Krementz building at 49 Chestnut Street. The Jones & Woodland line specialized in fine jewelry.

KELLER JEWELRY MANUFACTURING CO.

In January 1901, the firm of Keller & Henerlau Co. was incorporated, with Otto L. and Henry A. Henerlau of Newark and Adolph and Hugo P. Keller and John Garland of New York as incorporators. In June 1903, the Henerlaus left the firm to form the O.L. Henerlau Co. at 93 Chestnut Street.

The company was again incorporated under the name of Keller Jewelry Manufacturing Co., with a factory at 359 Mulberry Street and an office at 64 Nassau Street in New York City. By 1903, the factory had moved to 8 Lum Street, remaining at this location until 1907, when the firm reporedly moved to New York City. In the 1934 edition of *The Keystone Jewelry Trade Mark Book*, the listing is given as The Keller Manufacturing Co., Inc., at 74 West 46th Street in New York City. Keller went out of business in the late 1930s.

The Keller Jewelry Manufacturing Co. specialized in 10- and 14-carat gold ladies' rings, brooches, link buttons, scarf pins, lockets, fobs, neck chains, lorgnette chains, and tie clasps.

CHARLES KELLER & CO.

In 1865, Alexander Charles Keller and David Untermeyer joined into partnership in the firm of Keller & Untermeyer in New York City. This company imported watches as well as conducted a general jewelry jobbing business. In 1880, the name was changed to Keller & Untermeyer Manufacturing Co., specializing in watch cases. In 1885, the firm began to manufacture jewelry under the name of Charles Keller & Co. That same year, Charles Keller & Co. took over the factory of Charles Schuetz & Sons, located at 211–213 Mulberry Street in Newark; this concern had been founded in 1876.

In 1900, David Untermeyer died. The following year, the Keller & Untermeyer Manufacturing Co. was liquidated. In 1902, the Untermeyer-Robbins Co. was established by Henry, Emanuel, and Charles S. Untermeyer and Meyer L. Robbins. By 1917, Edmund Untermeyer was recorded as president and Meyer Robbins as treasurer of Charles Keller & Co., which remained at its original Mulberry Street address until 1926, when it moved next door, to 209. By the 1930s, both companies maintained the same New York office at 136 West 52nd Street. Charles Keller & Co. remained in business until 1931.

Charles Keller & Co. specialized in lockets. In 1901, the company patented the Apex Stud, which was constructed without a spring. Keller products were offered in 10- and 14-carat gold as well as platinum.

WILLIAM B. KERR CO.

William B. Kerr began his career in the jewelry trade as a salesman with Alling & Co. and, in 1881, was admitted as a partner. In January 1884, he withdrew from this company and, in 1885, formed a partnership with Sylvester S. Battin, Jr., as Kerr & Battin at 338 Mulberry Street. When Battin retired in 1888, his father took over his interests, with the name of the company remaining unchanged. Two years later, the elder Battin left the firm and Kerr took in a new partner, Paul L.V. Thiery, and the firm became William B. Kerr & Co., which, in January 1904, was changed to Kerr &

Thiery. Upon Thiery's departure from the firm in December 1905 to pursue a separate business in gold jewelry, the name became the William B. Kerr Co. On February 27, 1906, Kerr died, and that same year the firm was purchased

Chesney was president, with R. Edgar Kirk, vice president and treasurer.

In January 1891, Kerr opened an office at 860 Broadway in New York City and, in 1903, relocated the factory to 144 Orange Street. In 1924, the factory moved to 263–273 Washington Avenue. In 1927, the entire business was transferred to Providence, Rhode Island, where the firm continued to produce sterling silver and gold toiletware, cigarette cases, and other small articles. Kerr continued to be included in *Trade-Marks of the Jewelry and Kindred Trades* through 1950.

In 1893, William B. Kerr & Co. promoted itself as a manufacturer of artistic jewelry in gold and silver. A specialty at that time were bas-relief matchboxes reproducing the paintings *Psyche and Love* and *Satyr and Nymphs* by the French artist Bouguereau; the latter design was patented by Thiery in 1895. At the turn of the century, the firm featured sterling silver hollow ware, desk sets, toilet sets, novelties, and jewelry in the Art Nouveau style. In 1903, it introduced three new patterns in toilet ware: "Florodora," "La Favorita," and "American Beauty."

Although most of Kerr's offerings were small in size, the firm was often commissioned to produce important presentation pieces, such as the gold loving cup made in 1903 for the Gentlemen's Driving Club of Cleveland, which, at the time, was touted as the largest solid-gold cup made in America. It stood 13 inches in height, measured 21 inches from handle to handle, and weighed 9 pounds.

The William B. Kerr Co. contributed a display at the 1916 Newark Industrial Exposition of toilet sets finished in gold and French enamel of period decoration; it was greatly admired by those attending the exhibition.

KOLLMAR, RAUCH & CO.

In 1905, Eugene, Henry, and Otto Kollmar were working at a jewelry concern, located at 23 Mulberry Place. At the same time, Julius C. Rauch, who had formed Julius C. Rauch & Co., maintained a shop at 50 Columbia Street. By 1907, they had formed a partnership, Kollmar, Rauch & Co., taking William E. Kollmar, Jr., into the firm. By this date, the firm had relocated to 306 Market Street. In 1918, Julius Rauch was president; Henry C. Kollmar, secretary; and Robert Kollmar, treasurer. The firm employed twelve workers in the factory. Kollmar, Rauch & Co. produced moderately priced gold jewelry, set with seed pearls and small gemstones. The firm was listed in the Newark Directories until 1920 when, it is believed, it went out of business.

KREMENTZ & CO.

George Krementz was born in 1837 in Weisbaden, Germany. His parents emigrated to the United States when he was an infant, settling on a farm in New Albany, Indiana. On a visit to his relatives, the Lebkuechers, in Newark, he became fascinated with his uncle's jewelry business and, upon returning home, decided to forsake farming for a career in the jewelry industry. At the age of eighteen, he apprenticed to Alling, Hall & Dodd, after which he worked for eight years with Smith & Ford, a New York jeweler, eventually becoming foreman of the factory. On April 1,

1866, he went into business with Stephen Alling, the business known as Alling & Krementz, with a factory located on the second floor of 14 Oliver Street. This arrangement terminated one year later when Krementz entered into a partnership with Alfred Van Cleve Genung, who remained for only a short time. In 1869, he established Krementz & Co. with his cousin, Julius A. Lebkuecher.

Julius Lebkuecher (pronounced Lĕb'-kĕ-cher) was born in 1844 in Germany, coming to this country as a child. His jewelry career began with an apprenticeship with his father, Francis, a manufacturer of chains, after which he went to work for Smith & Ford and, later, with Leonard Decker, before forming a partnership with Krementz. Francis Lebkuecher's business, located on Broad Street, was consolidated with Krementz & Co. in 1872, the elder Lebkuecher remaining with the company until his retirement in 1885.

Lebkuecher and Krementz brought to their new business complementary abilities: Lebkuecher was in charge of sales as well as business management; Krementz invented new articles and the machines with which to produce them. In 1884, he secured patents for the Krementz one-piece collar button and the necessary machinery. By 1900, most of the collar buttons produced in the world were made at Krementz. Krementz also invented the one-piece bean-and-post cuff button and the Krementz bodkin clutch vest button. The development of these lines brought international fame to the house. In 1894, Lebkeucher served a term as mayor of Newark.

In 1875, Krementz & Co. purchased a factory at 49 Chestnut Street, expanded and remodeled to accommodate a growing business. The firm moved into its new quarters in the spring of 1876. Two years later, Krementz opened a New York office at 182 Broadway to service the retail trade. On June 1, 1894, this operation was moved to the Newark factory until November 1905, when the business had grown to such an extent that a New York office was reopened, at 1 Maiden Lane.

1892 was a year of growth for Krementz & Co., when several new partners were admitted into the firm, among them John N. Taylor and Thomas and Frank Krementz, brothers of the founder. Taylor became a traveling representative for the firm, covering the eastern district and, after leaving the firm, opened his own business, Taylor & Co. Frank Krementz worked for Krementz & Co. for thirty-eight years before opening his own business, the Frank Krementz Co., to manufacture 14-carat gold jewelry. Thomas Krementz remained with Krementz & Co. until his retirement.

Krementz & Co. was among only nine Newark manufacturing jewelers to contribute an exhibit to the 1916 Newark Industrial Exposition. The display included 14-carat gold and platinum bracelets, cuff buttons, scarf pins, enameled baby pins, cuff links, lavalieres, bar pins, link bracelets, and pendants, set with gemstones and diamonds.

Upon the death of Lebkuecher on May 13, 1913, and Krementz on March 5, 1918, their sons, Carl H. Lester (in April 1918, probably as a result of anti-German feeling in the United States, the family name was changed from Lebkuecher to Lester), and Richard and Walter M. Krementz took over the firm. Carl Lester had joined the business sometime in the mid-1890s and Richard and Walter Krementz in 1898 and 1902, respectively. In 1922, Krementz & Co. incorporated, with the Krementz and Lester families each having a fifty percent share.

In 1936, the company was divided into two parts, one for each of the owner families. Lester & Co. took over manufacturing most of the gold jewelry. Krementz & Co. continued to make some 10- and 14-carat gold jewelry, but its major emphasis turned to the gold-clad metal line. Their 10-carat gold line was known as "Diana" and sold mostly through department stores. Both concerns still manufactured their goods at the 49 Chestnut Street address; however, each company maintained a separate entrance. In 1946, Lester & Co. moved its facilities to 131 Ogden Street.

Krementz & Co. first used clad metal (fusing gold onto a base metal) for its collar buttons in the late 1890s. The success of this product encouraged the firm to develop a full line of man's jewelry using this technique. This division became the forerunner of the Krementz 14-carat gold-overlay division. Under the direction of Harrison D. Simpson, who later became president of the company, a ladies' clad metal line developed during the late 1930s; by 1940, it had become a significant part of the firm's business.

During the 1930s, Krementz & Co. dominated the jewelry industry in Newark, acquiring several important firms, including Bippart, Griscom & Osborn; Carter, Gough & Co.; Eckfeldt & Ackley; and Jones & Woodland. The acquisition of the latter firm enabled Krementz to enter the precious stone jewelry business.

During World War II, the New York firm of George O. Street was purchased, primarily for its gold license. In the early 1950s, the corporate name of that company was changed to Krementz Jewelry Co., under which the firm sold carat-gold jewelry. Gold-overlay jewelry continued to be sold by Krementz & Co.

In 1940, Krementz bought Abelson & Braun, a firm that specialized in bridal jewelry; in 1956, Allsopp-Steller was acquired for its expertise in medium-priced gold jewelry. Other acquisitions, made to obtain specific skills, included the M. & N. Co. for its ring manufacturing.

In 1965, George Schuler & Co., a small manufacturing firm in Pleasantville, New York, became part of the Krementz company. This firm provided the expertise to produce expensive handmade jewelry. Soon afterwards, Herbert Cockshaw & Co. was acquired and became part of the Schuler line, moving its manufacturing and sales activities to Pleasantville.

Upon the death of Carl Lester in 1966, Krementz Jewelry Co. acquired the stock of Lester & Co. The sales force and stock of both companies were combined and all products sold under the Krementz name. This new consolidation was the basis for Krementz's development of a new line in the medium-priced gold jewelry market. The following year, the Frank Krementz Co. was purchased. In the late 1970s, Krementz also purchased a Providence manufacturer that specialized in precious-metal wire, Improved Laminated Metals Co.

In 1975, Krementz & Co. became the first American jewelry manufacturer to show at the Basel Fair in Switzerland, exhibiting its gold overlay line. This initiative proved successful and companies were formed in Frankfurt, Brussels, and Paris; the Frankfurt firm closed after a few years. 1975 also saw the acquisition of another firm, McTeigue & Co., which provided an 18-carat gold and diamond jewelry line. This company had a small factory in New York City which was moved to the Pleasantville facility, the name becoming Schuler-McTeigue, Inc. The McTeigue line, which sold higher-priced rings, was kept separate, operating under the name of McTeigue & Co. In 1982, Shiman

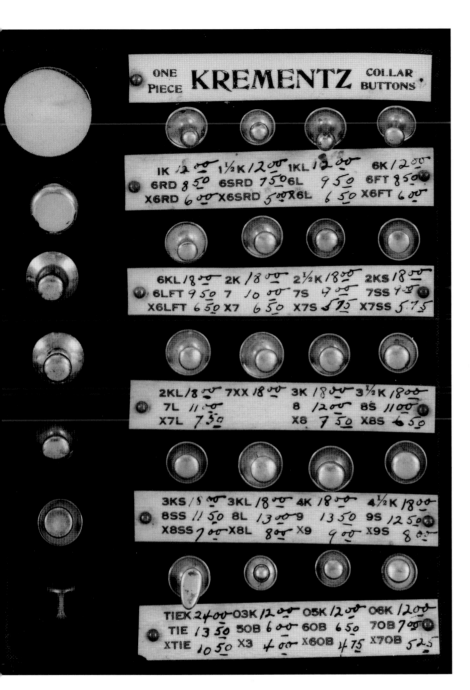

in 1947, learning the basics of the jewelry business, from goldsmithing and engraving to management, eventually assuming the role of gemstone buyer in the 1960s. Today, Krementz employs more than three hundred workers in its factory, many of whom live in the surrounding area.

Frank Krementz Co.

Frank Krementz worked for his brother's firm, Krementz & Co., for thirty-eight years, becoming a partner in 1892. In February 1910, he filed articles of incorporation to establish the Frank Krementz Co. for the manufacture of 14-carat gold jewelry. Officers in the company were Frank Krementz, Ida Krementz, and Harry Higham. The factory was located at 532 Mulberry Street and, by 1918, had moved to 164 Emmet Street. According to the 1918 *Industrial Directory of New Jersey*, it employed sixty workers. The Frank Krementz Co. produced lorgnettes, eyeglasses, children's sets, handy pins, bar pins, pendants, and pocket knives. By the 1960s, the company was producing eyeglass frames and lorgnettes. In 1967, the business was acquired by Krementz & Co.

LaPierre Manufacturing Co.

LaPierre Manufacturing Co. was founded in 1885 by Frank H. LaPierre at 18 East 14th Street in New York City, with the purpose of manufacturing novelty items. In 1893, the factory relocated to the Carter-Howe building on Park Street in Newark and, in 1900, to 58 Columbia Street. The firm filed articles of incorporation in 1895, with LaPierre as president and G.H. Henckel as secretary. Five years later, new papers for incorporation were filed, with LaPierre and H.C. Brown as officers. They maintained offices in New York City at Union Square and then moved to 7 Maiden Lane.

LaPierre produced silver hollow ware, toilet articles, and novelties. The company achieved success with the manufacture of a silver bangle bracelet, decorated with quotes from Shakespeare. By 1925, the firm consisted of the founder and C.M. Weston. In 1929, the company was purchased by the International Silver Co. and was relocated to Wallingford, Connecticut.

Larter & Sons

Larter & Sons dates its inception to 1865, when the firm of Davis & Elcox was established. In 1869, the name was changed to H. Elcox & Co., with partners Henry Elcox, his brother-in-law, Frederick H. Larter, and Horace Bedell operating the company. At that time, the company maintained an office at 41–43 Maiden Lane in New York City and, in 1873, opened a factory at 363 Mulberry Street in Newark. In 1892, the offices moved to 21–23 Maiden Lane.

Upon Elcox's death, on January 1, 1890, the name was changed to Larter, Elcox & Co. and its members included Frederick Larter, his sister, Annie Elcox, William H. Jones, and Theodore M. Woodland; the latter two later left the firm to establish their own company, Jones & Woodland. In 1895, Harry C., who had worked with Hayden W. Wheeler & Co., and Halsey M., sons of Frederick Larter, were admitted into the firm. In 1905, Larter and his sons became the owners of the business, changing the name to Larter & Sons. That same year, the firm moved its premises to 49 Chestnut Street and, in 1909, relocated to 88 Parkhurst, remaining there until 1986. By 1910, A.I. Hall & Son represented the firm in San Francisco, located in the Jewelers' Building on Post Street.

242. Demonstration panel showing collar button styles and steps in the manufacturing process, collection of Krementz & Co., Newark.

Industries was purchased, providing Krementz with a 14-carat gold religious jewelry line.

In 1988, Krementz & Co. moved into a new administrative and manufacturing facility at 375 McCarter Highway to house the following five divisions: Krementz Gold, Krementz Wedding Rings, Shiman, Krementz Gemstones, and the Traditional (Overlay) division. The McTeigue & Co. division remained in Pleasantville, New York. This division was sold to Tiffany & Co. in 1991.

Today, Krementz jewelry is sold under three names: Shiman produces 14-carat gold religious jewelry; Krementz & Co. makes the gold-overlay and electroplated brass line; and Krementz Gemstones produces the 18-carat gold and platinum colored-gemstone jewelry. In 1994, Krementz made an arrangement with Bill Blass, Ltd. to produce 18-carat gold and sterling silver jewelry bearing the designer's name. Richard Krementz, grandson of the founder, is the chairman of the board. He began working in the company

Larter & Sons specialized in gentlemen's seals and fancy rings, ladies, and children's rings, sleeve buttons, and lockets. In the early 1890s, the firm patented a spring link for its sleeve link buttons and, on December 13, 1898, Halsey Larter patented the spring-back stud, which the firm advertised extensively for many years.

Larter had a display at the 1916 Newark Industrial Exposition featuring jewelry made of 14- and 18- carat green gold or platinum, including rings set with kunzite from California; peridots from Egypt; pink tourmalines from California; and green tourmalines, aquamarines, and pink amethysts from Brazil. There were gold-handled pocket knives, platinum cuff buttons set with diamonds and other precious stones, green gold cufflink buttons, signet rings set with diamonds, pearls and other gemstones. A special exhibit of the Larter automatic vest buttons and the Larter automatic shirt studs was displayed at either end of the exhibition.

By 1917, Larter & Sons had taken over Barry & Co., located at 10 Austin Street, which offered a general line of jewelry, Halsey Larter becoming president until the firm was evenutally absorbed within the company. By 1922, other Larters, including Frederick and Warren, were also involved in the business, along with Halsey and Harry.

Harry Larter operated the business for many years, becoming the president until his death on December 7, 1931. He was very prominent in the field and was known as the "Mayor of Maiden Lane." He had also served terms as president of the Jewelers' Twenty-Four Karat Club and the Brotherhood of Traveling Jewelers. In October 1931, the business was incorporated, with Warren R. Larter as vice-president and H. Monroe Larter as treasurer. By the 1930s, the New York office had moved to 15 Maiden Lane.

In 1935, the firm was still operated by Larters, Warren and H. Monroe, but by 1943 only H. Monroe was on the executive board as president, with George A. Schuetz as vice president, Maurice Spain as secretary, and Jonah J. Newton as treasurer. Schuetz, who had been a salesman for the company, eventually gained control but retained the Larter name.

In 1986, Larter & Sons moved its business to 10 Industrial Drive in Laurence Harbor, New Jersey. Today, the business is run by Stephen Schuetz, grandson of George Schuetz, who continues the firm's tradition of specializing in men's jewelry and rings, as well as ladies' jewelry, including earrings, pins, charms, bangle bracelets, pendants, and a selection of enamel jewelry.

LESTER & CO.
Carl Lester was the son of Julius A. Lebkuecher (the family changed its name to Lester during World War I). He joined his father's firm, Krementz & Co., sometime in the 1890s and, upon the death of his father on May 13, 1913, inherited his interests in the company. By 1936, Lester had a fifty per-cent share in the business, and the descendants of Krementz, Richard and Walter, had an equal share. At about this time, Carl Lester formed Lester & Co. to manufacture gold jewelry, while Krementz & Co. continued to make the clad-metal line. The new business maintained its office and factory within the Krementz facility at 49 Chestnut Street, each company having a separate entranceway. In 1946, Lester & Co. moved its facility to 131 Ogden Street.

Lester & Co. attempted to compete with Krementz's overlay line, producing gold-filled, and then electroplated jewelry, but this proved unsuccessful. The firm eventually gave up manufacturing, moving to Springfield, New Jersey, and continuing in business as a wholesaler.

After the death of Carl Lester in 1966, Krementz Jewelry Co. bought the tools, molds, and jewelry stock of Lester & Co. Within a year, the sales forces and stock of the two companies were combined and this new division was absorbed within Krementz Jewelry Co.

LINK & ANGELL
John M. Link, brother of William, was listed in the city directory in 1872 as a jeweler at 21 Green Street, the same address as William Link. He worked at this address for two years. His name did not appear in the directory again until 1878, when he was listed as a jeweler. In 1886, he was a

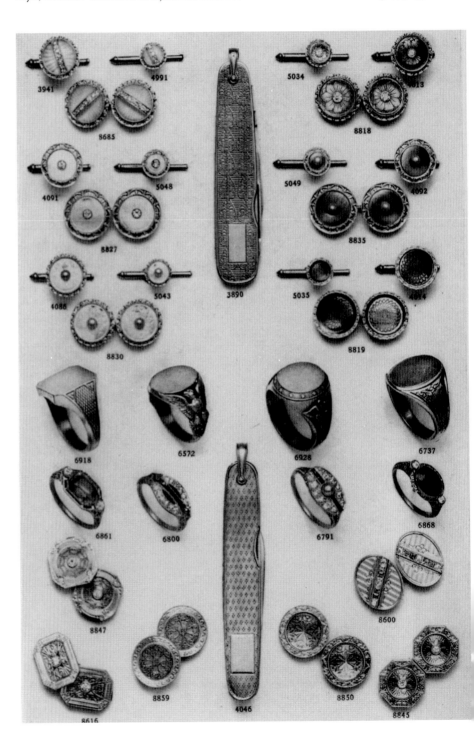

243. Advertisement for Larter & Sons in *Jewelry Fashions* 1917, p. 53.

partner in the manufacturing jewelry concern of Alexander, Milne & Co. at 19 Ward Street. Sometime in the next few years, he left this company and established Link & Co. This company was succeed by Link, Angell & Weiss in 1893, the partners being John Link, John Angell, and Fred Weiss, with a factory at 13–15 Franklin Street. Sometime around 1900, Weiss left the firm and the name became became Link & Angell. In 1918, twenty workers were employed in the factory at 71 Austin Street. In 1923, Link & Angell and William Link Co. seem to have consolidated their businesses, since the directory lists both firms at 407 Mulberry Street. Thereafter, only Link & Angell are recorded in the directory. In 1930, the company moved to 68 Orchard Street. It went out of business between 1933 and 1934.

WILLIAM LINK CO.

On August 1, 1871, William M. Link established a jewelry concern at 21 Green Street. Four years later, John D. Nesler entered the firm and, upon his retirement in 1882, Addison Conkling became a partner and the name became Link & Conkling. By this time, the company had relocated to 61–63 Hamilton Street. When Conkling left the company in 1886, William Link continued to operate the business, with the name reverting back to William Link Co. In 1890, he moved the factory to 61–63 Mulberry Street. In the 1890s, the firm offered solid-gold wire chain bracelets in five different sizes. In 1911, William Link died, but the company continued to operate. In 1912, the city directory lists William Link Co. at 407 Mulberry Street; in 1917, this company was run by J. Porter Russell of Boston as president and John Drake as secretary and treasurer. They employed twenty workers in their factory. In 1923, William Link Co. and Link & Angell must have consolidated since the directory lists the two firms at 407 Mulberry Street. Thereafter, only Link & Angell is listed.

MOORE & SON

Arthur W. Moore founded Moore & Hoffman in 1886. By 1901, he and his son, Arthur H. Moore, had gained control of the business, renaming it Moore & Son, with a factory at 22 Green Street. In May 1903, they incorporated, taking in William F. Weber as an officer. In 1904, they opened a branch office and sample room at 3 Maiden Lane in New York City. Moore & Son was a small firm, employing fourteen workers in 1918. In 1923, the factory moved to 34 Court Street which, by 1937, had expanded to 30–34 Court Street. In 1941, Arthur H. Moore was listed as president of the company and Joseph J. Chessman as vice president, at a new location, 9–11 Franklin Street. The last listing of Moore & Son appeared in the 1950 edition of *Trade-Marks of the Jewelry and Kindred Trades*. Arthur H. Moore, who had run the business for fifty years, died on November 5, 1965. Moore & Son manufactured a general line of jewelry.

NESLER & CO.

Nesler & Co. was founded in 1869 as Nesler & Redway, with a factory at 14 Oliver Street. In the 1870s, when Redway left the company, the name became J.S. & C.L. Nesler, then Nesler & Bioren and, finally, Nesler & Co. When Charles L. Nesler died in 1907, the company continued in operation under his son, Charles F., at 38 Crawford Street. In 1913, the company incorporated with the following officers: Charles F. Nesler, president; Edward Heyeck, treasurer; and William C. Schaef, secretary. In 1916, Fred

Nesler succeeded his brother as president. Nesler & Co. went out of business in 1923.

Nesler & Co. produced rolled-gold plate, 10- and 14-carat gold earrings and ear wires. In *The Industrial Directory of New Jersey* for 1918, the firm was listed as specializing in hoop earrings, with a staff of thirty workers.

PRYOR MANUFACTURING CO.

In 1902, three brothers, John A., Thomas F., and Joseph E. Pryor founded the Pryor Novelty Co., with a factory at 473 Washington Street and a New York office at 7 Maiden Lane. The firm specialized in sterling silver wares, including belt buckles, mesh bags, and other novelties such as bib clips. It also made hollow ware items. By 1908, the firm's name had changed to Pryor Manufacturing Co. The following year the factory moved to 11 Governor Street. In 1918, the company was consolidated with the B.M. Shanley, Jr. Co. at 11 Governor Street.

JOHN W. REDDALL & CO.

In 1891, John W. Reddall, together with Henry D. Hastings, established John W. Reddall & Co., with a factory at 60 McWhorter Street, moving to 107 Hamilton Street in 1893. Upon Hastings' death three years later, Reddall continued the business. On March 1, 1895, William A. Seidler, who had been superintendent of the factory, was admitted as a partner. Shortly after, J.J. Greenwood became a partner, until his retirement on January 1, 1902. By 1901, the firm had a salesroom at 41 Union Square in New York City. In July 1903, the company incorporated under shareholders Mary E. Reddall, Charles R. Hansel, and Marshall O. Wells. In 1905, the firm was called Reddall & Co., with a factory at Camp and Orchard Streets. This was the last year the company was listed in the Newark Directories.

John H. Reddall & Co. manufactured sterling silver wares, including toilet articles, hollow ware, as well as mounted cut glass, leather and steel goods. The company specialized in belts in 14-carat gold and sterling silver, and produced a line of gold jewelry, including side combs, hatpins, scarf pins, link buttons, brooches, bib pins, seals, and lockets. In 1895, Reddall produced two nautical-style belts, named the "Defender" in reference to the yacht that competed in the America's Cup. In 1898, the firm was making patriotic jewelry, including silver American and Cuban flags and a badge in the shape of a gun, from which was suspended a piece of silk with "The Star Spangled Banner" woven into the fabric.

ERWIN REU, INC.

Erwin Reu was born in Pforzheim, Germany, the son of a gold engraver. Before learning the jewelry trade, he attended the local design and jewelry school. In 1923, Reu emigrated to the United States and, after settling in Newark, worked for Davidson & Son in New York until 1931, when he joined Jones & Woodland as a designer.

In 1936, Reu opened his own business at 68 Orchard Street for the manufacture of fine gold and platinum jewelry. August Stark took an interest in the company in 1940, remaining with the company for twenty years. In 1965, Reu's two sons, Ronald and Edgar, joined the business. Ronald had apprenticed with Burgen & Burdett in Newark as a stone setter before entering his father's firm. In 1966, the company moved to a new location at 1020 Springfield Road in Union, New Jersey, where they are still located today.

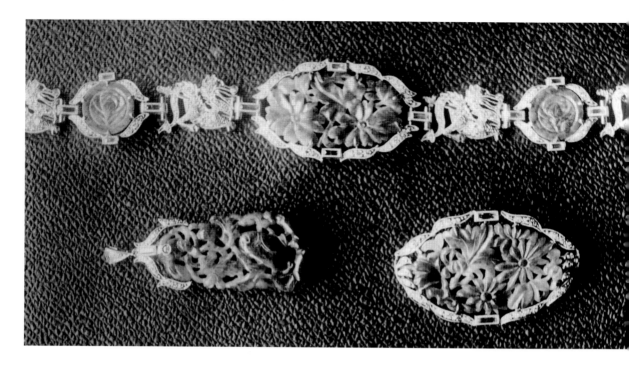

244. Richardson Manufacturing Co., photograph of platinum and diamond jewelry set with carved Chinese jade, 1920–1930, The Newark Museum, Gift of the Estate of Gertrude L. Grote, 1987, in memory of Herman E. Grote (87.41c)

After Erwin Reu's death in December 1985, his sons continued to manage the business until Edgar's unexpected death in 1989, at which time the business was sold to Lutz and Uve Jesse, skilled craftsmen from Germany. In 1990, the company expanded its operation by purchasing the signet ring line from Krementz & Co. Erwin Reu, Inc., has increased its sales operation from the East Coast to the Southeast and Midwestern territories.

RICHARDSON MANUFACTURING CO.

Enos Richardson was born in Attleboro, Massachusetts. He served an apprenticeship in Philadelphia before opening his own business in 1841 under the name Daggett, Richardson & Co. and, in 1843, Daggett & Richardson. In 1849, he formed a partnership with John B. Palmer, who had been a jeweler in Warren, Rhode Island. They opened an office in New York City at 23 Maiden Lane and a factory at 52 Columbia Street, Newark. A booklet, authored by William R. Bagnall in 1882, *The Manufacture of Gold Jewelry*, described the four-story building in detail. At this time, the firm employed about four hundred workers. When Palmer retired from the firm in 1865, the name was changed to Enos Richardson & Co. By 1882, the partners consisted of Richardson, his sons, Frank H. and William S., Leonard P. Brown, and William P. Melcher. In 1896, the firm's name was Enos Richardson Manufacturing Co. and, in 1898, the name was changed to Richardson Manufacturing Co., with Frank H. Richardson as president.

In the nineteenth century, Enos Richardson & Co. produced a full line of gold jewelry and chains as well as silver jewelry and desk sets. In 1885, it advertised the "Dicksonite," the trade name for the perfect imitation diamond. Richardson was the sole distributor of the "Benedict" patent collar buttons, which were offered in 10- and 14-carat gold, sterling silver, and rolled-gold plate. Several members of the firm secured patents for inventions, including Albert W. Turton for a jewelry holder, Edward B. Aiguier for a link button, and another employee for a combined key ring and cigar cutter.

In 1900, the factory at 52 Columbia Street was expanded with the addition of two floors. When advertising for prospective renters for the extra space, the firm proclaimed that its building was the only strictly fireproof manufacturing building in the city of Newark. It was equipped with the latest in services, including an elevator, electric power, steam heat, compressed air, hot and cold water, and a telephone pay station.

Enos Richardson remained as head of the company until his death in 1895, when the business was taken over by his son, Frank, who ran it until his death in 1907. The firm was incorporated that year with George V. Tucker, W. E. Reeder, and Mrs. Frank H. Richardson as officers. In 1932, the officers were Harriet M. Richardson, president; S. R. Burns, vice president; and Fred R. Keller, treasurer. Along with its New York office, the firm maintained an office in San Francisco at the corner of Post Street and Grand Avenue. Richardson Manufacturing Co. closed in 1969.

RIKER BROTHERS

William Riker was an heir to an old New Jersey family, founded by Abraham Ryker, who came from Holland in 1636 and settled at Newtown, Long Island. His father moved to Montclair, New Jersey, where, in 1822, William was born. At the age of fifteen, Riker began an apprenticeship with Taylor & Baldwin, continuing there until he left to work with Downing & Hoyt in New York. In 1846, he entered into partnership with George H. Tay, opening a shop on Quarry Street in Newark, the firm known as Riker & Tay. The firm grew to such a degree that, within a year, they bought the tools and fixtures of Bliss & Dwight at 379 Broad Street, where they relocated the company.

In 1849, Tay left the company to pursue gold prospecting in California, eventually opening a stove manufacturing business in San Francisco. Shortly after his departure, Horace Goble became a partner and the name was changed to Riker & Goble. In 1859, they moved their factory to Green Street, where they worked together until Goble retired in 1864. William Riker continued the business under his own name until the 1870s, when his sons, William Jr., Joseph M., and Cortlandt, joined the firm in 1871, 1873, and 1875, respectively, and the name became

Riker & Sons. In 1870, Riker purchased a schoolhouse at 42 Court Street, which he enlarged to accommodate his business.

During the 1870s, William Riker patented a number of successful mechanical processes for the manufacture of jewelry, including two for ornamenting the surface of jewelry and finger rings, and another for an improved sash fastener. In 1892, William Riker and his son Cortlandt withdrew from the company, Cortlandt becoming secretary of the Newark Rapid Transit Co. On May 1 of that year, the house became known as Riker Bros. and, on that same day, the selling office at 860 Broadway in New York City was closed, that division moving to the factory building, which had relocated to 42–46 Hill Street. On December 29, 1898, William Riker died. William, Jr., continued as supervisor of the office and factory while his brother became president of the Newark Manufacturing Jewelers' Association and assumed the duties of president of the Merchants National Bank.

William Riker originally offered gold fob chains and charms, and was one of the earliest manufacturers to offer Masonic goods of all kinds. In the 1870s, the company also sold onyx and cameo lockets and cameo rings. Its stock eventually included a full line of high-quality jewelry in gold and platinum. Riker was one of only a few firms working in *plique à jour* enameling. At the 1916 Newark Industrial Exposition, Riker Brothers exhibited eighteen pieces of platinum jewelry, set with diamonds, pearls, sapphires, and other precious gemstones.

Riker Bros maintained a factory at 42–46 Court Street, and was there listed in the city directories until 1926. It is believed that at this time the firm moved to 546 S. Meridian Street in Indianapolis, Indiana, remaining there until the mid-1940s.

Harry C. Schick, Inc.

On March 1, 1919, Harry C. Schick, Inc. opened a business at 99–105 Chestnut Street with only three other employees. By the end of the fourth year, the company had expanded to 128 workers and, by 1925, was selling its jewelry throughout the United States, Canada, Cuba, England, France, India, and the Phillipine Islands. James E. Wordley, formerly with Wordley, Allsopp & Bliss, was president, and Harry C. Schick, secretary and treasurer. Offices were maintained offices in New York at 170 Broadway, in Toronto at 13 King Street West, and in Chicago at 29 East Madison Street. Harry C. Schick offered such items as sautoirs and bracelets and was noted for its spring rings and snap clasps, known as schicksnaps. The factory was at 105 Chestnut Street; this address is still given in the last listing for the company in the 1984 edition of the *Jewelers' Circular/Keystone Brand Name and Trademark Guide*.

Shafer & Douglas, Inc.

Frederick S. Douglas was born in 1841, spending his boyhood years in Newark. After finishing his education, he entered the mercantile business, working for the DeWitt Wire Co. In January 1867, he left this concern and went to work with Swinerton & Shafer, a partnership established in 1855. When Swinerton retired in 1869, Joseph H. Shafer took Douglas in as a partner, under the name Shafer & Douglas. The two partners divided the responsibilities of the company, with Douglas assuming the office and selling duties and Shafer taking charge of the manufacturing functions.

All aspects of the business were at first conducted at the Newark factory; however, the firm soon opened an office on Broadway, in New York City. Subsequent moves included 11 Maiden Lane and, then, in 1893, to the Havemeyer Building at 26 Cortlandt Street. The factory was originally located on Green Street, later moving to Hamilton Street, 355–357 Mulberry Street, 42 Court Street, 9 Franklin Street and, finally, 68 Orchard Street.

A year after the death of Frederick Douglas on June 7, 1898, the business incorporated. The following year the officers were listed as Joseph H. Shafer, N.C. Barnum, Delancey Stone, C.L. Graham, and J.C. Heddenberg. Stone retired in 1911 and Heddenberg died in 1916. In 1919, Shafer and Barnum were still members of the board. Other members who had been taken in as partners were C.Z. Barnum, F.J. Orchard, and W.E. Shafer, son of the founder, who had entered the business in 1904. The company went out of business in 1931.

When Shafer & Douglas was founded, the firm manufactured a general line of jewelry. By 1895, it was specializing in rings.

B.M. Shanley, Jr. Co.

B.M. Shanley, Jr. Co. was founded in 1908 by Bernard Michael Shanley, Jr., its factory located at 11 Governor Street, with a sales office at 527 Fifth Avenue in New York City. In 1918, the firm merged its operations with the Pryor Manufacturing Co., with the following officers: Bernard M. Shanley, Jr., president; Thomas F. Pryor, Jr., vice president; John A. Pryor, secretary; and Joseph E. Pryor, treasurer. That year, forty workers were employed in the factory. Shanley went out of business in 1937.

In 1910, B.M. Shanley, Jr. Co. advertised 14- and 18-carat gold jewelry and fine mesh bags. It also made silver, gold, and platinum belt buckles, vanity cases, photograph cases, platinum and diamond sautoirs, and pocket knives.

Shiman Manufacturing Co.

In 1865, Marcus Shiman emigrated to the United States, seeking his fortune in the California gold fields before settling in Syracuse, New York, as a wholesale jeweler. In 1876, his son, Abraham, was born; the family moved to Pearl Street in New York City in 1888. It was there that Abraham learned the jewelry trade. In 1893, he and his three brothers, Moses, Nathan, and David, purchased the firm of Stern Metals and, four years later, organized Shiman Bros. to manufacture diamond rings and mountings. This business was located in New York City.

In 1906, Abraham formed a separate business with Simon Miller under the name Shiman-Miller Co. to make gold rings and jewelry (his brothers were silent partners). His first factory was located at 102 Mulberry Street in Newark and, the following year, moved to 45 Austin Street. The firm manufactured an assortment of gold jewelry, including crystal and onyx bracelets, brooches and pendants, flexible watch bracelets, earrings, and cameo brooches. In men's jewelry they made link buttons, scarf pins, belt buckles, tie clasps, cigar cutters, and Elks jewelry.

In 1914, Nathan Hayman was employed at the New York office, located at 87 Maiden Lane. He rose from office boy to sales manager and vice president, working in the New York offices at 15 Maiden Lane and, later, at 35 West 53rd Street. In 1925, Shiman-Miller changed the name of the company to Shiman Mfg. Co. That same year the company moved into a specially built facility at 113 Astor Street in

Newark. Another move occurred in 1935 to 113 Monroe Street. During World War I and II, Shiman Mfg. Co. converted its manufacturing capabilities to the production of surgical instruments and other wartime items.

In 1946, Abraham Shiman died, and his sons, Leonard and Daniel, took over the company along with their three sisters, Ruth Stein, Adele Trobe, and Bobby Felstiner. In 1969, H. Alan Stein, grandson of the founder, entered the firm as vice president of marketing. In August 1971, the name was changed to Shiman Industries with the following operating divisions: Shiman of Newark, The Craft Co., F.J.E. Fine Jewelry Exclusives, and Golden Era. In 1982, the firm was purchased by Krementz & Co. to form Krementz's 14-carat gold religious jewelry line.

SINNOCK & SHERRILL

In 1870, the firm of Tingley & Sinnock opened a jewelry shop at 23 Lawrence Street for the manufacture of seal rings. In 1875, Horace D. Sherrill joined the firm and, in 1878, Sherrill and Sinnock bought out the interests of Tingley, and the name became Sinnock & Sherrill. In 1880, the company moved to 46 Green Street while maintaining an office in New York City at 3 Maiden Lane. It was about this time that the firm began to manufacture the first Knights Templar charms. It also made stone rings; the "Princess" interchangeable rings were first introduced in 1890. Sinnock & Sherrill specialized in gold and platinum emblematic jewelry such as charms, rings, pins, and buttons.

Upon the death of Sinnock in 1909, the partners in the business were Horace Sherrill, Henry W. Sherrill, Joseph N. Sinnock, Frederick E. Sinnock, and George G. Ackerman, who was superintendent of the factory for seventeen years. In 1911, the company moved to 126 South Street and opened an office in Chicago with Henry Sherrill in charge. The New York offices included locations at 3, 21, and 15 Maiden Lane. The Chicago office closed after the death of Horace Sherrill in 1921. Joseph Sinnock remained in the business until his death in 1924. In 1933, Frederick E. Sinnock and Henry W. Sherrill were running the company. In 1935, they moved their premises to 30 Court Street. The firm's last listing appeared in the 1938 Newark Directory.

SLOAN & CO.

John Alexander Riley was born in New York City in 1828. He worked in this city throughout his career in the jewelry trade, entering the business as a young man and later becoming foreman for Chattellier, Dominge & Spence. About 1857, he left to establish Riley, Douglas & Williamson at the corner of Broadway and Cortlandt Street. After Williamson and Douglas withdrew from the firm, he continued alone, moving to 18 John Street. A few years later, he went into partnership with Charles F. Freer and George Valdran under the name John A. Riley & Co. Five years later, Valdran left and Riley and Freer continued the business, moving to 7–9 Bond Street and, later, to 860 Broadway. When Freer withdrew from the company in 1887, Riley renamed it John A. Riley.

In February 1891, Frank T. Sloan and Allen A. MacDonald entered the business and the name was changed to John A. Riley & Sloan & Co., with Riley as president, Sloan as treasurer and MacDonald as secretary. In 1893, James M. Bennett, who had been with Krementz & Co., joined the organization as vice president. Upon Riley's death on June 3 and Bennett's in September of 1895, Sloan took over the business, renaming it Sloan & Co. On January 1, 1896, his father, Augustus K. Sloan, who had retired from his long association with Carter, Sloan & Co., assumed the presidency of Sloan & Co.

Frank T. Sloan was born in Brooklyn on November 2, 1869. In September 1887, he went to work in his father's firm, Carter, Sloan & Co., as an office boy, and had risen to the level of stock clerk when he left in 1891 to become treasurer of John A. Riley & Sloan Co. For the first few years, he also served the company as a salesman, visiting the western territory.

In May of 1896, Sloan & Co. relocated its factory to 106 Ogden Street in Newark and opened a New York office at 23 Maiden Lane. The factory moved to 160 Mt. Pleasant Avenue in 1907, while the office was transferred to 15 Maiden Lane in 1911. In 1922, when Augustus Sloan died, the officers were Frank Sloan, president; Allan A. MacDonald, secretary; and Lewis J. Donniez, treasurer. In 1943, the principals were Louis J. Donniez, president, and George Kirschner, treasurer. In 1951, John Babcock was president and Julius Guth, secretary and treasurer. In 1952, the latter patented a device for non-piercing earrings. The last listing found for Sloan & Co. was in the 1984 *Jewelers' Circular/Keystone Brand Name and Trademark Guide*.

STRAUSS & STRAUSS

In December 1909, two brothers, Norman L. and William L. Strauss, opened the firm of Strauss & Strauss with offices at 9 Clinton Street. Norman had been a salesman with Louis Kaufman & Co. for nine years and, later, with Jacob Strauss & Sons for four years. William succeeded his brother at the Kaufman firm, working for the company for four years. In January 1910, the brothers incorporated with an authorized capital of $15,000, with Norman and William Strauss and Frederic L. Johnson as officers.

The firm specialized in gem-set rings in 10- and 14-carat gold and platinum. An office was maintained at 10 West 47th Street in New York City. The last listing of the name appeared in *The Keystone Jewelry Trade Mark Book* in 1934, with a New York address, 10 West 47th Street.

STROBELL & CRANE

In 1883, the Newark Directory listed Charles H. Crane as a jeweler and recorded that George H. Strobell worked for Block & Bergfels. In 1885, the two men established Strobell & Crane for the manufacture of jewelry. At first, they were located at 119 Chestnut Street. In 1886, they moved to 211 Mulberry Street and, in 1896, to 44 Hill Street. Ten years later, they erected a four-story building at 33 East Kinney Street, known as the Strobell & Crane Building. This facility cost $35,000 and was equipped with a power plant and a freight elevator. In 1926, the firm's office was listed as 68 Orchard Street and the East Kinney Street address was recorded as the Strobell & Crane building. By 1935, the company was no longer in existence.

In 1895, Strobell & Crane produced a photograph-and-French-mirror locket, made in either sterling silver or 14-carat gold. It also manufactured link buttons, link and bangle bracelets, bar pins, and rings.

TAYLOR & CO.

John N. Taylor began his long tenure in the jewelry trade in 1862. In 1871, he entered the employ of Krementz & Co. as a traveling representative, covering the eastern territory and

245. Sloan & Co., page
from a design scrapbook,
ca. 1900, showing the pendant in Fig. 16, private collection.

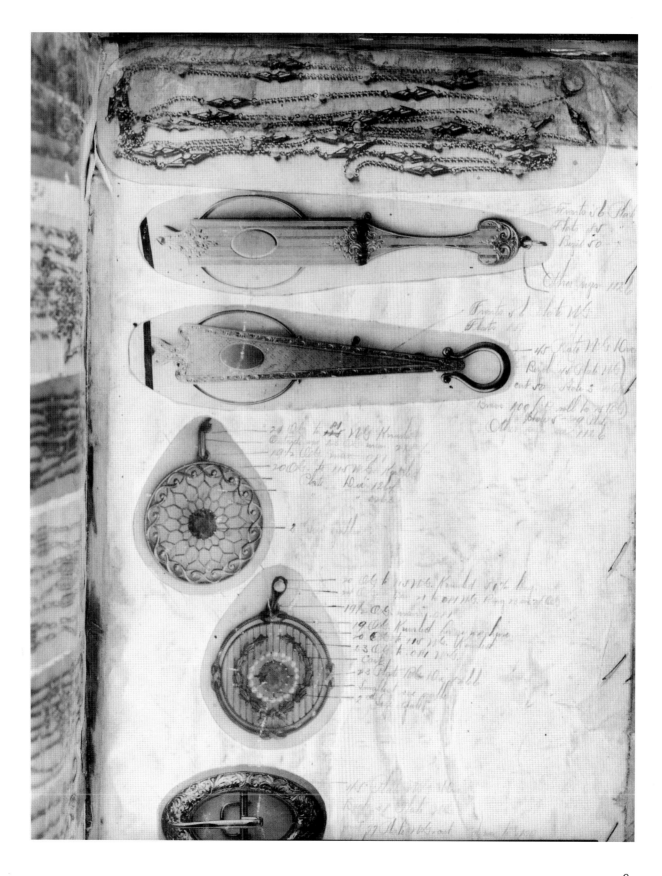

eventually rising to a partnership position in 1892. In 1906, he embarked on his own business, known as Taylor & Co., at 47 Chestnut Street, specializing in gold and platinum brooches, bar pins, sleeve links, scarf pins, and lorgnettes. In 1925, the officers were John Taylor, president and treasurer; Archibald Rutherford, vice president; and Adelaide V. Wright, secretary. In 1951, the factory was located at 131–45 Ogden Street.

TAYLOR & BALDWIN

Taylor & Baldwin dates the origin of the company to Epaphras Hinsdale who, with five other goldsmiths, left New England and settled in Newark in the 1790s. By 1801, Hinsdale is reputed to have established the first factory for the exclusive manufacture of jewelry, located in a small schoolhouse at the rear of 922 Broad Street, offering rings, watch charms, seals, and brooches. In 1804, John Taylor, Jr., entered into partnership with Hinsdale, the firm known as E. Hinsdale & Co., with a New York office conducting business under the name of Taylor & Hinsdale, adding the manufacture of necklaces, earrings, bracelets, and chains to its stock. By the time of Hinsdale's death in 1810, his company had grown to a substantial size, and the business continued under the partnership of his son, Horace Seymour, and Taylor. In 1818, Horace Hinsdale retired, relocating to New York, where he opened a retail establishment.

Around this time, John Taylor admitted Isaac Baldwin into partnership and the firm became Taylor & Baldwin, continuing to offer the same line of jewelry with the addition of silverware and gold watch cases. By 1821, business had grown and they were able to contribute a display in the Newark Industrial Parade on July 4. In 1842, when John Taylor retired from the firm to assume the presidency of the Newark Banking Co., the name was changed to Baldwin & Co., with the following partners: Isaac Baldwin and his sons, Horace and Wickliffe E., and C.E. Chevalier, a noted buckle maker. After Chevalier's retirement, Elihu Bliss was admitted into partnership. Upon the deaths of Isaac Baldwin in 1853 and Horace in 1855, and the subsequent retirement of Elihu Bliss, Wickliffe was the sole remaining partner. In 1860, the business was transferred to Thomas G. Brown, who conducted business at the corner of Halsey and Marshall Streets under the name of Thomas G. Brown & Sons.

The firm of Taylor & Baldwin served as the shop where many prominent jewelers apprenticed. Included in this illustrious list were James Madsion Durand of Durand & Co.; Aaron Carter of Carter, Gough & Co.; and William Riker of Riker Bros.

THEBERATH & CO.

Theberath & Co. was founded in 1908 by J. Henry Theberath, with a factory at 13 Franklin Street. In 1910, the firm moved to the third floor of the Herpers building at 480 Washington Street. The company was small, employing only five workers according to the 1918 edition of *The Industrial Directory of New Jersey*. Instead of maintaining a separate office in New York City, Kent & Woodland served as Theberath's selling agents through its 12 John Street office.

When Theberath & Co. was founded, it manufactured a selection of exclusive designs in 14-carat gold in brooches, festoons, handy pins, barrettes, pendants, and veil pins in either plain patterns or set with colored gemstones. The firm also produced platinum and diamond faced 10- and 14-carat gold jewelry. The last listing of the company was found in the 1926 Newark Directory.

THIERY & CO.

Paul L.V. Thiery began his jewelry career in 1877 as a designer for Durand & Co. After leaving Durand & Co., he worked for other jewelry manufacturers until 1890, when he became a partner with William B. Kerr in William B. Kerr & Co., located at 338 Mulberry Street. The following year, the partners opened an office in New York City at 860 Broadway. In January 1904, the company's name was changed to Kerr & Thiery, manufacturing sterling silver hollow ware, toilet articles, and novelties. In December 1905, Thiery left this concern and entered into a partnership with Harry B. Rogers under the name of Thiery & Rogers, at 306 Mulberry Street, specializing in gold jewelry. In 1907, Rogers left the firm and the name became Thiery & Co. This business remained open for only one year.

CHARLES L. UHRY & CO.

In 1888, Charles L. Uhry and Henry A. Alioth founded Uhry & Alioth at 336 Mulberry Street for the manufacture of jewelry. By 1891, Alioth had left the company and, with the addition of a new partner, Charles F. Tinckler, the name was changed to Charles L. Uhry & Co. In 1898, the firm moved its factory to the corner of Halsey and Marshall Streets and maintained an office in New York City at 189 Broadway.

Charles L. Uhry & Co. remained in business until 1905. Two years later, Charles Uhry formed another partnership with Henry Grasmuck, a jewelry designer, under the name of Grasmuck & Uhry at 9 Franklin Street. This partnership lasted for only a year. In 1909, Charles Uhry was listed in the Newark Directory as a jeweler.

In the 1890s, Charles L. Uhry & Co. produced 14-carat gold jewelry, specializing in fancy enameled jewelry in brooches, scarf pins, charms, neck chains, chatelaines, and novelty fobs. In 1892, the firm made a line of autumn leaf and green enameled wreath brooches.

UNGER BROTHERS

The Ungerer family emigrated from Germany, settling in Newark in 1849. One son, Herman, had been born before the move and, after establishing themselves in this country and shortening their name to Unger, four more sons were born to the family, including Eugene in 1850. One son, William, was a partner with Thomas A. Edison in the Newark Telegraph Works for two years.

Although sources record that Unger Brothers opened its business in 1872, the firm's advertisements from the 1890s cited a date of 1870 for its establishment. This earlier date may allude to Herman Unger, who was then listed in the city directory as an engraver at 5 Baldwin Street. Two years later, his brother George was listed as a jeweler at 242 Walnut Street. From April 17, 1872 to October 3, 1873, Herman Unger, William C.J. Keen, and Oscar Keen are listed as manufacturing jewelers at the corner of Marshall and Halsey Streets, the partnership of Unger & Keen lasting for only one year.

By 1874, Herman Unger's occupation was not listed, but he was working at 20 Governor Street, the same location as his brother Eugene, an engraver. The following year, Herman was recorded as a manufacturing jeweler at 36 Crawford Street and, in 1876, Eugene and Frederick joined him under the company name H. Unger & Co. In 1879, William joined the company and the firm moved to 18 Crawford Street. That year, a tragedy befell the family with the deaths of William, George, and Frederick. The two remaining brothers restructured the business, renaming it Unger Brothers.

In 1882, the brothers moved their business to 26–30 Beecher Street, a location maintained until at least 1910, while also opening a factory at 412–418 Halsey Street. They remained at the latter address for the duration of their business operation. They also maintained an office at 192 Broadway in New York City, but this site was closed on January 1, 1897, and all business was transferred to the Newark factory. By 1901, Unger Brothers had opened a retail outlet at the 416 Halsey Street address, offering all their wares including cut glassware. The firm did not produce glass but did the cutting at the factory. On January 21, 1904, the firm was incorporated.

In 1880, Eugene Unger married Emma L. Dickinson, the sister of Philemon Olin Dickinson. The latter was born in 1857 and, at the age of seventeen, entered the firm of Unger Bros. During his thirty-year tenure with the company, he held several positions, eventually rising to become the chief designer; on January 1, 1895, he and Edward P. Beach, a painter, became partners in the company. For several years until his death on June 19, 1905, Dickinson supervised all the designs that were produced at Unger Brothers, and he is credited with the Art Nouveau designs for which the firm became famous. Another designer who worked for the company was Otto Leigh.

When the company was first established, its trade was largely in gold jewelry but, as the silverware trade developed, it became more interested in this product and built up a large business, specializing in hollow ware, flatware, novelties, and silver jewelry. In 1881, Herman Unger patented a new technique for bangle bracelets by which two ends overlapped with a lateral pivotal action. By 1898, Unger Brothers listed itself in the city directory as manufacturing jewelers and silversmiths.

Eugene Unger represented the firm on the road for a number of years. His district included Baltimore, Washington, D.C., Philadelphia, and New York State. In 1906, he was vice president and treasurer of the company and, from 1906 to 1909, president of Unger & Christl, a jewelry firm in which he went into partnership with J. Victor Christl and George W. Hagney; the firm's factory was located at 165 Clinton Street. In 1907, Eugene's son, Raymond, became treasurer of Unger & Christl, which had moved to 60 Arlington Street. In 1908, Raymond left this firm, joining his father's company. Eugene Unger had also been director of the Manufacturers' National Bank. On November 20, 1909, Eugene Unger died and the business passed to his son, Raymond, who became president. Herman had died a few years earlier.

By 1910, Unger Brothers had ceased making jewelry and objects in the Art Nouveau style. The dies were destroyed and the company began to make simpler designs more in keeping with the emerging rectilinear style. By 1916, Unger had stopped making jewelry and was producing toilet articles, advertised in *Vogue*, as well as airplane parts. By this date, the Unger family was no longer running the business. G.L.R. Masters, an Unger inlaw, was the president and Clarence A. Leonard, secretary and treasurer. In 1918, Unger Brothers was listed in the Newark Directory as "mfg. metal parts." However, in *The Industrial Directory of New Jersey*, the firm was listed as specializing in sterling silver novelties, with seventy-five employees, still located at 412 Halsey Street. The business was sold in 1919.

UNGER & CHRISTL

At the turn of the century, J. Victor Christl was foreman for Alling & Co. In June and July 1900, he traveled to Paris, visiting the Exposition Universelle where, it is assumed, he saw the displays of the French jewelers. After leaving the Alling firm in 1905, he went into partnership with Eugene Unger and George W. Hagney under the name Unger & Christl. The factory was located at 165 Clinton Street. In January of the following year, the firm incorporated with a capital of $125,000, with Eugene Unger, president; Christl,

246. Unger Brothers, cover of *Holiday Suggestions 1901–1902,* based on an 1896 painting by Alphonse Mucha entitled *Summer.* New Jersey Historical Society, Newark.

vice president; and Eugene's son, Raymond, treasurer. That year, they relocated their factory to 60 Arlington Street. In December 1908, Raymond Unger withdrew from the firm to join his father's business, Unger Brothers. Christl continued in the business until it closed the following year.

WHITEHEAD & HOAG CO.

Benjamin S. Whitehead opened a business in 1879 as a job printer at 19 Arlington Street. In 1880, the name became B.S. Whitehead & Co. and, in 1883, his brother, Edmund B., joined the company. In 1884, Benjamin F. Clark became a partner and the name was changed to Whitehead & Clark, with a factory at 96 Market Street. In 1890, the firm relocated to 167 Halsey Street and was listed in the Newark

Directory as job printers and badge makers. In 1892, Chester R. Hoag became a partner and the name became Whitehead & Hoag. Four years later, the company relocated to 161–163 Washington Street, with another factory at 28–34 Warren Street.

Whitehead & Hoag advertised itself as "The Largest Business Devoted to the Manufacture of Badges in the World." It specialized in flags, banners, novelty advertising jewelry, celluloid novelties, badges, and emblems—the latter two products in 8-, 10- and 14-carat gold, sterling silver, gold plate and gold-filled. Benjamin S. Whitehead, Augustus J. Keil, William Hornich, and George B. Adams are credited with patenting various badge designs and key rings as well as a clamping device. The firm contributed a display

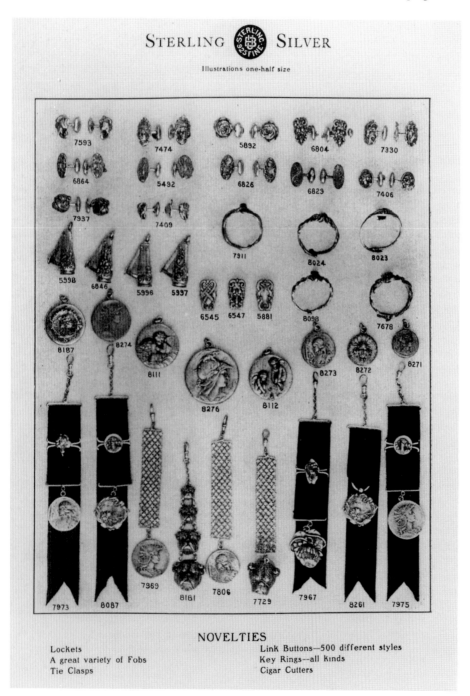

STERLING SILVER

Illustrations one-half size

NOVELTIES

Lockets
A great variety of Fobs
Tie Clasps

Link Buttons—500 different styles
Key Rings—all kinds
Cigar Cutters

247. Unger Brothers, silver novelties from *Holiday Suggestions 1901–1902*, p. 15. New Jersey Historical Society, Newark.

of badges at the 1901 Pan American Exposition in Buffalo.

In 1918, Whitehead & Hoag was the thirteenth largest manufacturer in Newark with 750 employees. By that date, the firm had relocated to First Street and Sussex Avenue. In 1939, the officers of the company were Herman C. Page, president; Philip O. Hoag, vice president; Raymond D. Whitehead, secretary; and Oscar H. Wheeler, treasurer. Whitehead & Hoag went out of business in the early 1960s.

WORDLEY, ALLSOPP & BLISS/ALLSOPP-STELLER

James E. Wordley, Edmund A. Allsopp, and Frank A. Bloemeke founded Wordley, Allsopp & Bloemeke Co. in 1907, with a factory at 101 Lafayette Street. The firm moved the following year to 33 Kinney Street. In 1909, Bloemeke left the firm and, with the addition of another partner, Harry A. Bliss, the name was changed to Wordley, Allsopp & Bliss. In 1915, Wordley left the company and the name became Allsopp & Bliss. The principals in the company were Harry Bliss, president; George A. Bliss, vice president; and Edward E. Allsopp, secretary and treasurer.

In 1922, George A. Allsopp, who was president of Allsopp Brothers, took control and became president of Allsopp & Bliss. In 1929, the factory was moved to the Allsopp facility at 26 Camp Street. In 1937, the two firms merged, with Edward E. Allsopp, president; Arthur Steller, vice president and treasurer; and Clifford Allsopp, secretary. The following year, the name was changed to Allsopp-Steller and the factory moved to 81 Warren Street.

The firm was acquired by Krementz & Co. in 1956 and moved to Krementz's Chestnut Street building. This division was operated separately under the direction of Arthur Steller, maintaining its own manufacturing and sales facilities. It remained independent from its parent organization until the late 1960s, when it was closed. Selected jewelry lines were added to the Jones & Woodland, Krementz 14-Carat Gold, and George Schuler divisions.

Afterword

By 1925, there were as many as 144 manufacturing jewelers working in Newark. The ones listed above, many of which had closed their doors by the 1920s, were chosen for their distinct historic role in the industry. Some created innovative production techniques that set a standard in the business, while others produced jewelry of special artistic merit. Also included are those manufacturers who made products that were mass-marketed all across the country.

Whether their shops were large or small, celebrated or relatively obscure, most of the founders of these firms started as bench workers. They either apprenticed with or worked as journeymen for established jewelers before forming their own business—often in partnership with another individual of similar background. Names reappear in different businesses, and often whole families were involved in the jewelry-making trade—although not always in the same company at the same time. Tracking the partnership changes and name changes proved to be one of the most challenging pieces of this biographical puzzle.

The preceding biographies summarize the available information on selected manufacturing jewelers. For some makers there was not enough material to create even a rudimentary biographical sketch. For many of Newark's manufacturers, no marked or documented examples of their products are yet known. Of course, this is just the beginning; it is to be expected that, as more material comes to light, the information in these entries will be updated. It is hoped that these biographies will tantalize, and open up new avenues of research, shedding more light on the remarkably complex fraternity of entrepreneurs and journeymen who made up Newark's great jewelry industry.

Most of the information in these entries was obtained from advertisements, notices, and obituaries appearing in *The Jewelers' Circular and Horological Review* (its name changed over the years) between 1878 and 1925. The Newark City Directories from 1858 to 1964 were also a rich trove of information.

Frequently Cited Sources

BOOKS AND CATALOGUES

Bagnall, William R. *The Manufacture of Gold Jewelry.* Illustrated by R.T. Sperry. Newark: Enos Richardson & Co., 1882.

Cunningham, John T. *Made in New Jersey: The Industrial Story of a State.* New Brunswick, New Jersey: Rutgers University Press, 1954.

Fales, Martha Gandy. *Jewelry in America, 1600-1900.* Woodbridge, Suffolk, England: Antique Collectors' Club, 1995.

Jewelry Fashions: The Authoritative Style Book. New York: Bureau of Jewelry Fashions, 1917.

Rainwater, Dorothy. *American Jewelry Manufacturers.* West Chester, Pennsylvania: The Schiffer Publishing Company, 1988.

Shaw, William H. *History of Essex & Hudson Counties, New Jersey.* Philadelphia: Everts & Peck, 1884.

Smith, Julia B. *The Jewelry Industry in Newark* (exhibition brochure). Newark: The Newark Museum, 1929.

TRADE JOURNALS AND PUBLICATIONS

Jewelers' Circular—Weekly (so called from 1900 on, before which it is *The Jewelers' Circular and Horological Review;* In 1918 it becomes simply *The Jewelers' Circular*). Abbreviated *JCW.*

The Jewelers' Circular and Horological Review (so called through 1899, after which it becomes *The Jewelers' Circular—Weekly*). Abbreviated *JCHR.*

Jewelry Workers Monthly Bulletin. Abbreviated *JWMB*

National Jeweler and Optician, called after 1920 *National Jeweler.* Abbreviated *NJO* or *NJ,* depending on date.

SELECTED ARTICLES

"A Fine Jewelry Exhibit," *JCW,* vol. 72, May 24, 1916, p. 71.

"Jewelry Industry in Newark," *The Keystone Weekly,* vol. 43, January 30, 1917, pp. 31-32.

"Newark The City of Gold and Platinum and Precious Stones," *The Keystone,* vol. 52, May 1925, pp. 161-192.

"Newark as a Jewelry Center," *JCW,* vol. 44, February 5, 1902, pp. 32, 34.

"Newark Sparkles Among Cities as Home of Gold and Platinum Jewelry," *Newark Evening News,* January 9, 1917, p. 14.

"Progress of the Jewelry Trade in Newark, N.J.," *JCHR,* vol. 26, February 8, 1893, pp. 82-85.

"Seed of Newark's Fame as Jewelry Center Sown More Than a Century Ago," *Newark Evening News,* January 18, 1917, p. 14.

William Wagner, "The Jewelry Industry in New York and Newark," *The Keystone,* vol. 59, April 1932, pp. 58-66.

Index of Names and Jewelry Forms

BOLDFACE NUMBERS REFER TO PAGES WITH ILLUSTRATIONS